B+T 14⁹⁵

Confidential Information Sources: Public & Private

Confidential Information Sources: Public & Private

John M. Carroll

Security World Publishing Co., Inc.
Los Angeles, California 90034

First Edition 1975

Library of Congress Catalog Card Number: 74-20177

ISBN 0-913708-19-4

Security World Publishing Co., Inc.
2639 South La Cienega Boulevard
Los Angeles, California 90034

Printed in the United States of America

To my wife, Billie, and our children:
Jack, Bill, Rob, Rick, Sandi, Alex;
and posthumously to Jim.

vii

Contents

Foreword and Acknowledgments

The hardest part of a book to write is that part where the author gives credit to all the people who have helped him gather material.

It is particularly difficult when the book represents a lifetime spent in gathering and analyzing information.

In the long view, one incident tends to dissolve into another and all sources no longer remain clearly in focus. It is all too easy to overlook someone's important contribution. For this I am sorry.

Some authors begin by thanking their mothers. But, although that fine lady was, in fact, an unerring human lie detector, she had little to do with the substance of this book.

Probably the principal credit should go to some unknown yeoman deep in the bowels of BuPers who, more than thirty years ago, yanked me out of an instructor's billet at Sonar School and posted me to the Navy Security Group.

However, what got it all together was the eighteen months I spent as chief investigator for the Canadian Privacy and Computers Task Force. For this singular opportunity, I want to thank Richard Gwyn, syndicated columnist, formerly Director-General of Socio-Economic Planning, Department of Communications.

For stimulating discussions, thanks go to the other members of the task force, especially John M. Sharp, Legal Research Institute, University of Manitoba (author of *Credit Reporting and Privacy*); and Professor C.C. Gotlieb, Computer Science Department, University of Toronto.

For making our investigation a success, thanks go to my fellow investigators: Professor J.I. Williams, Department of Sociology, University of Western Ontario; Carol Kirsh, Management Consultant, Toronto; Dr. Jean Baudot, Centre du Calcul, Universitie de Montreal; and Edward F. Ryan, Counsel, Ontario Law Reform Commission.

To all my associates in the Canadian Standards Association and especially to: David Balmer, Canadian Bankers Association (Chairman, Committee on the

Representation of Data Elements, Standards Division, Canadian Standards Association).

For the international flavor: H.P. Gassmann, Directorate for Scientific Affairs, Organization for Economic Cooperation and Development; Mme. F. Galluodec-Genuys, Director, International Institute of Administrative Sciences; Dipl. Ing. Gerhard Choust, IBM Vienna Laboratory; and Dr. Lance J. Hoffman, Department of Electrical Engineering and Computer Science, University of California, Berkeley (editor of *Security and Privacy in Computer Systems* and my liaison with Professor Alan Westin's group).

For the special focus on security: Director Clarence M. Kelley, Federal Bureau of Investigation; Assistant Commissioner A.C. Potter, Royal Canadian Mounted Police; Secretary-General J. Nepote, International Criminal Police Organization; Dr. Robert J. Gallati, Director, New York State Intelligence and Identification System; Inspector A. Dyce, Records and Inquiry Bureau, Metropolitan Toronto Police Department; Inspector Laverne Shipley, Inspector of Personnel, London (Ontario) Police Department; Ernest A. Côté, Deputy Solicitor-General of Canada; Col. Robert Diguer, Director, Security Services Branch, Department of Supply and Services; Major Douglas Dawe, C.D., Security Consultants of Canada, Limited, formerly Security Programs Manager, Department of Supply and Services; J.P. Crogie, Assistant Chief Secretariat, Canadian Penitentiaries Service; Dr. Rein Turn, Rand Corporation; George E. Stinson, Stinson Security Services (formerly with the British Security Services); Col. Robert Collins, Dektor Counterintelligence and Security Inc.; Daniel J. Reid, Vice-President, John E. Reid and Associates; J. Kirk Barefoot, Cluett Peabody and Co. (editor of *The Polygraph Technique*); Sgt. Lee Kirkwood, Los Angeles Police Department; Peter Marshall, Chief Superintendent, Chelsea Police Station, and Commander R.L.J. Ashby, Criminal Record Office, Metropolitan Police Office, New Scotland Yard; and Patrick J. Collins, General Manager, Insurance Crime Prevention Bureaux.

And the many sources who were interviewed or contributed material, especially: J.S.W. Aldis, M.D., Executive Director, Ontario Health Insurance Plan; W.J. Bell, Clarke Institute of Psychiatry; A.J. Bray, Executive Secretary, Canadian Consumer Loan Association; Maurice Clennett, Deputy General Manager, The Royal Bank of Canada; R. Melville Cox, President, Credit Bureau of Greater Toronto; William Denton, Director of Administrative Data Processing, University of Western Ontario; Walter E. Duffett, former Dominion Statistician; P. Dygala, Registrar of Motor Vehicles, Province of Manitoba; Frank Field, Bell Canada; Hugh Graham, Manager, Winnipeg Office, Retail Credit of Canada; H.F. Herbert, Assistant Deputy Minister,

National Revenue/Taxation; Gordon Kennedy, Regional Vice-President (Operating), Retail Credit of Canada; W.T. Lalonde, Hickling-Johnston Limited; M.D. Ledoux, Assistant Director General, L'Hopital Notre Dame; Margery C. Lucy, Chief, Division of EDP Service, California Department of Motor Vehicles; D.B. Mastin, General Manager, Royal Insurance Group; J.O. Miller, Director of Computing and Operations Research, MacMillan-Bloedel Ltd.; Dr. Howard B. Newcombe, Chalk River Nuclear Laboratories, Atomic Energy of Canada, Ltd.; A.I. Ormand, Director of Data Processing, General Motors of Canada; T. Overton, Head of Data Processing, North York Board of Education; M.T. Pearson, Managing Director, Associated Credit Bureaus of Canada; William Pollard, Vice-President and Secretary, London Life Insurance Co.; A.J. Smith-Windsor, Assistant Director—EDP, Avco Financial Services; William H. Thomson, Director of Data Processing, London Life Insurance Co.; and S.T. Vince, Manager of Administrative Services, Supertest Petroleum (now British Petroleum).

Thanks are due to Mrs. Jo Moore for typing and manuscript and especially to my wife, Billie, who shared in the typing chores and contributed in a great many special ways.

Finally, I want to thank Ray Farber, President of Security World Publishing Co., for his faith in the project; Louis Charbonneau for his superb job of editing; and Mary Margaret Hughes, Vice-President, Security World Books, who opened many doors for me.

I hope this book will help open many doors for you, too. That, after all, is half the job of gathering information.

The other half is compounded of healthy skepticism and dogged determination. And this, you have to supply.

John M. Carroll
London, Ontario, Canada
1974

Chapter 1

INTRODUCTION

"And the Lord spake unto Moses . . . saying,
Take ye the sum of all the congregation
of the children of Israel, after their
families, by the house of their fathers,
with the number of their names, every
male by their polls. . . ."

—Numbers:1:1, 2

Every time you have tried to cash a check, applied for credit, purchased insurance, sought employment, or attempted to enter a facility with controlled access, you have become a security problem—one of the most basic problems faced every day by every business, large or small, as well as by public and private investigators of every description.

Each of these activities compels the security officer, the investigator, or the businessman concerned with loss prevention to ask some fundamental questions. Who is this person? Is he simply making a purchase or a legitimate application, or is he out to cause some loss? What kinds of identification will serve the applicant's purpose while protecting the company's or society's? What records are available to verify the facts, and how can they be obtained?

The answers to such everyday questions link security, records and identification in an essential chain.

1

SECURITY

Security has been aptly defined as *protection from loss* due to any cause. It may be your loss, or loss suffered by the organization, employer or client you are engaged to protect.

More specifically, in the context of a study of identification and records systems, security is concerned with the prevention of loss caused by *people*.

People may cause loss either accidentally or on purpose. Some individuals are accident-prone, and their accidents can prove costly. Others may attempt to steal— money, goods, or even valuable information—or to commit acts of sabotage or vandalism.

The only sure way to protect against such losses is to identify potential loss-causing individuals and to keep them out of positions or situations in which they will be able to bring about that loss. It follows that, for the sake of effective loss prevention, any business or organization must exert some degree of control over the selection and activities of its employees, vendors and customers. (For specific types of organizations, the term *customer* may be understood as equating with students, policyholders, creditors, depositors, members or clients.)

Learning and specifying what controls to use to this end in day-to-day operations is one of the most important security functions.

Elements of Loss Situations

Three ingredients are invariably present in any loss situation caused by people: motive, opportunity, and risk.

1) *Motive* or *predisposition* includes criminal inclination, where the loss arises from theft or other deliberate action, or propensity, where the loss arises from accident.

   In any given group of people, a relatively small percentage will be either totally trustworthy or totally untrustworthy. The process of evaluating predisposition, therefore, involves answering a question of probability: "What are the chances that a particular person, given the opportunity, will steal from you or cause an accident for which you may be held responsible?" And, by extension, "What fraction of all the people having access to your property in some given period of time will be predisposed to cause you loss?"

2) *Opportunity* must be present for loss to occur. The task of security is to determine where such loss-causing potential may exist and to take necessary steps to prevent or frustrate it. The question is again one of probability: "What are the chances that a particular person, given the

predisposition toward accident, theft, or other loss-causing action, will be *able* to commit such action?"

3) *Risk* is the dollar value of property subject to loss and accessible to a person predisposed to cause you that loss.

To these basic ingredients of a loss situation must be added two other loss factors, both related directly to security:

- The cost of installing and maintaining controls.
- The cost of lost business opportunity arising from restrictions imposed in the name of security.

Evaluating Security Measures

While good security economics dictates that an attempt should be made to minimize the three cost-of-loss components, it is also necessary to strike a balance between (1) security or screening measures that are not sufficiently discriminating, and (2) measures that are overly restrictive. It can easily be demonstrated that, under the right conditions, overly restrictive measures can sometimes contribute more to loss than less rigid security.

In the first instance, where inadequate security permits an employment or business relationship with a person who is either dishonest or accident-prone, the potential loss for a given period can be measured by a simple equation:

$$\text{Cost of Loss (\$)} = \text{Motive} \times \text{Opportunity} \times \text{Risk}$$

Suppose that you are investigating the problem of loss to a retail store arising from cashing worthless checks presented by customers. You find that the store has established a policy of accepting any kind of check—personal, payroll, or whatever. Under these conditions, the probability of a cashier being presented with a worthless check is one in ten (0.10 probability, or a ten percent chance).

Suppose also that the store's security controls (a file describing prior worthless check offenders, say, and measures for collecting such checks) are such that the store can recognize or subsequently collect on one bad check in every five presented. Loss will then be suffered on eight worthless checks out of every ten presented (0.80 probability, or 80 percent chance).

Suppose, finally, that the store cashes a total of $100,000 worth of checks in a year.

You now have the three ingredients of the loss equation: predisposition is equal to 0.10; opportunity is equal to 0.80; and risk is equal to $100,000. The cost can thus be measured:

$$\text{Cost of Loss} = \text{Motive} \times \text{Opportunity} \times \text{Risk}$$
$$0.10 \times 0.80 \times \$100,000 = \$8,000$$

The expected annual cost to the store arising from worthless checks, under a check- screening process not sufficiently discriminating, is $8,000.

You can apply this kind of arithmetic to almost any conceivable loss situation as long as you can intelligently estimate the value of each of the three terms of the cost-of-loss equation.

Overly Restrictive Measures

On the other side of the coin, let's examine the consequences if the store's security measures overreact to the threat of loss arising from worthless checks and become too restrictive, excluding from an employment or business relationship persons who are neither dishonest nor accident-prone.

The store in our example could eliminate its losses from worthless checks by simply refusing to do business with *all* potentially loss-causing customers.

Assume that a study of such checks for the year disclosed that all of them were personal checks. A drastic solution would be to change the store's policy and refuse to cash all personal checks. What would be the cost of lost business opportunity from such a restrictive policy?

That cost can be measured by an equation parallel to the one used above. Suppose that seven out of ten checks cashed in the store (0.70 probability, or 70 percent) are personal checks. Suppose, further, that if these customers are denied the privilege of cashing personal checks, half of them (0.50 probability, or 50 percent) will react to the new policy by taking their business elsewhere.

You then have the ingredients for estimating the cost of overly discriminating check- screening procedures:

$$\text{Opportunity Cost} = \text{Probability of exclusion}$$
$$\times \text{Probability of lost business}$$
$$\times \text{Access}$$
$$0.70 \times 0.50 \times \$100,000 = \$35,000$$

In other words, policies designed to save $8,000, the estimated cost of loss due to worthless checks, would have cost the store an estimated $35,000 in lost business opportunity, resulting in a net expected loss of $27,000.

In other situations, the cost of lost business opportunity might prove harder to estimate— but potentially even more damaging to an organization. For example, overly restrictive screening measures in the selection of new employees might deny to the company the opportunity to hire talented people who, if hired, could conceivably have led the company to new heights of achievement.

When shotgun-like restrictions laid down in the name of security cost an organization more than they save, they cease to contribute to security and instead contribute to loss—the exact opposite of security.

A cost/effective screening procedure works like a sniper's rifle rather than a shotgun. But every experienced rifleman knows that he has to define his target.

Defining the target means acquiring information about it. Records on file become the security officer's "eight-power scope" when he goes about bringing the loss-causing individual into the cross-hairs.

RECORDS

A *record* is a collection of assertions called data elements. These data elements describe states of being or historic events.

A *file* is an ordered collection of records, each of which contains the same set of data elements.

A *personal record* is a set of assertions concerning or describing an identifiable individual.

The value of personal records in preventing loss caused by people rests on the assumption that the future behavior of a person can be predicted accurately from knowledge of what he is and what he has done or experienced in the past.

To put it another way, in the absence of better information the events of the past provide the single best guide to the future.

The general applicability of this presumption might be questioned from either a liberal or conservative point of view, the former pointing out that criminally inclined individuals can reform, the latter arguing that an unblemished record may simply mean that its subject was never unlucky enough to be caught. These, however, are exceptions rather than the rule. For most persons, the pattern of behavior woven in the fabric of his life will provide a reasonable guide to his future behavior.

But it may require a sharp and practiced eye to discern the deviant threads.

What a man is can be as important as what he has experienced. Consider the extreme example of an applicant for a highly sensitive position of trust with the government who has close relatives living in a foreign and potentially hostile country. It is readily conceivable—the situation has become a staple of television drama—that these relatives could be held as hostages to compel the subject to commit disloyal acts. Although the chances of this happening may be small, the stakes may be altogether too high for the government to risk employing the applicant.

Omissions from Records

Records will not always tell the whole story of a subject's past life. The concept of introducing some measure of forgiveness into personal records is becoming institutionalized in our society. As a result, some organizations now "seal" or refuse to disclose certain unfavorable events on individual records, provided that a stipulated period of time has elapsed during which the subject has not been observed to do anything of a questionable nature.

Practices vary widely among organizations, and there is no universal agreement as to how many years of responsible conduct must elapse before the notation of an unfavorable event is expunged from a personal record. Nevertheless, here are a few common guidelines:

- Bankruptcy: fourteen years after discharge.
- Defaulting on a bank loan: seven years.
- Criminal conviction: five years after release from custody, probation or parole.
- Motor vehicle accident: three years.

The alert security officer will bear these possible omissions in mind when evaluating personal records.

False or Misleading Records

Aside from administrative non-disclosure of certain events, records in general are not completely trustworthy. They can and frequently do contain false or misleading information. These shortcomings are normally traceable to one of five problems:

1) Inaccuracy
2) Imperfect rationalization
3) Bias
4) Error
5) Incompleteness

Inaccuracy occurs when the recorded assertions concerning or describing an individual are incorrect. They may have been based upon unfounded gossip or rumor. Witnesses may have lied, been honestly mistaken, or misinterpreted what they thought they saw or heard.

Imperfect rationalization is frequently encountered in computerized or other machine-readable files. It occurs when the person recording an event or condition is presented with only a limited number of fixed choices and is so constrained that he can make no qualifying statements.

Consider, for example, a hypothetical data recording form containing this question:

"Uses drugs?   Yes_____ No _____"

If the recorder checks the box labeled "yes," anyone subsequently perusing the record would have no reliable way of knowing whether the subject has a $40-a-day heroin habit or has simply had antihistamines prescribed for him by his physician to control some chronic allergic reaction.

Such rationalized information is common in computerized files, obscuring a wealth of relevant detail.

Bias arises from the frame of mind of the person entering information in a record. It can tend either to discredit the subject unfairly or to depict him in a more favorable light than the circumstances warrant.

Contrary to belief cherished in some quarters, bias most often works in the subject's favor, contributing to the concealment of unfavorable events. A sympathetic physician, for example, may report a case of gonorrhea as "ureteritis." Or an embezzler may, subsequent to discovery of his crime, be allowed to resign from his position of trust "for reasons of health," perhaps to spare the organization he victimized the embarrassment of public disclosure that would ensue if he were prosecuted, or perhaps in exchange for restitution of misappropriated property.

Error here refers principally to clerical or computer errors. Even the substitution of a single letter—for example, mistyping "now" for "not"—can materially affect the sense of a record.

Such errors are also common. In fact, when one state police organization converted its file of criminal records from manual to computerized format, thirty percent of the records were found to contain significant errors. The experience of other organizations during similar changes in information-handling policies indicates that the thirty percent figure is widely representative of manual files.

Incompleteness means simply that important material is missing from a record. It normally arises from failure to bring a record up to date, either because of delays in data processing or from neglect. But it may also indicate that certain relevant facts were never recorded or that portions of a record were at some point in time removed from a file.

Its effects can be far reaching. A record containing a notation regarding criminal involvement, for instance, may fail to show that subsequent to his arrest the individual charged was tried in court and exonerated. Or a delay in data processing might permit a motorist whose operator's license has been revoked for some driving infraction to report his license as lost and succeed in obtaining a replacement before the notice of revocation is posted to his driving record.

Frequently an employee's derelictions come to light only after he leaves his place of employment. By that time his personnel record may already have been transferred to the company's archives, with the result that no derogatory observations are entered in his record. With the passage of time and turnover of management personnel, a future manager might subsequently write a glowing letter of recommendation—based upon incomplete information.

Records, then, are not gospel. They are composed of entries made by fallible human beings. They are stored, managed, and manipulated by other fallible human beings. Recognizing these shortcomings, what can you rely on?

The answer is *consistency*. Don't put all your eggs in one basket. Don't place all of your faith in one source of information. You must cross-check and verify, and to do this you must become familiar with the wide range of information sources available to you.

IDENTIFICATION

The problem of personal identification is simply stated: How do we know we have the right man?

Unfortunately, there is no infallible method for making a unique identification that is satisfactory for all purposes. Nor is there a Single Identifying Number (SIN) that is completely satisfactory for the purpose of tagging an individual and linking him to a particular record or chain of records. Social Security (or in Canada, Social Insurance) numbers have been proposed for this purpose, but they contain several serious deficiencies, as we shall discover.

In the absence of any such panacea, there are three ways to identify an individual: by what he has (documentation); by what he knows (privileged information); or by what he is (physical and other personal characteristics). Let's examine each of these methods.

Identification By What He Has

Documents an individual produces are the most widely accepted method of identification, but these should be subjected to skeptical examination. Documents have always been the target of forgery, and no longer is forgery an art requiring talent and practice. Today it has been made easy by reproduction technology readily available to anyone.

Many legitimate documents—including birth certificates, marriage certificates, divorce decrees and university transcripts—are now issued in the form of certified photocopies of originals retained in the files of the issuing agency. The forger need only obtain a copy of someone else's document and alter it to contain his own name and description. He can then make a new photocopy to obliterate evidence of erasure or whitening out and certify the copy himself with a notary's raised seal—or find a notary willing to certify it for him.

Every pulp magazine carries advertisements for blank birth certificate forms and similar documents that, filled in in a believable manner, might easily pass cursory inspection.

The kinds of I.D. most commonly presented—driver's license, Social Security (Insurance) card or permanent voter's registration card—can often be acquired by making a simple application or passing a test of skill. A person seeking to establish a false identity can then attest to it by perfectly valid documents issued and validated by the proper authorities. And he can use these documents to obtain others, such as credit cards or a passport.

When obtaining documents for identification purposes, it is always best to have the subject sign a document release form and have the copy sent directly to you by the issuing agency. This is customarily done in the case of university transcripts.

Identification By What He Knows

What a man knows is usually the most reliable way to identify him. Since what he should be required to know depends on what he is seeking, this method of identification might best be exemplified by a brief examination of its use in governing access control to a secure facility. (It is not our purpose here to attempt a definitive explanation of such controls, but rather to suggest some of the principles and methods in typical use; these will naturally be adapted or modified to suit specific needs.)

Access control is typically implemented by personal identifiers, passwords, or personal assessment.

Personal Identifiers

Personal or organizational identifiers may be universal or local, and they may be used alone or in combination.

1) *Universal personal identifiers* include Social Security numbers, birth registration numbers, driver's license numbers, and passport numbers. Because they are easily obtained from public records and often quoted on documents having wide distribution, they make poor access control devices.

2) *Local personal identifiers* include student numbers, employee numbers,

depositor numbers (bank accounts), and programmer numbers in computer systems. They are often serially issued or they may represent some numeric rendering of the subject's name or other data. Because they are widely disseminated on time cards, registration cards, invoices and the like, they make poor access control devices. They are used for convenience, not security.

3) *Universal organizational identifiers* include employer numbers, Dun and Bradstreet numbers, Standard Industrial Classification numbers, census list numbers, or sometimes a unique postal code number. Like universal personal identifiers, they are widely quoted and easily obtained from public records documents. They are not intended as access control devices, nor are they generally used as such.

4) *Local organizational identifiers* include location numbers, branch (or bank) numbers, transit numbers (for check-clearinghouses), area numbers, dealer numbers, department numbers, account numbers, or project numbers (for computing systems). They are assigned for accounting convenience, not for access control. They usually have a mnemonic significance. These are a few examples:

• Location and department numbers are often hierarchically assigned. 01 may signify the comptroller's department, 0101 the accounts receivable branch, 010103 the retail accounts section.

• In right-of-way companies like pipelines or railroads, local organizational numbers may signify outward distance from the terminal. On the Polar Bear route of Canada's Ontario Northland Railway, for example, 183 means Moosonee, because Moosonee is 183 miles from Cochrane, the terminal of the Arctic tidewater division.

• Area numbers are often widely used as a shorthand designator within an organization. The French equivalent of the CIA, the SDECE (*Service de Documentation Exterieure et de Contre-Epionage*) uses R-designators (for *renseignement*, or intelligence): 2 = Eastern Europe, 4 = Africa, 7 = the U.S. and Western Hemisphere. The British SIS (Secret Intelligence Service) uses country numbers; 12 used to mean Germany. Kim Philby tells how German agents in Turkey used to try to annoy their British counterparts by sitting near them in a cafe and singing, "*Zwoelfland, Zwoelfland uber Alles.*"

• Transit numbers are made up of a bank number and a slash followed by, in the United States, the number of the Federal Reserve District in which it is located (that is, its check-clearinghouse).

With organizational identifiers as with personal identifiers, wide publicity, comparative ease of access, and the tendency to use them for a long time render them poor access control devices.

Passwords

Passwords can be used to control either physical access (as with code-operated locks) or access to files in a computer system. They may be randomly assigned or selected by the individual they identify. A weakness of the latter procedure is that the individual often selects a password with a high mnemonic content, such as his date of birth, license plate number, telephone number, or a permutation of his name and initials. This gives a potential infiltrator the basis for making a good guess at the password.

Passwords can be given to individuals or to groups of individuals possessing similar access privileges. The latter procedure is poor from a security point of view; one careless individual can compromise an entire group. However, group passwords sometimes become necessary as an operational measure, as when push-button, code-operated locks are in use.

The more frequently a password is used, the greater its susceptibility to compromise. There are, however, a number of protection measures that can be adopted, including frequent change of passwords (the one-time password is the extreme example) and the use of countersigns to which a particular response must be given from a previously distributed list. Of course, the process of distributing lists of passwords in itself constitutes some hazard to security.

In computer systems a password may be protected by typing it over a *mask,* so that it cannot easily be recovered from the hard or paper copy made by the terminal teletypewriter, or by *inhibiting* the printing of the password at the terminal, so that it never appears on the teleprinter record. Even in such systems, however, the password is still vulnerable to possible wiretapping. A more elaborate protective measure is *authentication,* in which the user adds his password to a random sequence of numbers sent by the computer or, in some cases, performs some other transformation, such as adding without carrying. The computer, which has stored the random number, simply reverses the transformation and recovers the user's password. This measure affords some limited protection to the password against wiretapping.

There can also be hierarchies of passwords. For example, a password may enable a user to gain access to a special group of files, with a second password, sometimes called a *lockword,* being required for the user to get into any particular file within the group.

Another backup protection for the password is an *authority code.* Such a code determines what a user is privileged to do once he gains access to a facility. If the user tries to exceed his authority, he will be challenged as an impostor, on the theory that a legitimate user would know the extent of his authority while an impostor would not. The password itself gives no hint of the level of authority it conveys, although this information is available to the access controller, which may be human or mechanical.

It is essential, of course, that any access control mechanism deny admission to a facility if a user cannot provide the right password. It is also good security practice to make a permanent record of all unsuccessful attempts to gain access to a secure facility, and, where possible, to apprehend and interrogate the person seeking unauthorized access.

Personal Assessment

In addition to personal identifiers and passwords, direct interrogation and assessment by the security officer may be required for identification purposes.

Border control officers and customs officials have a deserved reputation for a sometimes uncanny ability to identify and thus clear their own nationals by nuances of accent or to recognize subtle symptoms of guilty behavior. In personal assessment there is no substitute for experience and judgment—but these, after all, are the security officer's stock-in-trade.

For personal assessment it is good security practice to collect several items of identification and check them against each other for consistency. Ask the applicant questions about himself (address, phone number, date of birth) and check his answers against the entries on his I.D. Have him write his name and compare the signature against that on his I.D. card.

Preferred I.D. for access to a secure facility would include:

1) Police, military or government I.D. or an I.D. card issued by some recognized organization, such as a computer manufacturer, telephone company, public utility or defense contractor. These cards are usually printed on laced background, watermarked stock. They contain photo, fingerprint(s) and signature. A police officer should also be able to produce a shield, and its number should match that on the card. In many forces he will also have a police driver's license. A military man or government officer should also have a military or government driver's license.

2) A valid national passport.

3) A bank courtesy card (photo I.D. card that conveys check-cashing privileges).

4) An age-of-majority card (youth I.D.) or senior citizen's card.

5) A valid driver's license.

6) A card identifying bearer as a registered American Indian or welfare recipient (its account number should agree with that on his check).
7) Permanent voter's registration card, alien registration card, or landing card (Canada).
8) Insurance cards—principally auto, medical or hospital insurance.
9) Assorted plastics—Social Security (Insurance) cards, travel and entertainment cards, air travel cards, bank charge cards, oil company and store credit cards.
10) Membership cards to professional societies, fraternal organizations or social clubs.

Look upon such I.D. not as an open sesame, but rather as a source of information that you can put together with what you learn from the subject to make your own personal assessment.

Remember, too, that all I.D. is to be scrutinized, not just saluted. An officer in U.S. Naval Intelligence once boasted in the author's presence that he had been able to get into every secure facility in Washington by flashing his membership card from the Boston Athletic Club!

Computerized Assessment

It is sometimes possible to mechanize the process of personal assessment for computerized access control. A number of facts about each user, contributed by the individual or extracted from his employee data sheet, are stored by computer. During the access control procedure the computer will ask such questions as:

"WHAT WAS YOUR WIFE'S MAIDEN NAME?"

"WHAT WAS THE NAME OF YOUR HIGH SCHOOL FOOTBALL COACH?"

"WHAT ELEMENTARY SCHOOL DID YOU ATTEND?"

Failure to give the correct answer to these and similar questions results in denial of admittance.

The computer may also interrupt the user at work after he has gained access and ask additional questions. Again, failure to supply the correct answers means denial of access.

Since performing a large number of checking operations quickly and accurately is something a computer does remarkably well, it is possible to employ several access control measures to safeguard entry to computer systems. Moreover, all the bonafides furnished—name, programmer number, account number, password, lockword, personal facts, and processing authority—would have to be consistent before access would be granted.

Systems security officers have not in general implemented all the measures available. Owners are often apathetic about security. Users tend to become impatient with the rituals of access. For such measures to be successful, management support is essential.

Identification By What He Is

Identification by physical characteristics usually implies fingerprinting. Voice prints, handwriting, lip prints, dental work, blood samples, and even samples of semen have been used for identification. However, positive identification will usually require classification and comparison of fingerprints.

It is true that a classification of single fingerprints exists. However, most fingerprint classification systems require that prints of all ten fingers be present before the file can be searched. Furthermore, unambiguous comparison with similar prints found in the same classification group requires that they be properly rolled.

Other Physical Characteristics

Photographs and physical descriptions are less useful today for identification purposes than in the past, principally because of the everyday use of highly disguising cosmetic practices by persons of both sexes.

Styles in wearing hair and beard are continually changing. Devices such as hairpieces, skin tint, hair dye, colored contact lenses, platform shoes, constraining undergarments, and even crash diets can contribute to significant changes in a person's appearance.

Even features once thought to be dependable for identification, such as the hairline or the shape of eyelids, nose and ears, are subject to dramatic alteration by hair transplants or cosmetic surgery. Practically the only features that cannot be perceptibly altered are the general contour of the skull, the interocular distance, and the shape of the face. These too, however, can be disguised by capitalizing on the phenomena of camouflage and optical illusion.

EMPLOYMENT APPLICATIONS

What information is required from an applicant for employment and how it is validated will depend on the position being filled. An application for a manual or laboring job will require less background information than that of a managerial trainee. Similarly, more data is sought concerning executive personnel than for the young professional. (We are not here considering highly sensitive positions for which background investigation would be appropriate —see Chapter 10.)

All employment applications cover personal data, educational history, work history, special training, and skills. The differences are of degree and emphasis. All forms should collect enough information to put the new employee on the payroll, pay him, collect his payroll deductions and social benefit premiums, and contact his next of kin in event of emergency.

Manual Worker's Application

A typical manual worker job application stresses skills, such as typing, shorthand, or machine operation. Salary data is not required, presumably because the wages are fixed by collective agreement. No references are requested.

It is unlikely that any checking will be done except with the applicant's former employer to establish his level of skill and reliability.

Professional Application

An application at the young professional or managerial trainee level stresses education. It asks about salary—in fact, it may require the applicant to indicate what he is looking for in the way of compensation. It requests data of a professional nature (patents, publications, etc.) and calls for several references.

For such positions a prospective employer will normally contact former employers as well as the named references. Quite likely, transcripts of academic records will also be requested, or at least confirmation that the applicant did attend and acquire the degrees, diplomas or credits he claims.

Executive Application

The executive application form is the most exhaustive. It will concentrate heavily on recent work experience. Prior salary information will be requested even though salary for the position sought is left open for negotiation. It will look for a history of steady promotion, increased earnings and responsibility, as measured by the number of employees supervised and the dollar amount of business handled. Four or more references will be requested. And an effort will be made to probe the applicant's health status, since an older age group is here under consideration and a long-term relationship is normally being contemplated.

SAMPLE EMPLOYEE APPLICATION AND DATA SHEET (INDUSTRIAL)

A. Personal

Name (Mr. Mrs. Miss), Employee Number, _____
Citizenship, Seniority Date, Previous Hire Date, _____
Date on Salary, _____
Address, Telephone Number, Area Code _____
Social Security Number, _____
Case of Emergency: _____
Name, Relationship, _____
Address, Telephone Number. _____
Male/Female; Unmarried, Married, Widowed, Divorced, Separated. _____
Spouse, Dependent Children (Number), Independent Children (Number). _____
Other Dependents (Number), Handicap, Date of Birth. _____

B. Education

	Course	Grade	Credits or Diploma	Year
High School;				
Trade School;				
Junior College;				
College;				
Post-Graduate;				

Educational objective of further course of study and expected completion date.

C. Training Courses

Presented by, Title, Duration (days), Year. _____
_____

D. Skills

☐ Certificate or ☐ License, ☐ State or ☐ Province, Year _____.
Languages:

       ☐ English, ☐ French, ☐ Three (3) Others.
       ☐ Read, ☐ Write, ☐ Speak.
       ☐ Nil, ☐ Limited, ☐ Fair, ☐ Fluent.

Words per minute: _____ Typing, _____ Shorthand,
Other skills, qualifications, machines operated _____

E. Work Experience (including armed forces)

Employer and Type of Business, Occupation, Dates. _____
_____

F. Additional Information

1. Comments. _____
2. Notations by Manpower Planning and Selection. _____
3. Product Group or Staff Department. _____
4. Division, Section or Unit; Code. _____
5. Manager, Date. _____

Figure 1-1

In addition to professional activity, information at the executive level is sought regarding professional, civic and military honors. Questions concerning social relationships and family background, especially the socio-economic level of parents, spouse and siblings, may reflect employer concern about how the new executive will fit into the company establishment. A totally self-made man might not be desirable in all instances.

When an important executive is hired—say, at the middle management level—references and former supervisors will probably be contacted personally, perhaps over lunch. It is also quite likely that a report will be ordered from an investigatory credit-reporting agency to look into the stability of the applicant's marital situation and his general reputation in the community.

These are minimal measures—yet there is abundant evidence that the most basic security precautions are overlooked in many instances, even where the legitimate interests of stockholders and the public at large should have dictated that care be exercised. There are cases on record where

- A convicted forger and confidence man was able to become president of a large drug firm.
- Several New York clinical psychologists were found to have obtained mail order Ph.D's from a college which was merely a superannuated grade school in London, Canada.
- A military surgeon was unmasked as a former meat-cutter's apprentice.
- A school psychologist was discovered to be a convicted confidence man with only an eighth-grade education.

EXECUTIVE SEARCH

High paying positions in the private and, to a lesser extent, in the public sector are often filled with the help of an executive search consultant. Such firms—unlike most job placement agencies—charge the client for their service regardless of whether a candidate is successfully placed or not.

The service is initiated by an order placed by a company client. No telephone orders are accepted.

The consultant assigned to the case visits the company and reviews its basic performance. He discusses the company's requirements with the personnel manager and interviews the supervisor of the position to be filled. If the client's expectations are unrealistic in terms of qualifications required and remuneration offered, the order will be refused. If it is accepted, its terms are written down and formally accepted by the consultant and the client.

Candidate Search

Three steps are taken in preparing the initial *long list* of candidates: search of the consultant's files, advertising, and contacts with industry. (Here search consultants must be careful to avoid charges of raiding.)

The long list may include twelve to 1,000 candidates. It usually averages thirty to fifty names. These candidates are invited to complete the consultant's application form. A dozen candidates are selected from the long list on the strength of their appraised applications.

To reduce the remaining candidates to a final *short list*, interviews are arranged. Basic information about the candidate and the position is exchanged, although the name of the client is not mentioned. The consultant looks for personality hangups, social and emotional problems. Approximately half of the candidates take an intelligence test and undergo technical interviews to assess their competence.

During all interviews the candidate is rated on appearance, oral expression, responsiveness, poise and manner, interest and motivation, and job knowledge. Additional comments may be added by the interviewer, and an over-all rating is given. The interview rating form is added to each candidate's file.

The client reviews these files and picks the short list of two or three candidates.

Investigation

The consultant now verifies the educational, technical, and professional qualifications of these final candidates. References are checked out. Normally the references are contacted by phone although the call-back system is not generally used. The interviewer may take notes or record the conversation. The tapes are usually erased, but the transcripts are retained. The client and candidates may receive summary statements of references without the source being identified.

The client may obtain his own references as well, and the candidate is made aware of this possibility.

The candidate's current employer is not contacted until the job offer becomes contingent upon that reference alone.

Once the final candidate is picked, a complete credit check is undertaken. Consultants do not normally engage private investigators, but a local file-based credit bureau and an investigatory credit-reporting agency may both be asked to verify information given to them. Where permissible, police records are checked.

The candidate is also asked for the results of his last medical examination, but this report is usually not verified. Candidates are made aware that they will usually have to take company medical examinations if hired.

Executive search consultants commonly keep two sets of files. The successful candidate file contains the resume, interview results, short list data, and information on final placement. This information is kept indefinitely. The unsuccessful candidate file is really the basic search file. It contains resumes received over the previous eighteen months, typically including 3,000 names on file. After a resumé has been kept for eighteen months, it is pulled and burned.

Employee Services

In addition to providing executive search services for employers, some consultants also offer psychological services to job seekers. These services include interviews, biographical profiles, and a complete range of psychological testing.

Such job seekers range in age from 16 to 65 years, although most are under thirty. They may come on their own or their parents' initiative, or be sent by employers when a manager asks for assistance in making a decision regarding appointment or promotion.

Normally the candidate controls the information, in that he may review the findings, designate distribution, or ask that the files be destroyed. Where an employer pays for the services, he may ask that the candidate be given no feedback. However, the employer is encouraged to discuss the findings with the candidate.

If a person receives career development services, he may not be considered as a candidate in the consultant's executive search activities until six months after leaving career development. In some areas this time lag is required by law.

File Security Problems

Executive search consultants share many problems of file security with other professionals. Some have reported instances in which their files have been disturbed.

A typical search consultant has 25 professional workers and ten supporting staff. The professional workers may include psychologists and search consultants. The latter usually have a background in business administration. Generally, all company personnel records are available to all employees, and all are informed of company policies and guidelines.

The use of computers is not viewed as feasible in executive research work. The volume is too low and the record length too great. All files, therefore, are manual. Typically there is one general filing system for all company activities.

Except for individual files that may stay in a consultant's office, or sensitive, government-client files that may be stored separately, the files are generally kept in open cabinets in a room occupied by company employees during working hours. Security procedures both during and after hours vary with local conditions.

Most consultants take reasonable measures to protect the security and confidentiality of records. There is, however, a point at which many of these records are vulnerable, as are the records of many companies.

Consultants, like lawyers and other professionals, lease offices in general office buildings. The owners of these buildings contract with cleaning services to clean the offices. The cleaning personnel are provided with a set of master keys which they use to gain entry to the offices while working at night. More often than not, their activities are not monitored.

Most building tenants know little about the cleaning personnel and have no say in their selection—even though cleaners often have access to the records of the tenants.

EVALUATION OF PERSONAL DATA

Considering all reasons for which personal information regarding a subject may be sought, the following breakdown[1] indicates the frequency with which various sources are utilized:

- Interview subject - 72 percent.
- Check medical records or medical information - 28 percent.
- Check references - 25 percent.
- Contact former employers - 21 percent.
- Contact present employer - 18 percent.
- Check educational institutions attended - 16 percent.
- Interview immediate family - 10 percent.
- Check for criminal record - 4 percent.
- Interview neighbors (investigatory credit report) - 3 percent.

These figures should give many security officers nightmares. They suggest that, if someone wants to misrepresent himself, there are three chances in four nobody will check the references he lists, four chances in five nobody will check to see if he ever did the work he says he did, better than four chances in five nobody will find out whether he really has the degrees he claims, and 19 chances in 20 that he can successfully conceal a criminal record.

All in all, his chances of pulling something off are somewhat better than for getting away with burglary—and the prospective return is infinitely greater.

While it is unlikely that you will be your own investigator—that is something like acting as your own lawyer; usually you have a fool for a client—here are a few suggestions for evaluating personal data:

- Redundant references have no plus value. If a subject is asked, for example, for five references, don't permit him to list five former employers or school principals, because these individuals will be named in other elements of the questionnaire.
- In checking out references or other sources, nothing beats face-to-face contact. Some security specialists are skeptical of "telephone patrols." People tend to censor what they say over the telephone and especially in letters; such replies will tend to be bland and inoffensive. You may get a totally different picture of the subject in a face-to-face interview. (Incidentally, letters of recommendation presented to you by the subject aren't worth the paper they're written on.)
- It may be better to interview a fellow employee who had day-to-day contact with the subject, than some remote, high placed manager who knew him slightly if at all. A credible reference should (1) positively identify both subject and referee, (2) clearly establish the working relationship between them and its duration, (3) define the nature and scope of the work accomplished and the subject's role, and (4) assess the subject's competence, dependability, loyalty, interpersonal relationships, leadership ability, and potential for future development, each illustrated with first-person experiences and anecdotes.
- Confirm all significant information that has a subjective content, either favorable or derogatory, by reports from two *independent* sources.
- Try to reduce subjective content by asking the source to cite *critical incidents* rather than giving personal evaluations. "John Doe is a drunk" is, for example, a personal evaluation. A critical incident might be, "John Doe rolls in drunk at 2 A.M. every Saturday night. Last Saturday he came home so smashed he fell on his face in the petunias."

SUMMING UP

This introduction may seem overly pessimistic. It isn't meant to be.

The great majority of people you meet will be honest, respectable citizens. As for the "bad actors," there are very few international spies or master criminals among them. Most of your potential troublemakers will turn out to be unsophisticated individuals habituated to antisocial behavior who have been in and out of trouble most of their lives and are well known among former teachers, employers, neighbors and local authorities.

In an interview situation people like this will generally wilt before an interviewer with a steady eye and a firm voice. They will become unresponsive, evasive, defensive, or offer self-serving excuses when specific, detailed information is demanded of them. Usually they will break off the interview if you mention the possible necessity for fingerprinting or bonding the successful applicant.

There is, however, no magic touchstone that will enable you to identify in advance that rarer bird, the sophisticated criminal who could take your organization for a mint. You must know where and how to look for the right information that will identify and expose him.

SOURCES OF INFORMATION

The sources of information available that can help you protect your client or company from the loss-causing individual are many and varied.

Newspapers and Periodicals

Your local newspaper is one of the best information sources. News stories, public notices, and advertisements (both classified and display) provide a rich and continuing panoply of personal intelligence. In particular look for:

- Crime, accident and court reporting. (Note, however, that a growing tendency of suspects and defendants to report "no fixed address" is making it more difficult to link newspaper reports to particular individuals with common names.)
- Reports of marriages and engagements.
- Obituaries, memoriams, and probate notices.
- Public notices of birth, death, divorce, and change-of-name.
- Divorce advertising and non-responsibility notices.
- Bankruptcy petitions, announcements by bankruptcy trustees, and discharges from bankruptcy.
- Incorporation announcements, doing-business-as notices, and tenders.
- Hospital admissions and discharges.
- Real estate advertising, tax sales, delinquent tax notices, auctions, and even "garage sales."
- Social news: parties, luncheons, travel and vacations, banquets, community meetings and awards, and the activities of private and public charities.

Specialized newspapers addressed to the legal or financial communities provide a more convenient collation of news reports, notices and advertising having a legal or financial import than do general newspapers.

Business and trade newspapers and periodicals provide useful information regarding hiring, promotion and transfer of personnel as well as new business ventures, contracts awarded, new plants and facilities, mergers and acquisitions, business meetings, new products, and business failures.

Directories in Print

A whole host of useful directories can help you piece together biographical background information. In many cases, however, the information is supplied by the subject. Take this into account when assessing its reliability. Fortunately, the large number of directories in print affords a good opportunity to check for consistency. Among them:

- Local and out-of-town telephone directories (white and yellow pages).
- General and specialized city directories issued by local chambers of commerce, church councils, public libraries, municipal tourist and convention bureaus, and private firms.
- Business and trade directories.
- Society and association directories, membership lists, and nomination slates.
- Professional directories and registries.
- High school, college and university catalogues and yearbooks.
- Vanity directories: *The Social Register, Burke's Peerage,* various *Who's Who* directories, *American Men of Science, Contemporary Authors, Books in Print,* and many more.

Clipping Services

So many and varied are the sources of published information that a private security organization may find it worthwhile to retain a good clipping service. A corporate security officer can often accomplish the same end by developing a good working relationship with the company's public relations director or advertising manager.

Annual and quarterly reports of corporations, supplied by a friendly local stockbroker, frequently contain information of interest regarding corporate officers, managers and directors. Some proxy solicitations even contain income data relating to key personnel. In a corporate setting, the company's secretary or comptroller may be best able to obtain this information for you.

Vital Statistics and Other Public Records

Local courthouse and "county seat" records offer a valuable source of public information generally open to anyone. The county recorder's office (or corresponding local registry office) has information openly available on *vital statistics,* including births, deaths, marriages and divorce records.

Municipal offices also maintain open public records on:

- Land titles and mortgages.
- Chattel mortgages and liens.
- Tax assessment rolls.
- Land tax rolls.
- Voters' lists.

It is possible to check such public records, for instance, to ascertain what real property an individual owns. In each county in each state there is a Register of Deeds office. There the various documents affecting title are recorded—e.g., deeds, mortgages, death records, affidavits, land controls, etc. (This question of determining land ownership is considered in more detail in Chapter 3.)

Court records are public information. These include records on filings for bankruptcy proceedings, as well as the records of civil and criminal suits, failed or adjudicated.

County or city Health Department records are, in some instances, matters of public record. Examples are records of mental petitions filed, and information concerning rare or communicable diseases. The matter of personal medical records is examined in Chapter 8.

Searching public records, although privileged to any citizen, is usually best done by someone with legal training and experience. A private security organization might well retain the services of a resourceful law firm for this and other reasons. A corporate security officer can accomplish the same purpose by establishing a good working relationship with his company's legal counsel.

You may experience more difficulty in getting to see incorporation papers, business license files, and registries of tradesmen and professionals than in getting into files of liens, mortgages, land titles, and vital statistics. Access to this information is sometimes restricted, but it can be gained if the investigator is able to advance a plausible reason for requiring it. Here, too, your cooperative lawyer may prove to be helpful.

Criminal Records

Access to arrest records and records of criminal convictions in some jurisdictions is readily available to private investigators and security officers. In other jurisdictions it is easier for a lawyer to obtain this information. This situation is highly variable; in some places no private citizen can obtain access. Your practice will have to be consistent with local conditions.

Motor Vehicle Records

Motor vehicle registration information is, in most jurisdictions, freely available. In some a small fee may be charged. In general, if you have the license plate number, you can obtain the name and address of the owner and confirm the description of the vehicle. And if you have the name and address of the owner, you can get the license plate numbers and descriptions of vehicles registered to him.

It is somewhat more difficult to get the transcript of an individual's driving record showing convictions under the motor vehicle code, accidents, suspensions, and revocations. However, this information is generally available to persons connected with the insurance industry. A cooperative insurance broker can thus be helpful to the private security organization, and a corporate security officer can work profitably through the corporate officer who places the firm's insurance, usually the company secretary.

Information-Gathering Agencies

A background investigation cannot always be carried out on a do-it-yourself basis. And there is no reason why it has to be. In addition to published sources and public records, there is a plethora of information-gathering agencies whose services are available to investigators with a valid business reason for pursuing information. Some charge a fee—usually not large—by the case. Others serve members of the business community on a subscription basis. Your company or client may already have the necessary connections to make their services available to you.

In subsequent chapters we will discuss several of these agencies in detail with a critique of their methods. Here we will simply list the types of information-gathering agencies, indicate their clientele, and show parenthetically which officer in a typical business organization would be most likely to have a working arrangement with each agency.

- File-type credit-reporting agencies; general business. (Credit Manager.)
- Banks: other banks, some general business firms. (Loan Officers, Credit Manager, Comptroller.)
- Investigative credit-reporting agencies: insurance companies, general business. (Underwriters, Personnel Managers.)
- Mercantile credit-reporting agencies: financial institutions, some general business. (Loan Officers, Credit Managers.)
- Lender's exchanges: small loan companies. (Branch Manager.)
- Credit indices: general business. (Credit Managers.)

- Employment agencies: general business. (Personnel Manager.)
- Central Registries to protect the integrity of credit cards:
  1. Travel and entertainment cards: franchise holders. (Clerks.)
  2. Petroleum products: dealers. (Attendants.)
  3. General merchandise: franchise holders. (Clerks.)
- Special registries serving the insurance industry:
  1. Medical Information Bureau: life insurance companies. (Underwriters.)
  2. Insurance Crime Prevention Institute: fire insurance companies. (Underwriters.)
  3. Casualty Index: casualty insurance companies. (Underwriters.)
- Educational institutions: other educational institutions, prospective employers. (Admissions Officers, Personnel Manager.)
- Former employers: general business. (Personnel Manager.)
- Medical institutions and practitioners: other medical institutions and practitioners, life insurance companies, prospective employers—patient's consent required. (Medical Officer.)
- Welfare agencies: other welfare agencies. (Case Officers.)
- Police Forces:
  1. Interpol: national police forces. (National Central Bureau.)
  2. National police forces: other national police forces, state and local police. (Central Records Officer.)
  3. State police: national, other state and local police. (Central Records Officers.)
- Telephone companies: other telephone companies. (Security Officer.)
- Power utilities: other power utilities. (Credit Managers.)
- Internal Revenue Service/National Revenue-Taxation: internal use, other national revenue services under treaty. (Auditors, Investigators, District Directors.)
- Social Security/Social Insurance: internal use, other national pension plans under treaty. (Case Officers.)
- Civil Service Commission/Public Service Commission: internal government use. (Personnel Officers.)
- Bureau of the Census/Statistics: internal agency use, some information furnished to IRS/National Revenue and HEW/National Health and Welfare. (Statisticians and Planners.)

The information you need to help you identify individuals who, given the opportunity, might cause your company some loss most certainly resides in the files of at least one of these agencies. It may be made available to you or to some surrogate you engage to help you in your investigations.

The amount, kind, and reliability of personal information varies widely from agency to agency, and each has its own rubrics as to what information can be released to whom and under what circumstances. Whether or not you can make use of this information depends upon whom you represent and, to some extent, upon where and how you go about seeking it.

But in every case you first have to know:
- What information is on record?
- Who has custody of those records?
- How can I or my surrogate get it?
- How much faith can I place in what I get?

Helping you find the answers to those questions is what this book is all about.

Chapter 2

PERSONAL RECORDS: AN OVERVIEW

FILES AND RECORDS DEFINED

A *personal record* is a collection of data elements concerning or describing an identifiable individual. There are two kinds of data elements: standing elements—for example, the legend *name*; and active elements—for example, *Jones, John J.*

A *file* is an ordered sequence of records, each of which contains the same collection of standing data elements. A file is ordered on a sequence of *keys*, a key being an active data element that uniquely identifies the subject of the record. It is usually the name of the subject, although it might be a unique identifying number, such as his Social Security number.

- A *serial* file is keyed on the subjects' names, sequenced by arranging the records in alphabetical order of those keys.
- An *inverted* file consists of a list of keys whose subjects share a common set

29

of characteristics—e.g., a list of blond, left-handed bank robbers, all of whom are under 35 years of age.

- A *hashed* file is based on an artificial key obtained by assigning to each record a unique random number. The records are arrayed in ascending numerical order of the artificial keys. Such a file is entered by means of an *index*, consisting of an ordered list of natural keys—for example, subjects' names in alphabetical order—and a list of corresponding artificial keys.

Types of Files

A file made up of records in manila folders, on sheets of loose-leaf paper, or on cards is called a *manual* file.

A file made up of records on punched cards or on magnetic tape is called *machine-readable*. Files on magnetic tape are additionally known as *computerized* files.

The contents of a manual file may be photographed in sequence on a long roll of 35 or 16 millimeter film. Such files, called *microfilm* files, can be read with the aid of an optical device known as a viewer.

Both microfilm and magnetic tape afford a large reduction in storage space over that required for manual files. Two thousand cards can be photographed on a single reel of microfilm. A single inch of magnetic tape commonly holds 856 characters of data.

When files are computerized, it is the usual practice to store only the active data elements. Standing elements are stored within the computer itself and reproduced only when a readable record is required.

Computers can search files extremely rapidly. A 2,400-foot reel of magnetic tape, capable of holding nearly 30,000 records, can be searched in a little over three minutes. And when the information is stored on magnetic disks, the computer can retrieve any desired record in a fraction of a second without running through the whole file as it must do when files are stored on magnetic tape.

A computer delivers readable records by means of a printer or a visual display, which resembles a television set. The printer or visual display may be located many miles from the computer and connected to it by telephone lines or radio. These remote printers or visual displays are called *terminals*.

Copies of computerized records obtained from a printer are called *print-outs* or *hard copy*. If a print-out is made of an entire file of records, it is known as a dump. High-speed printers can reproduce 600 lines a minute. Smaller printers, usually used as terminals, commonly deliver 30 lines a minute.

If desired, some computers can also make microfilm copies of computerized files.

FILE PRACTICES

A profile[2] of the average file containing personal information reveals the following characteristics:

- Average *size* is 72,000 records.
- Average *density*, or amount of information contained in each record, is 520 active characters.
- Average *age*, or time a record is kept on file, is 67 months.
- Average *activity*, or number of times the file is entered in a year, is 1,300 times.

It is interesting to observe that, on the average, ten times more work is done putting information into files than is done getting it out. Putting it another way, there is only one chance in ten that any particular record will ever be seen again once it is filed. (Averages can, of course, be misleading. There is an old story about a statistician who drowned in a creek whose average depth was three feet.)

There are nearly five billion personal records on file in the United States. The bulk of these are concentrated among a relatively small percentage of file-keeping organizations. To illustrate:

- While the most commonly encountered file has less than 5,000 records, one-fifth of the organizations who maintain personal records keep 90 percent of them.
- While the most commonly encountered records contain less than 300 active characters, 7-1/2 percent of the record-keeping organizations maintain records whose density exceeds 2,000 active characters.
- While two-thirds of all organizations keeping personal records consult their files less than 100 times a year, 4 percent of these organizations respond to more than 10,000 requests for information a year. This latter category includes police forces, motor vehicle bureaus, credit bureaus, and mailing-list suppliers.

Categories of Files

File practices vary depending upon the relationship of the record-keeping organization to the individuals whose records they keep. There are three basic categories: employees, customers, and subjects.

The first category is self-explanatory. The second includes clients, patients, students, policyholders, and members as well as customers in the strict sense of the term, depending upon whether the records are kept by professional firms, hospitals, schools, insurance companies, associations, or stores. The third category implies a different sort of relationship between the organization and the individual. It encompasses prospective customers, persons upon whom credit or criminal records are held, automobile owners and drivers, subjects of research studies, welfare recipients, veterans, immigrants, and job seekers, among others.

A given individual may, of course, fall into all three categories. Although the average American has only one organization that regards him as an employee, fifty-four organizations look upon him as a customer, and twenty organizations record him as a subject.

In each category the pattern of a few big fish and a lot of small fry can be observed.

- *Employees:* The average employer has 980 employees on whom records are kept. The most commonly encountered employer has less than 100. But less than one-fourth of all employers employ 80% of all workers.
- *Customers:* The average organization has 61,000 customers. The most commonly encountered organization has less than 25,000. But 14 percent of the organizations have 87 percent of all customers. (Note: These figures are based, not on the corner store but upon some 75,000 to 80,000 large and medium-sized organizations, both public and private.)
- *Subjects:* The average organization that keeps records on subjects—some 32,000 organizations—has 70,000 records. The most commonly encountered organization has less than 100. But seven percent of these organizations (2,500) maintain over half of the records in the subject category (734 million).

Laxity in Handling Information

Organizations generally are surprisingly lax in their handling of personal information. Nearly half of them have no policy, written or unwritten, specifying how such information will be handled and to whom and under what conditions it may be released. One quarter of all organizations do not police the actions of their data-processing staffs. And only ten percent have ever taken disciplinary action against staff members who misuse personal information in the files.

With a few notable exceptions, organizations in the public sector are nearly twice as likely as those in the private sector to take effective action to discipline staff members for misuse of personalized information on file. The types of organizations most likely to take such action are motor vehicle bureaus, police forces, public utilities, credit bureaus, and medical institutions.

FILE PROCEDURES

Most information is first taken down on a printed *form* containing the standing data elements. If a manual filing system is in use, this data-collection form is simply inserted in the subject's file folder, which is then interfiled alphabetically in a filing cabinet.

Critical data elements may be transcribed on a file card which can then be interfiled in a catalog file drawer, a visible index, or an open tub file.

Machine-Readable Files

If the record is to be maintained by machine, several additional steps are required. To begin with, the blanks on the data-collection form will probably have been assigned *field* numbers by printing these numbers on the form. A field is a set of machine readable characters used to hold an active data element.

The data in the numbered fields is transcribed by hand printing them in correspondingly numbered fields on a *coding form.* In some cases, a data element must be truncated or shortened to fit the number of characters provided for it. For example, usually only 14 characters are allocated to the subject's last name.

The coding forms are next given to a *key-punch* operator who uses a typewriter-like keyboard to punch the information into business machine cards—80 characters to a card. The information is then said to be in machine-readable form. Indeed, there are electro-mechanical machines available to sort, sequence, and search files of punched cards and print summary reports from them.

Computer Files

To create a computer file, a batch of punched cards called a *deck* is fed into the computer, which arranges the information in the desired sequence and stores it on a magnetic tape or disk. This operation produces what is called a *transaction* file.

At this time, hard copies of each new record are printed out and sent to the originator for verification. These printed records are called *confirmation copies.*

The next step involves using the computer to merge the transaction file with the existing *master* file, during which process a new or *updated* master file is created. Each successive updated master file is called a generation. The most recent is referred to as the *son*, the next older the *father*, and the next older the *grandfather*.

The usual practice is to retain the three most recent generations of each master file so that if a processing error is detected, the operators can "fall back" and recreate the information from earlier generations after the error has been corrected.

Variations from this basic procedure for updating a master file are possible. For example, in some installations a typewriter-like keyboard is used to create a magnetic-tape file without first having to create an intermediate punched-card file. Two such systems are known as *Key-Edit* and *MTST*.

When it is necessary to retrieve a record stored on magnetic tape, special punched cards called *control cards* must be created or withdrawn from a *program library*. The most recent version of the master file also must be withdrawn from the *magnetic tape library* and mounted on the computer. The computer is then run under direction of the control cards and the desired record is printed out on the high-speed printer.

Requests for information are usually batched or accumulated until a periodic updating run of the master file is scheduled. Some organizations update their files daily, some weekly, some monthly. During an update run, new records are added to the master file, over-age or redundant records are deleted, erroneous records are corrected, new information is added to existing records, and requests for information are fulfilled.

It should be apparent that there are several shortcomings inherent in the batch processing system of handling records. The most serious is that at any given time a significant proportion of records are incorrect or outdated. Furthermore, these records cannot be accessed except at the cost of disturbing the routine operation of the data-processing center.

The usual solution is for each executive to receive a personal dump of the master file, which, of course, is accurate only as of the last update run. The executive answers inquiries by manually searching his personal dump of the file.

DATA SECURITY

Computerized file systems create a number of security problems. Several clerical employees, for instance, must handle the records during processing. These clerks necessarily come into possession of confidential information, and gossip is not unknown.

The practice of distributing confirmation copies may also contribute to leaks. What's more, the recipients often retain these confirmation copies and photocopy them in order to build up *ad hoc* files, which frequently contain uncorrected information.

In addition to the computerized master file, the original data collection form is frequently retained for legal reasons, and copies of it may be retained on microfilm. Thus there is a minimum of four copies of the master file that have to be safeguarded.

Garbage Disposal

In records processing, several intermediate files are produced: coding forms, punched-card decks, intermediate magnetic tape files—usually referred to as *scratch tapes*—and often print-outs of the files created as part of the update procedure for reference between updating runs. These intermediate products, except for the magnetic tapes that can be electrically erased and reused, are usually looked upon as "garbage."

Disposal of paper residue is a major problem at data-processing centers and within executive offices. Along with the intermediate products of file processing and personal print-outs, this paper residue includes used carbon ribbons from printers and carbon interlayers of multi-part forms.

Where the volume of paper to be disposed of is too great to be handled by the usual electric shredders, most of the waste is incinerated in batches, except for punched-card stock that is collected for recycling. The important point from the aspect of loss prevention is that waste awaiting destruction or recycling is frequently stored under conditions of dubious security.

Tape Erasure

There is an ongoing debate as to how effective is electromagnetic erasure of scratch tape. At one time the CIA had reached the conclusion that it wasn't effective at all and called for tapes to be overwritten fourteen times with random characters before being wiped for reuse. Even then some doubts remained as to whether the secret material had been completely obliterated.

The matter is even more serious when magnetic tape is considered surplus and released for sale to jobbers. A similar dilemma arises when data-processing equipment containing magnetic disks on which secret data has been recorded is consigned to be traded in on new equipment.

There is as yet no answer to the quest for a way to sanitize magnetic media formerly used to store highly sensitive material that completely satisfies all security specialists.

Real-Time, On-Line Processing

The shortcomings of batch processing have led the computer industry to begin moving over to real-time, on-line processing. This kind of data storage requires bigger and more expensive computers. It requires that the master files reside on magnetic disks usually kept permanently within the computing equipment. And it is more expensive than storing data on magnetic tape.

On the other hand, real-time, on-line processing offers several advantages. Each user is afforded immediate access to the master file at any time. This is accomplished through a mechanism called *time sharing*, in which each user is given a slice of time in round-robin fashion so that each perceives himself to have exclusive use of the computer. Any authorized user, including users at remote terminals, is able to call up and display on his personal terminal at will any desired record in his file. Because modern computers can perform several million operations a second, a large number of users can be accommodated simultaneously on time-shared systems.

Theoretically each user could have the capability of adding, deleting or altering records from his remote terminal. In this way all records could be kept continually up to date. However, for security reasons the ability to *update-in-place* is utilized sparingly, if at all.

Indeed, the security problems surrounding real-time on-line computer systems are many times more difficult to solve than those surrounding batch systems. Among these problems:

- The master file resides permanently within the computer and can easily be compromised by computer operators and programmers.
- There is much less of a visible audit trail than exists in batch operations and less accountability than when each file has to be withdrawn from a vault for regularly scheduled update runs.
- It is difficult to monitor the actions of users at remote terminals. In fact, it is not easy to be sure that only authorized persons use these terminals.

For security reasons, therefore, update messages from remote terminals are normally accumulated in real-time on a separate *journal* file. The computer program to update the master file is run only once a day, and then under strict supervision.

In this way, organizations using real-time on-line computer systems sacrifice the potential of having a continually updated master file in the interest of security. They are thus able to preserve the integrity of the file with respect to unauthorized additions, deletions, and changes. However, they are still not entirely able to prevent unauthorized disclosure of information from the file.

It must also be appreciated that the telephone lines connecting remote terminals to a computer are as vulnerable to wiretapping as are ordinary voice circuits.

EXPERIENCES WITH COMPUTERS

Analysis of the previously noted Privacy and Computers Task Force Questionnaire provides the following profile of the uses of the computer in file keeping, and of practices among various organizations in the gathering of personal information.

Half of all organizations who maintain files of personal records keep such files on computers. By and large, the computer users are larger organizations having larger and more frequently used files.

Whether or not a file ever becomes computerized depends upon its size, structure, and degree of utilization. A rough rule-of-thumb is that a file consisting of 10,000 records, ten percent of which must be used or updated weekly, can be considered for computerization. However, trade-off between size and utilization must be included in the evaluation. A small file that is frequently used and a large file with infrequent access may both have equal potential for profitable computerization.

Files that are frequently used to retrieve collections of records sharing common values of selected data elements (that is, when inverted files must be created) are likely at some time to become computerized irrespective of their size.

Ninety percent of computer users back up their computerized files with manual files. These contain information which is more subjective, sensitive, narrative, or graphical in nature.

Kinds of Data

Fifty-five percent of the computerized files contain data on customers; 31 percent contain data on employees; and 14 percent contain data on subjects.
- The *customer* files contain records on three-fourths of the organization's customers and 40 percent of all the information the organization has about each of these customers.
- The *employee* files contain records on 58 percent of the information the organization has about each of these employees.
- The *subject* files contain records on only 30 percent of the subjects about whom the organization has information, and only 22 percent of the information the organization has on each.

Four out of ten organizations who use computers rent the services of computer bureaus who do their processing for them. Their processing is done principally in the batch mode. They experience all the special security problems that arise out of having sensitive work done off their premises by a third party.

Roughly half of the organizations who own or lease their own computers have configured them for real-time on-line data processing.

Five percent of organizations having their own computers have extensively decentralized systems with 200 or more remote terminals.

How Users Assess Computers

A survey of how computer users assess the results of computerization shows that three-fourths of these organizations detected errors in manual files at the time they went to computer processing. Typically thirty percent of the manual records contained errors. Other findings:

- 51% say the computer improves routine data handling.
- 45% say the computer provides more complete timely reports.
- Only 41% say the computer is essential to their operations.
- Only 32% say the computer permits better collation of data.
- Only 4% say that improved management planning is one of the principal benefits of computerization.

Most computer users say that after computerization they began to collect more data on each individual whose record was on file. However, only four out of ten report this was done because of the additional capability afforded by the computer. The rest say that it came about because of changes in organizational objectives or programs, or because of increasing government requirements for collecting and reporting information.

Security at Data-Processing Centers

The same survey indicates that, generally speaking, the security at data-processing centers is deficient.

- Only 73% have implemented physical access controls over spaces in which electronic data processing is conducted.
- Only 69% have implemented the use of secure disposal methods for sensitive waste.
- Only 58% utilize audit trails or monitoring logs to insure that only authorized persons have had access to files.
- Only 42% run checks on the integrity of data processing personnel.
- Only 39% have implemented the security measures provided by the manufacturers of their computer systems. And of these, only one in four

has sought to implement security measures that go beyond those furnished as part of the basic equipment package.

Altogether, present day data-processing procedures present a dismal picture from the point of view of the security specialist. However, the field is full of promising opportunities for a sales-oriented security man who can convince all these potential customers that it is well worth while to safeguard information. It is a valuable corporate asset.

ACQUISITION OF INFORMATION

One source of information used by practically all information-gathering organizations is the subject himself. This includes pursuing information sources nominated by the subject: personal references, former employers, present employer, educational institutions, hospitals and medical practitioners.

Information gatherers may also interview the subject's family or neighbors. They may consult published sources, retain private investigators, obtain information from police forces, employ investigatory credit-reporting agencies, or obtain information from other organizations of the same type as the one seeking the information, as when a merchant checks out a new account with another merchant.

Among organizations seeking personal information on a subject,

- 28% consult medical sources. The types of organizations in this group include other health services, insurance companies, social welfare organizations, charitable institutions, and regulatory (usually licensing) organizations.
- Only 25% actually check personal references.
- 21% contact former employers, against 18% who contact the subject's present employer. Organizations most likely to approach either of these sources include merchandising houses, employment agencies, insurance companies, police forces, and prospective employers.
- 16% approach educational institutions attended by the subject.
- 10% interview the subject's family. These include health service agencies, social welfare agencies, police forces, and charitable institutions.
- 8% utilize the services of investigatory credit-reporting agencies.
- 6% retain private investigators or obtain information from them.
- 4% check with other organizations in the same business.
- 4% obtain information from police records.
- Only 3% consult public records or published information.
- Only 3% talk to the subject's neighbors directly. Organizations that do so include health services, insurance companies (working through investiga-

tory credit bureaus as a general rule), police forces, and social welfare agencies.

The most prolific sources of personal information in order of their activity in dissemination are:

1) Motor-Vehicle Bureaus
2) Regulatory or Licensing Agencies
3) Educational Institutions
4) Credit Bureaus
5) Health Service Agencies
6) Insurance Companies
7) Oil Companies
8) Law Enforcement Agencies

In order of importance, the principal sources of information used by police forces are other police forces (including the FBI), regulatory agencies, private investigators, insurance companies, and the subject's present employer.

The principal sources of information used by private investigators are police forces, insurance companies, other private investigators, social welfare agencies, and regulatory agencies.

Information gatherers generally agree that in obtaining information regarding a subject from third parties, the single most important consideration is to give believable assurance that the source of the information will be protected by being kept confidential.

EXCHANGE OF INFORMATION

For the purpose of studying patterns of information exchange, it is useful to consider all organizations as falling into one of three categories:

1) Nurturing or subject-serving organizations. This category includes health service agencies, educational institutions, and social welfare agencies. These organizations obtain information from the individual and divulge a disproportionate amount of it to agencies in the same and other categories. For this reason, from the viewpoint of information exchange, they may be regarded as *sources.*

2) *Business* or self-serving organizations, principally employers and merchants. These organizations obtain information both from the individual and from other organizations. They appear to divulge about as much information as they obtain, principally to others in the same general category and, to a lesser extent, to those in the final category. Business-type organizations may be regarded as *dynamic storage* elements.

3) *Authoritarian* or society-serving organizations. These include private

investigators, investigatory credit-reporting agencies, and police forces. They obtain information from the subject and from organizations in the other two categories. However, they tend to divulge far less information than they acquire. Consequently, they may be regarded as information *sinks* where personal information tends to become concentrated.

Information-Generating Activities

There are seven activities in our society that account for most of the interchange of personal information among organizations. They are, in order of the amount of information interchange they generate:

- Determining an individual's worthiness to obtain consumer credit.
- Selection of individuals for employment.
- Administration of criminal justice.
- Testing an individual's means to determine his eligibility to receive social-welfare benefits.
- Determining an individual's eligibility to purchase insurance.
- Social planning.
- Ascertaining an individual's right to operate a motor vehicle.

Determining *credit worthiness* helps credit grantors to avoid loss by refusing to extend credit to individuals unable or unwilling to pay. It generates information interchange among taxation offices, social welfare agencies, insurance companies, census bureaus, police forces, motor vehicle bureaus, credit bureaus, employers, health services, and potential credit grantors.

Employment selection helps potential employers avoid loss that could arise from engaging unsuitable employees. It generates information interchange among police forces, motor vehicle bureaus, credit bureaus, employers, educational institutions, census bureaus, and taxation offices.

Criminal justice helps identify actual and potential lawbreakers, select worthy candidates for probation and parole, and monitor their subsequent actions. It generates information interchange among police forces and other law enforcement agencies, motor vehicle bureaus, health services, census bureaus, credit bureaus, insurance companies, and regulatory agencies.

Means tests help avoid loss of social welfare funds by assuring administrators that applicants are truly deserving. They generate information interchange among taxation offices, social welfare agencies, insurance companies, census bureaus, police forces, motor vehicle bureaus, credit bureaus, employers, health services, and educational institutions.

Determination of *insurability* helps insurance companies avoid loss by avoiding customers likely to be poor risks. It generates information interchange among credit bureaus, insurance companies, motor vehicle bureaus, health services, employers, social welfare agencies, and educational institutions.

Social planning helps avoid loss of public resources that might arise as a consequence of improvident planning. It generates information interchange among census bureaus, health services, credit bureaus, employers, and educational institutions.

Ascertaining an individual's *right-to-drive* helps avoid loss by getting off the road drivers who are excessively prone to having accidents. It generates information interchange among police forces, motor vehicle bureaus, health services, census bureaus, and credit bureaus.

U.S. Fair Credit Reporting Act

The exchange of personal information is now constrained to some extent by the U.S. Federal Fair Credit Reporting Act. It is based upon Congress's power to regulate interstate commerce, and its applicability to credit-reporting agencies rests upon their interstate affiliations and the location of their information recipients.

The Act provides that if an applicant is refused credit, employment, or insurance on the basis of a report filed by a credit-reporting agency, the applicant must be informed of this fact and furnished with the name of the agency turning in the report. The applicant then has the right to visit an office of the agency and be informed of the basis for the unfavorable report. If he does not agree with the substance of the report, the agency is obliged to reinvestigate the case and issue a second report.

If the applicant believes that additional information is required to have his case understood in the proper light, he can submit a statement up to 100 words in length to the agency. The agency is then required to make the subject's statement a part of his file and to circulate copies of it to everyone who has received a report on that individual within the previous six months.

This law specifically excludes cases in which an applicant has applied for a job paying $20,000 or more a year, a life insurance policy with a face value of $50,000 or more, or a loan of $50,000 or more.

Credit-reporting agencies are allowed to charge individuals a fee for exercising their rights under this act. Charges now in effect range from $4 to $25.

Subject Complaints

Complaints from subjects, however, are seen to be the exception rather than the rule.

- 32 percent of organizations receive complaints regarding the inability of a subject to see his record. The organizations most likely to receive complaints of this kind include law enforcement agencies, credit bureaus, and health services.
- 31 percent of organizations receive complaints from subjects regarding the disclosure of personal information. These organizations include motor vehicle bureaus, credit bureaus, educational institutions, law enforcement agencies, social welfare agencies, and employment agencies.
- 20 percent of organizations receive complaints from subjects regarding their methods for collecting personal information. The organizations most likely to receive such complaints include law enforcement agencies, motor vehicle bureaus, credit bureaus, travel-and-entertainment credit card companies, and insurance companies.

With rare exceptions, most of the valid complaints arise because the organization has identified the wrong individual. This is bad business not only for the subject but also for the organization. It can lead to lawsuits and to constraining legislation when it entails denying a benefit to a deserving individual. It can lead to loss on the part of the organization or its clients and loss of credibility on the part of the information system when it entails granting a benefit to an undeserving individual.

Most organizations identify an individual by his surname, his first given name, initials, and lineal designation if any, together with his full address (apartment number, building number, street, city, state, and postal zone). This information will properly identify most individuals if it is complete and up-to-date, and if it is tied into a complete and accurate residence history in the case of historical data. Unfortunately, it is usually neither complete nor up-to-date.

Then, too, there are special problems. In one west coast city there are a surprising number of marriages in which a Mr. Singh marries a Miss Rau. It turns out that among members of the Sikh community (a Hindu sect) all men are called Singh and all unmarried ladies are called Rau.

Unique Personal Identifiers

These and other problems of identification have led information processing specialists to seek a unique numerical identifier for each subject. The Social Security number (Social Insurance number in Canada) has been proposed for this unique identifier, despite the fact that social security cards specifically say the number is not to be used for identification.

Social Security numbers present several problems as unique identifiers. Some individuals have more than one number. (In fact, the ease with which Social

Security numbers can be obtained makes it highly likely that many Americans have two or more.) Some individuals have no Social Security number, including those who have never worked, young people, housewives, and persons in the country on student or visitors' visas. And Social Security numbers are useless for establishing genetic linkages to persons who lived before advent of the Social Security program.

Some motor vehicle bureaus use an individual's surname, first given name, sex, and date of birth to generate a unique operator's number. In fact, in police-sponsored campaigns to have citizens use steel engraving pencils to make identifying marks on valuable items of personal property, the owner's driver's license number is given preference over his Social Security number.

The London Metropolitan Police in England use an individual's surname, first given name, date of birth, and height for identification purposes.

In Canada, the Department of National Revenue/Taxation formulates a taxpayer account number from the first five alphabetic characters of his surname, his Julian date of birth (number of the day of the year in which he was born, from 1 to 365 or 366) and a three-digit file sequence (tie breaking) number. Even so, problems remain in correlating the withholding statements of, for instance, strip teasers who perform in different cities under different names as well as different Social Insurance numbers.

CONTENT OF PERSONAL RECORDS

In modern society the life of virtually every individual is a matter of record. The rites of passage are celebrated by filling out a data acquisition form.

Life begins with registration of birth, which is filed at the local registry office. These files are now frequently consolidated on a state-wide basis.

Primary and secondary school records contain items relating to family background and subjective comments as well as academic marks. These are frequently consolidated on a district basis.

Vocational schools, community colleges and university admissions files frequently contain biographical as well as academic data, and scholarship applications require detailed financial information regarding the student and his family. Graduate schools frequently carry out extensive investigation into the backgrounds of applicants, including psychological testing, sometimes a psychiatric assessment in the case of medical schools, and a criminal records check in the case of law schools.

When a person gets his first job, the number of records kept on him jump dramatically. He will fill out an employment application, receive a Social

Security number, make an income tax withholding statement, and usually apply for group medical and hospital insurance. He will also begin filing federal, state, and in some cases local income tax returns. He may also become the subject of a life insurance policy, a bonding policy, and a personal security clearance.

With the acquiring of income, possessions and responsibilities, the invididual's life becomes increasingly documented. The purchase of an automobile necessitates obtaining a driver's license, car registration, public liability insurance (which entails the opening of a record by an investigative credit-reporting agency), and usually a loan, which in turn involves recording the lien with a state-wide personal property security registration system. The car owner will probably also obtain one or more oil company credit cards—and should he abuse this privilege, the facts will be recorded by a national data service.

If the individual marries, the fact will be recorded in a state-wide registry of marriage and divorce as well as in the local registry office. If he opens charge accounts, applies for travel or entertainment credit cards, opens checking or savings accounts, obtains a loan from a bank or finance company, or applies for a general credit card, he will become the subject of another file in each instance. And if he fails to handle his consumer credit privileges in a responsible manner, he may become listed on the credit index or become unfavorably identified by one or more service agencies established to ensure the integrity of credit cards.

Home ownership means the recording of a deed, a mortgage, a listing on the municipal land tax assessment roll, an application for fire and casualty insurance. If the home owner reports too many fires, he may become listed with the fire underwriters' investigation bureau. If he makes a questionable claim against his own or another's casualty insurance, he may become listed on the casualty index.

Our much-documented individual will doubtless also be enumerated by the school census and the national census, register as a voter, and obtain a passport and one or more foreign visas if he travels beyond his country's borders. Any episodes of illness will lead to the opening of new records by the hospitals and medical practitioners he selects.

His career activities will add to the record, whether he becomes listed among aircraft pilots, lawyers, security officers or zoologists. A businessman will probably be evaluated by a mercantile credit-reporting agency, and members of the armed forces and government employees will become subjects of special record-keeping systems.

Those whose lives deviate from the norm usually become subjects of specialized records—for example, files for recipients of workmen's compensation, unemployment insurance, or welfare benefits. And individuals whose activities bring them into conflict with the law incur arrest records, court records, probation, penitentiary or parole records.

The pattern continues to the end, when the last record is made with the filing of a death certificate at the local registry office, where the facts will likely be added to a consolidated state-wide file of vital statistics information. If he leaves an estate, probate records will also be created.

During his lifetime the average individual will become the subject of at least fifty files—and his activities might easily double this figure.

File Density

It is convenient to classify files by their information content as being sparse (an average of 16 items), medium density (an average of 48 items), or dense (an average of 72 items). Few records contain more than 100 items, and there are usually no more than 150 items that can be collected on one individual, if we consider repeated episodes as being a single item of information.

Dense files, decreasing from a density of 100 items, include: life insurance applications, applications for permanent residence in a country, automobile loan applications, mortgage applications, personal history forms, passport applications, bank loan applications, secondary school information, probation records (face sheet), and applications for welfare allowances on account of permanent disability.

Medium density files, decreasing from a density of 60 items, include: applications for welfare allowances on account of blindness, armed forces enlistment, applications for welfare family benefits, applications for general credit cards, marriage license applications, and oil company credit card applications.

Sparse files begin at around thirty items. They include employment applications, short-form tax returns, applications for telephone and power utility service, applications to open store charge accounts, and the like.

Looking at the whole range of questions that can be asked, 40 percent are concerned with identifying and locating the subject; 20 percent with his health, housing, prior residences, habits, and associations; 13 percent with his marital status and the names and addresses of immediate relatives; 12 percent with his occupation, educational history, and skills; 10 percent with his financial status; and 5 percent with his ancestry or religion.

A complete list of questions commonly asked to obtain information for personal records is appended to this chapter. The questions are ordered according to the percentage of files in which they appear.

Who Keeps Files

State governments maintain 25 percent of all files of personal information. These include driver's licenses, automobile registrations, social welfare files, files dealing with probation and parole, and criminal records.

The federal government maintains 20 percent of all files. These include criminal records, immigration and naturalization records, passport applications, social security records, income tax records, personal history statements, and armed forces enlistment records.

Banks and similar institutions maintain 15 percent of all files. These include checking, savings and trust accounts, loans, mortgages, and credit card accounts.

Local governments maintain 13 percent of all files. These include primary and secondary school records, statements of births, marriages and deaths, land tax assessment roles, and some hospital records.

Insurance companies maintain 12 percent of all files. These include applications for automobile insurance; bonding; group and personal hospital and medical insurance; life insurance; personal property, fire, and casualty insurance; group life insurance; and group and personal annuities.

Other businesses maintain 10 percent of all major files. These include charge accounts, credit card accounts, telephone and power utility service accounts, and credit records.

Employee files account for the remaining 5 percent.

PERSONAL INFORMATION AND CIVIL RIGHTS

Those who are concerned with designing, managing, or using personal records systems today become sensitized to the increasingly constraining requirements of civil rights and human rights legislation, such as the prohibition of job discrimination because of age, sex, color, creed, or national origin.

These requirements have presented the manager concerned with forms design and information handling with a dilemma: Should he studiously remove all data from files that might be used to perpetrate unlawful discrimination? Or should he carefully gather statistics based upon these data to prove discrimination does not exist?

Information handlers opting for the first choice have soon found themselves facing other difficulties. For example:

- Banning photographs of employees because they might foster racial discrimination makes it impossible to issue photo badges for security purposes.
- Without an indication of age, it is impossible to administer retirement and annuity policies.
- Without an indication of sex, it is impossible to furnish the proper salutation on letters or to plan sanitary facilities in new buildings.
- Without an indication of marital status, it is impossible to process income tax withholding statements.
- Without an indication of nationality, it is impossible to comply with security regulations requiring citizenship in various government positions or to answer questions posed by the federal census regarding the employment of aliens in certain occupations.

Many administrators argue that the way to comply with human rights legislation is not to purge blindly all items of personal information that might conceivably be used to violate such rights. Instead, these types of data should be collected where necessary for normal operation of the organization.

In some cases such data can be collected on an aggregate basis only. Sometimes a computer can be programmed so that print-outs of records furnished to individuals or committees making decisions relative to hiring, promotion, retention, or the award of some benefit are devoid of any data elements that might enable the recipient to discriminate unlawfully against any individual.

SUMMARY

The astonishing variety and extent of personal records keeping has become, in the age of the computer and the data bank, a subject of widespread interest and concern, generating an ongoing debate over the rights of privacy against the essential needs of business and government to keep pace with the affairs of a complex and mobile society. Aspects of this apparent conflict are discussed in greater depth in Chapter 11.

In this overview we have examined the nature and content of personal records and file systems. We have seen how information is acquired, who acquires it, and the major activities in society that lead to the acquisition and exchange of information.

In the following chapters, we will look in some detail at the content of records kept by credit-reporting agencies, police forces, motor vehicle bureaus, social welfare agencies, census bureaus, health services, educational institutions, and employers. We will examine their data acquisition practices and information handling procedures.

And we will see who can obtain what information from their files, and under what conditions.

Chapter 3

INVESTIGATORY CREDIT-REPORTING AGENCIES

"Curse not the King, no not in thy thought,
And curse not the rich in thy bed chamber,
For a bird of the air shall carry the voice,
And that which hath wings shall tell the matter."

— *Ecclesiastes*, Chapter 10, Verse 20

HISTORY OF COMMERCIAL REPORTING

The commercial reporting field can be traced back more than a hundred years to a modest beginning.

Before the mid-1880's there was little need in North America for credit bureaus. Credit was relatively little used in buying consumer goods. Most customers were personally known to the merchant. Most retail establishments were small. Customers tended to stay in one place.

However, the panic of 1837 rocked the finances of the United States and business needed a way to obtain information before entering contracts involving credit. On August 1, 1841, one Lewis Tappen established such a means when he founded the Mercantile Agency in New York City.

51

Lewis Tappen had been a merchant. More prudent perhaps than others of his time, he had compiled over a long period of time detailed records relating to his customers, on which he noted not only their transactions with him but also any other information about them that he was able to discover. After the crisis, Tappen found a ready market for the contents of his files.

Between 1841 and 1859 several changes took place in the ownership and management of the firm. A Benjamin Douglas became sole owner in 1854. Robert G. Dun joined the Mercantile Agency several years after it was founded, and in 1859 Dun bought out the company, renaming it R.G. Dun and Company.

By this time there was a competitor in the field, the Bradstreet Company. Since the late 1840's, John M. Bradstreet, a Cincinnati lawyer, had been operating from an office in New York a firm called Bradstreet's Improved Commercial Agencies. After competing for many years, the two firms merged in 1933 to form the well known Dun and Bradstreet Company.

The early firms specialized in credit reporting with limited service to fire insurance companies. Specialized insurance reporting began in 1895 when Mutual Life of New York, followed shortly by the Equitable Society and New York Life, established inspection reports.

Mutual of New York operated its inspection departments as a subsidiary, National Commercial Agency, until 1942, when it turned its inspection work over to independent companies. The Equitable Society still operates its own inspection department, although its overflow is handled by independent companies.

Meanwhile, a number of other reporting agencies were springing up. Some special mercantile agencies were formed which offered reporting services to specific trades. The Shoe and Leather Mercantile Agency Incorporated was founded in 1879 and the Lumberman's Credit Association in 1876. The first credit bureau reporting primarily on individuals, rather than businesses, was established in Brooklyn in 1860. By 1906 there were thirty such bureaus, and in 1939 the Associated Credit Bureaus Incorporated was established to assist in exchange of information between members.

The Retail Credit Company was founded in 1899 to supply merchants with reliable information about customers seeking to do business with them on credit. The company supplies personal history information, based on face-to-face interviews.

The Hooper-Holmes Bureau Incorporated was founded on March 6, 1899, in

New York City. At that time the Casualty Index (see Chapter 5) was its only function. In 1912 the company entered the commercial reporting business.

Kinds of Agencies

There are essentially two ways to develop information about consumer credit worthiness.

One way is to compile historical evidence of how a consumer has paid his bills in the past by collating the experiences of the various credit grantors with whom he has done business. A credit bureau that operates this way is called a *file-based credit-reporting agency.*

The other way to establish credit worthiness is to ascertain the individual's general reputation in the community and observe his life style, to determine whether patterns of behavior exist that might make him behave irresponsibly in discharging his future obligations. A credit bureau that functions in this way is called an *investigatory credit-reporting agency.*

Investigatory credit-reporting agencies can, in turn, be subdivided into two categories. One specializes in *personal credit reporting,* the other in reporting on corporations. The latter are known as *mercantile credit-reporting* agencies.

These distinctions are not clear-cut. Although an investigatory credit-reporting agency gathers the bulk of its information by face-to-face interviewing, critical incidents in an individual's life that profoundly affect his general reputation frequently become matters of record. Among these might be financial obligations that were written off by the credit grantor as "uncollectible."

Similarly, a file-based credit-reporting agency, although specializing in the collation of the collection experiences of credit grantors, could not be expected to overlook a criminal conviction, which obviously would affect the individual's ability to discharge his commercial obligations.

Nor is the line between personal and mercantile credit-reporting clear. In a one-man business, the individual and the business are the same entity.

It is becoming common for investigatory credit-reporting agencies to have affiliate organizations that specialize in file-based credit reporting.

There are two principal firms in the field of investigatory personal credit reporting: Retail Credit Company and the Hooper-Holmes Bureau Incorporated. There is one major company in the field of investigatory mercantile credit reporting: Dun and Bradstreet Inc.

The operations of the two kinds of investigatory credit-reporting agencies are revealed in a closer look at Retail Credit Company and Dun and Bradstreet Inc.

RETAIL CREDIT COMPANY

Retail Credit Company, which has its headquarters in Atlanta, Georgia, has over 300 branch offices and 1500 other offices located in every state of the United States. The company employs over 8500 investigative personnel who prepare approximately 35 million reports annually. Retail Credit Canada has 27 branch offices which have under their direction 81 sub-offices in the towns and cities throughout the country, employing, at the time of writing, a staff of nearly 700 full-time salaried employees.

The business of Retail Credit Company falls into two main divisions. The first is supplying personal history information dealing with life insurance underwriting, automobile and casualty insurance underwriting, and personnel selection. The second deals with credit reports.

It is particularly relevant to this study to describe what the company does *not* do:

- It does not operate a private detective agency.
- It does not undertake any assignments connected with gathering evidence for divorce or related to domestic affairs.
- It does not handle any aspects of industrial intelligence.
- It is not involved in the gathering of information on politicians or in political intelligence of any kind.
- In none of its business operations does it use eavesdropping or wire-tapping equipment of any kind.

Customers and Services

Who are the customers of Retail Credit Company, and how does one become a customer? The answers to these and other questions regarding the practices and policies of the company have been developed through personal interviews with a Regional Vice-President, headquartered in a city of two million population, and a Branch Manager located in a city with a population over 200,000. Where indicated by the question-and-answer format, the responses are those of the company officials interviewed.

An examination of the investigative activity of Retail Credit Company for the district reveals the following breakdown of business by category:

- Life and Health Insurance   26%
- Fire and Casualty Insurance   36%
  (including auto)
- Employment Services   8%

- Insurance Claims Services   11%
- Credit and Commercial Services   18%
- Management Information Services   1%

Investigations which Retail Credit Company is commissioned to make by its customers originate with an application by the person who is subsequently investigated. The kind of information sought is determined by the business needs of the customer, not by Retail Credit Company.

As a matter of policy, the company accepts assignments only from customers who have entered into a written agreement. This contract places stringent obligations upon customers to keep the information contained in the reports they receive in strict confidence. The company would terminate an agreement with any customer discovered to be using reports for any purpose other than the customer's legitimate business reasons.

Direct questioning elicited a clear picture of the nature of report requests received and acted upon by Retail Credit Company.

Q. Suppose someone wanted to find out what you had on some individual and came to you asking for information.

A. They couldn't get it because we will report only to established firms with whom we have an agreement. These firms must treat the information confidentially and must be using it for business reasons.

Q. If an established law firm with whom you had never done business before were to say, "We would like to know such and such," would you provide the information?

A. There are very few law firms that would use us, except in connection with insurance claims. However, I imagine that a lawyer being asked by one of his clients to look into a business for him to invest in might secure a credit report on that particular situation.

Q. So, in fact, if someone wanted to find out what you had on someone else, they could do so by subterfuge?

A. No, I don't agree with that. We are very careful about what customers we sign up. They're reputable firms. We investigate if we have any doubt about them. I don't think we would investigate a large oil company. But in the case of a small legal firm, we would do our own checking to make sure they're reputable, and would find out the reasons for which they would use our reports. They would have to be for business purposes. We don't involve ourselves in any divorce actions, or business espionage, or things like that. Strictly business relationships.

Q. Do you do market research?

A. We've done some of that. We've helped a couple of colleges in the States. It was a statistical survey. We have done image studies for a large insurance company that wondered why it was having a large turnover of personnel. We interviewed former employees and worked this up into a survey for them.

Q. Do you do security checks?

A. We don't do any. We just make employment reports, interviewing the man's previous employers and business associates who knew him, and this works into an employment report. As far as security, we can't check on it.

[Author's Note: In Canada, this statement would be entirely accurate. The Royal Canadian Mounted Police handle all security investigations and they do their own investigating. In the U.S., it is conceivable that an enforcement organization performing a security check might, if it had an existing relationship with RCC, order an investigatory credit report as part of or preliminary to its security investigation.]

Q. What is your relationship with law enforcement officers?

A. There is no relationship really. We're abiding by general principles embodied in the U.S. Fair Credit Reporting Act. If a policeman comes to see us, the best we can do for him is give the subject's name, address, and former address, and the officer has to do his own investigating.

Q. Do you do reports for government agencies?

A. We'll report to government agencies when there is a legitimate need for our services and where we have an established reporting arrangement with the agency.

[Author's Note: These agencies can, of course, include law enforcement agencies.]

Q. Do finance companies use your credit-reporting service?

A. No, I think because they know their business so well, they do their own checking up.

Q. Do banks use your service?

A. Some banks will use outside reports, but they use the file-based credit-reporting agencies to a larger extent.

Q. What about other lending agencies?

A. We're doing a reasonable amount of work for them at the acceptance or mortgage level, but not at the personal financing level—not where they take a general lien on a man's assets and property as collateral for a small loan.

Q. Do you work for mortgage lenders?

A. Yes, in mortgage work and car financing, where there is a significant transaction.

Q. Do you work for large employers?

A. Yes, the employer group that traditionally uses our services is the insurance-oriented market, because we're so well trained with it. The insurance companies use us in selecting agents. They are not using us routinely on staff jobs, but rather on the people in their field force that they have to license. The sales field generally seems to be an area of major concern. The insurance market is very conscious of this, and they do a lot of it. In the manufacturing, industrial and commercial fields we do a reasonable amount of employment reference checking for sales positions.

Q. What is your relationship with mercantile credit-reporting agencies?

A. It's our understanding that they haven't done any personal investigation work now for about a year and a half. If we were asked to do commercial reports, rather than personal, we'd have a problem. It's a different product. We're involved in personal reports on the one-man business level, where the owner's personal reputation and his business reputation are really indivisible. As soon as you get into the corporate entity, where one man is not recognizable as the firm, then our training does not gear us into it.

Q. Would you evaluate a neighborhood for buying real estate?

A. No, we don't sell that type of information. Our definition of reporting is reporting on people, not groups.

Q. Do you do reporting in connection with oil company credit cards?

A. We don't do a lot of oil company credit cards. Our operation is oriented towards the larger amount transaction, such as the long repayment mortgage, home improvement situation, purchase of a car, machinery or equipment. Where you have a two-year or longer repayment with a significant monthly payment factor. Then it's worth while spending a little more money to select the person you do business with.

Q. Are you doing any work in travel-and-entertainment cards?

A. I'm not aware that we are into any travel-and-entertainment cards.

Q. What about air travel cards?

A. Yes.

Q. Then is air travel the only credit card business you have?

A. I guess we are involved in oil company credit cards, but it is more the commercial user. The owner has a truck, as opposed to a car, and there is a volume factor. It could be a small commercial account which is a one-man operation.

Q. Do you ever carry out an investigation for training purposes?

A. We've got to have a request before we can order a report. I can't make one up to create work for the sake of work or experience. It could be disadvantageous to the organization.

Report Procedures

In order to insure that inquiries come only from a proper source, Retail Credit Company requires that each customer request any report using a pad of inquiries provided for him by RCC. The pad is imprinted with the customer's account number, which governs the mailing of the final report. The customer could not order a report mailed to someone's home address or to some other company.

The requisition form used by Retail Credit Company provides for the identification of the customer, the identification of the subject, and the situation for which information is desired (including a facility for indicating that the customer is interested in a particular factor). In some instances, particularly for volume customers, a requisition ticket is built into a reporting form for convenience in ordering. The act of typing the order automatically heads up the report, thus eliminating any opportunity for error in transmission.

Additional information on report requests was provided in interview.

Q. What information about the subject you are to investigate do you obtain from the customer?

A. He gives us the subject's name, address, and former address. On a routine life insurance investigation, we like to get two years of address history, his occupation, his employer, his date of birth.

Q. In employment investigations, what information would the customer give?

A. There is a place for them to list the former employers the man has had and the references he might have given. We will not contact the applicant's present employer unless we are informed that it is okay with the applicant. This would mean that the prospective employer has discussed it with the applicant and got his approval.

Retail Credit tries to clear the handling of reports within a few days of receipt. On a routine report by mail, allowing three or four days to act upon it, the customer would receive the completed report in a week's time. A more detailed investigation would take longer. The customer also has the privilege of ordering a wire report for faster service. A written report follows up any wire report.

Q. How do you charge?

A. We charge on a per-report basis on the smaller transactions. Probably the average is around $5.00 for a brief checkup. When it is a brief checkup, the hazard is on the insurance company, because chances are if anything is missed, it is probably unfavorable information. Now if you get in a million-dollar life insurance application, then our man will handle it on an hourly rate, because you don't know how far you will have to go to come up with a good story there.

Q. What is your hourly rate?

A. It runs about $10.00 an hour. Any extra expenses would be charged to the investigator's time. This includes mileage if it is a local case.

Field Representatives

In the United States the Retail Credit Company employs over 8500 investigative personnel handling approximately 35 million reports each year. The company's employment standards are high, and an investigation is made before hiring. Approximately 27% of the field representatives have had college training or hold a bachelor's degree, and each is subjected to a thorough course of training under a supervisor and branch manager for a period of a month.

Continuity of service is usually a reliable measure of the effectiveness of an organization and its work force. Among Retail Credit's full-time field representatives

- 25% have had more than five years experience.
- 42% have had five years of employment.
- 0.09% have had less than one year of service.

In addition to full-time investigators the company employs both part-time field representatives, to handle overflow volume, and rural correspondents, for whom the work is generally a supplementary income. The rural network is maintained through a continual process of referral-and-qualification, often relying upon businessmen who are working locally for national firms. A minimum of two rural correspondents is hired in any community where the company operates, in order to provide an alternate source of information.

Q. Do your investigators sign a confidentiality statement?

A. No, not a statement as such. We instruct them very carefully.

Q. What about training in covering the city?

A. We don't physically prepare them, but we require that it be done. A man gets familiar with a territory and his supervisor guides him in using his time.

Q. What about in-service training?

A. There isn't a set period, but at least twice a year one of our people re-checks behind each investigator to see what he's been doing. We can use what we find out for coaching. If we find something seriously out of line, then it would go beyond that. Every time you follow behind someone, you could find something wrong, but usually what you find wrong is that the man has not gone far enough with the investigation. When we get incorrect information, it's usually of the favorable type. We have to follow behind our men to make sure they are being thorough enough. Regarding serious disciplinary action on field representatives arising out of follow-ups, this would occur in something less than one percent of the instances.

Supervision

Branch managers and supervisors are frequently checked for the continuity and thoroughness of the supervision that they maintain over field representatives. In each branch office there are specially trained employees who review finished reports to make an independent evaluation for possible incompleteness or error. The level of report quality is also reviewed and analyzed by branch managers, regional vice-presidents, and the home office of the company.

In the branch office studied, supervisors included:

- A reports supervisor, overseeing as many as sixteen types of reports.
- A claims director, specializing in insurance claim reports.
- An "hourly rate" or "specials" supervisor, who spends all his time on hourly rate reports relating to insurance.

Q. How do supervisors function on a day-to-day basis?

A. The supervisor looks the tickets over and he assigns each one to the man who handles a given area within a supervisor's area. We discuss the cases with each man before he goes out on the street. They get together on what needs to be done. When the man gets back, he sits down again with his supervisor and goes over the cases. If the supervisor says that they are okay, the field representative dictates his reports and they're typed by the typing unit. Following this, the reports go to a reviewer to see that they meet the standards that we set. If he or she feels that the report is satisfactory, it is mailed to the customer, and our copy goes into the file.

Q. What kinds of standards?

A. Everything. Have enough sources been seen to confirm the information? I think that's one thing in which we're particularly interested. The company's training manual says that unfavorable information on habits, morals, or reputations should be confirmed with two or more sources or by record information. Rumors, gossip and scandals must be sifted. Where adverse information appears in a report, it should be substantiated by any visible dates, facts and circumstances. A field representative is told to report to his supervisor, if during his investigation he develops adverse information which he is unable to confirm. The supervisor is responsible for directing the field representative on the proper handling of the information.

Q. When you go on a case, do you pull the file if it exists?

A. Yes, every request that we receive in the morning is run through our files and the files are matched to the request. The file might help to limit the current investigation. This would be arrived at through discussion with the supervisor.

Q. What if the final reviewer is not satisfied?

A. If the final reviewer is not satisfied, she sends the report back to the supervisor, who will then re-handle it with the field representative. Probably a quarter of the cases go right to the manager for a final decision: "Do we need to do more work, or have we done everything we should?"

Q. Who does the follow-up?

A. In many cases, it is the supervisor. In some of our smaller offices the manager himself will do the follow-up.

Day-to-Day Operations

Retail Credit Company does its own investigating, rather than relying on information from sources. The company finds little need for cross-checking. While the occasional million-dollar life insurance policy might warrant a check on the credit record of the applicant, the time and effort involved would not justify such procedures on a small, routine policy.

Q. What about interviewing the subject himself?

A. In well over fifty percent of our reports the subject is interviewed.

Q. What about public records?

A. Yes, there are bankruptcy records, mortgages and motor vehicle records. Of course, you will have to buy these, but they are valuable.

Q. What are your policies on interviewing people?

A. In most cases we will only talk to people who are of mature age. But an under-age wife—in certain situations—we would talk to her. Neighbors and friends, of course.

Q. What about educational institutions?

A. Yes, we would get whatever information we could. Schools have become pretty cautious in recent years. The information is more negligible all the time.

Q. How do your investigators identify themselves?

A. Some of them have business cards. We do have identification and we try to assure people we are not just frivolously trying to get information. If we are asked to say who we are, we say "Retail Credit Company." In the vast majority of cases we introduce ourselves as "Retail Credit Company."

Q. Have you ever had trouble with people pretending to be from your company who, in fact, aren't?

A. Very rarely, but it has happened. We don't know of any instances where it was done in other than our own line of business.

Q. What information would you divulge during an interview?

A. We would not divulge information about the applicant. For example, we would know that it was a fifty-thousand-dollar life insurance application, but we would simply introduce ourselves: "My name is Kennedy and I wonder if you could help me with an insurance reference on Mr. Jones." We just say "insurance." We're very cautious about divulging anything we know to anyone we talk to.

Q. Then the investigator knows when he goes out that it is, say, a hundred-thousand-dollar life insurance policy?

A. Yes, we have to know that to categorize the extent of the investigation, because the customer sets a base with us and says that, under fifty thousand, they want just routine reports, above that they want the hourly rate, a thorough investigation.

Q. Do you promise to protect the identity of your sources?

A. We have never made any promises, but we would endeavor to protect our sources. We don't make promises. We just ask questions.

Q. Do you confirm negative information?

A. It would vary, depending on the nature of the facts. If you get into drinking habits, you have to go to several people. In some cases there may be record information to back up negative information. This would limit how many sources we would ask, but there would be at least two.

Q. Do you confirm positive facts?

A. Yes, it would depend on the nature of them.

Q. If an unfavorable fact is neither confirmed nor denied, would it be left in?

A. No, it would not. We won't report information from one source. However, here is a case you might run into: A former employer in a situation where there was only the boss and his employee, and the employer is the only person who knows about the subject's record. We would have to point out, however, that it came from one source, his former employer.

Q. What about telephone interviews?

A. Most credit work is handled on the telephone. Mostly we have girls doing the credit work, because that contact is with specific references that are given on credit applications: employers, and so forth. When we get into insurance and employment, we sell our service on the basis of face-to-face interviews.

Q. What if you were compelled by law to reveal the contents of a report to the subject?

A. It would limit the type of information you could report if you had to lay a copy of the report in front of the person. You would dry up the sources of information, and the people who could be hurt would be the 95 percent of people who today are getting favorable reports. When you are in the investigative field, you have to protect your source. If you get into a court case, that's another thing.

Specific Procedures

Retail Credit's Branch Manager provided a rundown on the typical case procedure.

Q. What's the first thing you do when you get a request for an investigation?

A. Run through the files. Corporate statistics suggest that we have a file in 25–30% of the cases, but ours is not a file service. We're selling and providing an information service. The file is only an aid to investigation.

Q. How do you find your sources?

A. On a routine requirement it doesn't create a problem. In a reasonable number of cases we learn the names of the people in the immediate neighborhood before we go out. This information is available from the street directory. You can't be sure, there might be a change of address.

Q. How many cases a day do your men handle?

A. It depends on what type of report, the territory involved, and the level of information required. There are some types of information requests of which a man could handle more than sixteen in a day. There are others on which he might spend all day and not complete a single one. There is a minimum of two interviews a case, and there is no maximum. The information contained has to be confirmable before it is reportable. . . . The average case load per man would probably be sixteen–seventeen per day.

Q. You are talking of about, maybe, forty interviews a day. That's about ten minutes of interview.

A. Right. That is what people looking for employment with Retail Credit wonder. It is necessary and there is no problem in accomplishing it. An effective interview of our type can be accomplished in less than ten minutes. This is the thing that makes our work proper and possible.

Q. And your men spend time writing up cases in the morning?

A. Right. The gathering of information is essentially done while the men are in the field. Communication is done back here in the office.

Q. How do you cover the territory?

A. The thing that makes it possible is this: If a man is working sixteen cases, he'll do it all in one geographical area in the city and he won't have to get out of the area. This is the only way we can do it. We can provide a minimum of non-productive time for him, a minimum of travel time, and we can orient his work so that there is a reasonable path for him to follow, eliminating double backs.

Q. How do you handle the average report?

A. The largest percentage of our reports confirm the application the man has made. They confirm that the man is an average, responsible citizen, a good risk for credit or whatever. If he falls into that category, then the communication needed back to the customer is minimal. If there is something unusual, some question mark about eligibility or conduct, or some record information such as a bankruptcy or a driving conviction, it has to be explained and that takes more time.

Q. How do you get motor vehicle records?

A. We don't make a motor vehicle record check unless the customer asks us to. If they ask us for one, then one of our clerical people would obtain the record from the Motor Vehicle Bureau.

Q. What about cases where there is a lot of geography involved?

A. We will have a second man who handles the other part. We wouldn't have a man go from one section of the city to another. You might find three or four men working on the same case.

Q. Do you send out tickets to rural correspondents?

A. Not the ticket. A questionnaire goes to them. Rural correspondents don't get to communicate directly with the customer of Retail Credit, nor do they see the customer's identification. The questionnaire is related to the type of inquiry involved. There is a specific questionnaire for each line of service.

The Investigative Process

In the course of a field investigation, Retail Credit Company's trained investigator

- Asks for specific examples of negative information, such as a report of drunkenness, in order to distinguish gossip from fact.
- Confirms such information through other sources, accepting it as probable only when several sources say the same thing.
- Seeks to develop only *relevant* information. What is pertinent to employment is different from what is pertinent to life insurance.
- Seeks to report the facts as they exist, not to make moral judgments.

Q. How do you know what to ask and to whom in a short interview?

A. If the source doesn't know the subject, we have used thirty seconds of interview time, and we'll end the interview there. However, you can get a lot of information from face-to-face interviews if you're talking to the right person.

Q. Then you don't have time to hypothesize about the subject?

A. Of course not. The only thing we're interested in is the man's record up to the present.

Q. How could you develop information about sexual morals and so forth in such limited time?

A. Do we? It is rare, if ever, that we get this kind of information from the type of interview we make. We're not directing questions to develop that kind of information. None of our customers have asked us to focus on that type of thing. It's a sensationalistic kind of communication. Ours is a mundane job. Our people are pretty well trained and continually upgraded. We can't afford to end up with impression type of information. We're looking for descriptions of conduct and accidents, not a person's judgment on a situation. If it is observable, I'll ask a person, "Did you see it? Do you know?" Confirmable, observation information. Then a customer can make a judgment on the basis of facts. This is perhaps why you can get a lot of information in less time, because it is not a matter of asking for judgment.

Q. Do you probe into the condition of the family?

A. Here is our guideline: Is it socially acceptable? When I'm talking to a prospective employee, I draw a line and say, "You can visualize a straight line as being average." Our job is to confirm where a person is. If he is average you don't have to say anything. If he lives where he says he does, he is average. If he doesn't live where he says he does, then there is some deviation. If a man is steadily employed, that's fine. If there are breaks of employment in the recent past—six months, twelve months, even up to two years—there might be a deviation. If a person has had a promotion in his firm, that is a deviation on the positive side, you can credit him. If he is active in community affairs of any kind, or in any socially recognizable activity, fine. If his conduct is such that it is anti-social, then that is negative. . . . Anything that is above average is reportable and ought to be said for him, and anything that is below average is recognizable and must be said as well. We tend to recognize the average for the community.

International Operations

Retail Credit Company will make an investigation for a customer in another country through the offices it maintains in the United States, in Canada, and in Mexico, or through its New York department which conducts overseas investigations through correspondents in England and Germany. In such cases, the report will be sent to the customer but the file will be maintained in the country to which it pertains.

When an individual for whom a file exists is transferred from one country to another, the file will be transferred on request either of the individual concerned or the company office in the new location.

Case Files

The case files of Retail Credit Company are maintained in hard-copy form at the various branch offices. The filing operation breaks down into three major categories:

1) Checking new requests against reference files;
2) Filing into reference files;
3) Removing obsolete files and maintaining files in good condition.

Only one file is kept on each subject, even where more than one report may occur, such as an insurance report and a later employment report. The original of any report is sent to the client; a copy goes into the file.

While most files result from requests for an investigation, some are opened on a speculative basis, principally from newspaper clippings. Such clippings are made either by the branch office's clerical staff or, in some offices, by a professional clipping service. Clippings are made only where there is sufficient information to provide reasonable identification of the subject—including an address, for instance, as well as the subject's name—and will include bankruptcy, fatalities, accidents, judgments, reports of self-inflicted wounds, and reports of criminal offenses.

Q. What about records of criminal involvement?

A. We would retain in file a newspaper clipping of someone who is convicted of armed robbery or some criminal offense. This is published information and we're going to retain it. If we've sold a report on that person, we would keep it in the files. It is entirely possible that we don't have a file. If there is a newspaper clipping or a record of judgment or bankruptcy or some matter of published record, we would put that in the file against the possibility of there being a report to be made. In the information business, we are expected to know some things.

Maintenance of Files

The majority of RCC's files are destroyed in thirteen months, with the exception of those that contain unfavorable information or certain evidence of fraud or serious crimes. Favorable reports—which account for nearly 95 percent of all files—are deemed obsolete after a year. Unfavorable records are also destroyed eventually—bankruptcy information after fourteen years, most other negative information after seven years.

A detailed explanation of these procedures was provided by the company's Branch Manager interviewed.

Q. Tell us about your file maintenance.

A. We have two operations: *destroying* and *experting*. Experting is alphabetizing. It is done to make sure that the files on John Smith are all together and that information on John A. Smith is not mixed with that on John B. Smith. Destroying is done on a twelve-month cycle, but we will retain for thirteen months. Each file drawer is destroyed and experted once a year. The program exists on a twelve months basis: 8-1/2 percent are done each month. We go through our files as a continuous daily process. It's just a built-in clerical function. We start at the A's and go right through to the Z's, then come back and start at A again. It's a continual process, and there is a point where all information will be dropped from a file when it is no longer of any value. The advantage for us is to have less information in the files. You need pertinent information. As soon as an automobile insurance company says, "We don't consider driving accidents after three years to be of value," that information is gone. It's not marketable information. The same thing is true of judgments and other categories of information.

Destruction Versus Retention

Q. The number of files tends to remain much the same, I think. We don't want any excess paper. We meticulously destroy and expert our files to contain only useful papers. We would retain information beyond thirteen months only if that information has a valid or significant importance. The man may have had an accident fourteen months ago. We would retain the file on him because an accident has a value to an automobile insurance company for three years.

It's a small percent that would be retained. We're dealing with a market where the large percentage of people are quite deserving and all we can do is to confirm their eligibility and confirm that they are responsible, normal people. There is a small percentage who would not deserve trust, but that smaller percentage is important to identify.

Q. If you keep the five percent, wouldn't that build up over the years?

A. That five percent is being dropped off the other end eventually, too. There is no sense keeping that adverse file after a period of time. In the States it is seven years—bankruptcy fourteen years.

Destroying Files at the Request of the Subject

Q. Are people given the right to request that their name be pulled out of the system?

A. If they don't make any demand on organized society, I think they should have that right. But, if they want an insurance transaction to go through, I think they necessarily have to give up a little of their privacy. You have a right if you want to disconnect, but don't ask me to put a million dollars on your life.

Security of Files, Office Spaces, and Information

Retail Credit Company places great stress on protecting the privacy of the individual on whom it reports. Every manager and employee is instructed that giving out information from the files to other than regular customers or recipients of reports may not be proper publication. Every such request, therefore, whether by letter or by telephone, is referred to the manager, who assumes responsibility for the release of information.

Office security is also the responsibility of the manager, and measures for the protection of office security during and after office hours vary accordingly in the light of local situations. There is no record of files having been destroyed by fire; and theft, destruction or alteration of records has never been a problem. Only one instance of a clerical staff member taking or mis-using records is known.

Every manager's office is constructed so that he can exercise close supervision of the floor operation, and access to the files is confined to a special file group and, where necessary, to field representatives in the absence of appropriate clerical staff.

Results of Information Supplied

Retail Credit Company analyzes its reports on a continued basis, according to well established statistical methods.

This analysis of records indicates that, having regard solely to the information contained in reports, approximately 4.4 percent of life insurance applications processed through the company might be turned down.

However, industry records indicate that the number of rejected applications is actually less than three percent overall. Of these approximately two percent are rejected for heart disorders or other health problems. Less than one percent are rejected because of information in RCC reports—known familiarly within the insurance industry as RCR's.

In automobile insurance, a survey indicates a rejection of about 5.3 percent of the applicants.

In personnel reporting, the comparable figure is 7.7 percent, and most of the unfavorable reports are on the person's employment record.

HOOPER-HOLMES BUREAU, INC.

Hooper-Holmes Bureau, the other major firm in the field of investigatory personal credit reporting, characterizes the average field inspector as being a full-time salaried employee, having 5-1/2 years experience, married, age 32, high school graduate, some college. (Fifty-eight percent are college graduates or undergraduates.)

They have normal appearance, better-than-average intelligence as determined through recognizable approved psychological tests, and they have satisfactorily completed Hooper-Holmes training and educational programs. Character and background are above reproach, as determined through close scrutiny and thorough investigation at the time of hiring.

The average field inspector owns and drives his car daily in his work. A total of 324 employees have had ten years or more of service.

DUN & BRADSTREET, INC.

Dun & Bradstreet, the only major firm engaged in investigatory mercantile credit reporting, is a national and international organization for the collection, analysis and dissemination of credit information and other business facts. It maintains 153 offices in the United States and Canada, with offices and correspondents in principal cities throughout the free world.

The company's subscribers are business concerns seeking information primarily for the purpose of determining whether to extend credit to commercial customers. It prepares no reports on consumers or individuals who are not engaged in business.

In business reporting, the primary source of information is the company which is being reported on. The report is available for review by the subject company.

Current information on business enterprises is obtained daily from a nationwide network of credit reporters and correspondents extending into every city, town and village in the United States and Canada.

The credit reporter interviews the merchant at his place of business, discusses his financial condition and sales trend, observes his merchandising methods, his stock, his location and his competition. He calls upon local sources of information, including the bank. He is constantly aware of local conditions affecting credit, such as employment, shifting of industry buying habits, and the like. He knows by experience where and how to obtain information which has significance to executives who must exercise credit judgment.

The record of the manner in which the businessman meets his obligations is obtained from the ledgers of his creditors, who may be located in various cities. Great numbers of responses to Dun and Bradstreet requests for ledger information are received annually from wholesalers and manufacturers.

Court house records obtained from every part of the country contribute data on suits, liens, chattel mortgages, writs, judgments, bankruptcies, and real estate transfers.

Content of Reports

A commercial credit report has six main sections:
1) The *rating* is in two parts: estimated financial strength and composite credit appraisal.

The following notation is used to indicate financial strength:

HH	up to	5,000
GG	"	10,000
FF	"	20,000
EE	"	35,000
DD	"	50,000
DC	"	75,000
CC	"	125,000
CB	"	200,000
BB	"	300,000
BA	"	500,000
A	"	750,000
AA	"	1,000,000
AAA	"	10,000,000
AAAA	"	50,000,000
AAAAA	over	50,000,000

The following notation is used to indicate composite credit appraisal:

1	High
2	Good
3	Fair
4	Limited

2) The *summary* section of a report brings out its highlights.

3) The *trade* section shows the paying record of the businessman, as reflected by tabulation of ledger experiences obtained from merchandise suppliers.

4) The *finance* section presents a financial statement, including operating details such as net sales, net profits, dividends or withdrawals, and gives other interpretive comments and explanations regarding the condition and trend of the business.

5) The *operation and location* section tells what the function of the business is, how it performs that function such as manufacturing, wholesaling or retailing. It lists products sold or manufactured, the trade to which distribution is made, selling terms, number of employees, facilities and locations.

6) The *history* section traces the background of the principals of the business and of the business itself from the start to the present.

Supplementary Services

Additional Dun & Bradstreet services for subscribers include the following:

• *Letters of introduction* enable subscriber's representatives when traveling to inquire for information at any of the agency's branch offices.

- *Service consultants* offer subscribers a more personalized relationship.
- The *business library* in New York provides reference facilities.
- The *mercantile claims division* provides to commercial credit grantors collection facilities designed to obtain results quickly without loss of customer good will.

Confidentiality Agreement

The importance which Dun & Bradstreet attaches to the confidentiality of the information which it obtains in the course of business is exemplified by the Confidentiality Agreement that must be signed by all applicants for employment with the company. It reads:

"I realize that if I am employed by Dun & Bradstreet, I may receive in the course of my employment information which is of a confidential nature and trade secrets, all of which are proprietary to Dun & Bradstreet.

If employed, I will treat such information and trade secrets which I receive as the property of Dun and Bradstreet and will not disclose them to any unauthorized person during or after my employment.

I understand and agree that if Dun & Bradstreet employs me, any violation of this agreement will entitle Dun and Bradstreet to terminate my employment without limiting any other remedies which Dun and Bradstreet may have."

Officially then, the extensive mercantile data collected by Dun & Bradstreet, which would obviously be of great value in any business investigation, is available only to subscribers, and the company does not condone or knowingly permit the release of the information to others.

THE PROBLEM OF OWNERSHIP

Investigations into the matter of credit worthiness, whether of individuals or corporations, often involve questions of holdings of value. It may be pertinent in many situations to learn just who owns a particular enterprise, or to determine what properties are owned by an individual or a company.

Stock Ownership

In general, information regarding stock holdings is considered to be a private matter. Some companies will divulge information concerning ownership, others will not. By way of illustration, a United States Senate Committee in 1974 investigated the ownership of banks and insurance companies. A number of the principals of major companies were called to give testimony before the Committee. Some volunteered the information regarding ownership, but others did not.

Often there is a great deal of "street information" of this kind, and a persistent investigator can learn much on an informal basis from business competitors and knowledgeable stockbrokers. However, other aspects of business ownership necessarily become matters of public record.

For instance, most businesses must have local licenses, and the license-holder's name will consequently be found on file with the city or county clerk. In the liquor business, the names of license-holders will be found to be on file with local, state or provincial liquor-control agencies.

In order to adopt a name as a trade style, the proprietor may be required by law to advertise the fact that he is doing business as (DBA) this-or-that name.

Corporations are fictitious persons; indeed, in much of the world they are known as anonymous societies (SA). Incorporation papers must be filed with the state or provincial Secretary of State, the Minister of Consumer and Commercial Relations, or with the Federal Department of Consumer and Corporate Affairs. Incorporation papers give the names of charter officers and directors and also the proportion of capital stock of various kinds owned by them.

Additionally, the secretary of each corporation must file annually a list of officers and directors with the number of shares held by each. And when a corporation sells its securities to the public, it must issue a prospectus that makes essentially the same information available to the investing public at large.

Each year the managing editor of every U.S. publication is obliged by law to publish the names of the officers and directors of the company that owns the publication and names of all persons having beneficial ownership of 1% or more of the equity (stock) or indebtedness (bonds) of the corporation. This publication is required as a condition for keeping the privilege to mail the publication at low second-class rates.

The names of all stockholders of a corporation are known to the corporate secretary or the corporation's stock transfer agent, usually a bank. These lists are regarded as private. The lists are used to mail out dividends and corporate reports and to solicit the proxy votes of stockholders on behalf of management.

Possession of a list of stockholders can be an asset to some dissident group which seeks to unseat the incumbent management.

Individuals who are elected or appointed to high government office are increasingly being required by Conflict-of-Interest laws to make public an exhaustive disclosure of their business holdings as a condition of obtaining the public office they seek.

Individual income tax returns need not contain an itemized list of the taxpayer's holdings. However, if the taxpayer wishes to avail himself of certain exclusions, like those on income from some Canadian mining shares, he must disclose his ownership. Otherwise it would suffice to say that he earned so much in interest and dividends and so much in capital gains from such-and-such a brokerage account.

American citizens must declare their holdings in foreign firms and pay a 15% interest equalization tax on them at the time of acquisition.

Annual reports of corporations are frequently illuminating, inasmuch as they sometimes list as balance sheet items the ownership of certain percentages of the stock of non-consolidated subsidiaries.

Foreign Holdings

The question of ownership has become particularly poignant in an age of resurgent nationalism. Just when does a corporation deserve to be classified as "foreign owned"?

It is not a question simply of *where* the firm is incorporated, since most "foreign" companies are, in fact, incorporated within the host nation.

The addresses of the officers and directors afford something of a clue to the nationality of ownership (or, more properly, to the locus of actual control), but the persons in question may have several residences and choose, quite properly, to list a local one. The author has yet to see a stock prospectus that gave the *citizenship* of corporate officers or directors.

The names of corporate management do not necessarily disclose where control resides, for the officers and directors may only be acting as agents for unnamed principals. Nor would the addresses of all stockholders tell much about either the source from which the control of corporate operations ultimately derives, nor the eventual destination of the profits desired from these operations.

In one recent case involving such considerations, the sale of locomotives to Cuba by a Montreal firm was held up because two directors of the firm were American citizens. These men did not wish to appear to violate the Trading With the Enemy Act by being party to the actions of the firm. The American directors thereupon resigned, were immediately replaced by two Canadians, and the deal went through. It is safe to assume that the actual "nationality" of ownership of the firm was not changed in the least by this game of "musical chairs."

Land Ownership

The Northwest Ordinance of 1787 established a coherent system of land division for most of the United States and, through imitation, in most of Canada as well.

Of course, land boundaries along the Eastern seaboard and in the Canadian province of Quebec seem to follow the ramblings of a drunken cow, and inchoate Spanish deeds have sometimes given rise to confusion in California. Elsewhere, states and provinces are rather neatly laid out, with their boundaries following meridians of longitude and parallels of latitude or prominent natural features such as rivers.

These senior subdivisions are further subdivided into a rough checkerboard pattern of counties, and the counties are in turn subdivided into townships bounded by townline roads.

Within each township, there are several sections or concessions of 640 acres each. They are bounded by secondary roads. Each section contains four 160-acre lots. Originally each lot was intended to be a single farm, although some large farms covered one or more whole sections.

As some of the original townsites subsequently grew to be cities, neighboring farm lots were subdivided, sometimes several times, into parcels.

Information regarding land ownership is to be found in municipal (city or county) registry offices. This information consists, in the first instance, of a registered map giving the meets, boundaries and benchmarks used to create each subdivision. These maps define the parcels of land. The fact of ownership of these parcels is authenticated by deeds recorded each time a parcel changes hands.

These records are indexed in two ways. One is by legal description; that is called a *tract index*. The other is a *grantor-grantee index* system, which exists in all counties. Starting with the original grant—the U.S. Government normally, in some cases the Kings of France, England and Spain—the names of all purchasers of land are entered in books. The names are arranged alphabetically and chronologically. In tracing the title back, the best way to use the system is to work backwards—that is, beginning with the most recent entry. To find out what property a person owns, it is necessary to go through the grantee book, looking for all entries of deeds wherein the person being checked appears as grantee.

Information regarding land ownership is also carried over into assessment rolls, where the parcels are recorded against the names of their owners. Assessment rolls are used in collecting local land taxes from land owners.

Title Searches

The procedure for establishing ownership of a piece of property involves locating the most recent applicable map. This is not always easy to do, as the maps are frequently filed chronologically. After the applicable map is found, a licensed land surveyor must physically locate an appropriate benchmark (usually a concrete marker) and lay out the meets and bounds (perimeter) of the parcel with reference to the filed map. This is done to see that existing fences, etc., conform to the specified boundaries.

It is a wise step to go back in time to prior maps to see that all easements, riparian (water) rights, timber rights, mining rights, and rights-of-way, etc., granted in the past, are brought to the attention of a new prospective owner.

Next it is necessary to follow the succession of deeds recorded subsequent to subdivision to see that the putative owner actually has title to the land he is attempting to sell. The deed the seller presents will provide an entry point to the file of recorded deeds, which is also in chronological order.

Records of tax liens and recorded mortgages must be searched to determine that there are no undisclosed encumbrances on the parcel. It is also necessary to discover whether the seller has any judgments against him personally, which would render him incompetent to sell the land or make the buyer liable for his debts were he to consummate the purchase of land.

In the United States there are abstract and title guarantee companies that will, for a fee, ensure the title to the land is clear and valid. These companies receive copies of all these public records. They may index them better, but the information is the same as the public records. In Canada such firms do not exist, although there is a statutory limitation on past claims.

Normally, title companies make records available to builders, real estate brokers, and attorneys—particularly the attorneys, because they are more likely to understand the system. In any jurisdiction it is advisable to have title searches done by an attorney who specializes in such matters.

In some cases, it should be noted, it may be difficult to ascertain the actual ownership of a parcel of land, since the owner of record may be a trust company or some other third party acting in behalf of the actual owner.

Computerized Land Records

The government of Ontario is currently preparing a computerized province-wide inventory of real estate, perhaps pointing in the direction of things to come in other areas. The initial input was the information previously contained in hand-written assessment records held by counties and municipalities.

The province assumed responsibility for real property assessment in 1970, but it inherited a number of problems:

- Records were incomplete. Municipal records listed 1,750,000 taxable properties. Current lists contain close to 2,600,000.
- Records were inaccurate. Roughly 270,000 properties were missing or incorrectly entered. Property descriptions were often incorrect.
- There were wide-ranging inconsistencies in valuation and taxation information.
- Changing and updating the original hand-written records proved to be costly, time-consuming and tedious.
- It is estimated that some four million assessable properties should be listed.

In addition to bringing the file up to date, supplementary information will be added to it. This will include:

- An inventory of existing housing in the province, categorized by type, age, number of stories, living space (square feet), and occupancy status.
- A permanent and regularly updated record of land holdings will be maintained.
- A record of the sales prices for all residential properties will be compiled. This record will be broken down according to regions and municipalities.

Assessors will use the data bank to:

- Develop opinions of the market value of property.
- Obtain property listings with relevant physical, financial and locational information. (This will be helpful when land is to be acquired for a new highway, park or other public improvement.)
- Retrieve groupings of properties for comparative valuation.
- Make statistical projections of future tax revenues.
- Identify market trends in properties of different types, such as two-story houses, three-bedroom bungalows, etc.

Typically, the information stored in the data bank will be the same as that previously available in physical records, but it will be more accurate, more up-to-date, and much more easily accessible.

Chapter 4

LAW ENFORCEMENT INFORMATION SYSTEMS

> "When bad men combine, the good must associate
> else they will fall one by one an unpitied sacrifice
> in a contemptible struggle."
>
> —Edmund Burke, *Thoughts on the Causes of
> the Present Discontents*, April 23, 1770

Law enforcement information systems are found on the international, national, regional (that is, state or provincial), and municipal (county, township, city or village) levels.

If a rationale for the existence of such systems is needed at all, it is simply stated. Few crimes occur in a vacuum; fewer still would be solved by the police investigator isolated from information—and none would be prevented.

It is the goal of law enforcement information systems not only to make pertinent information easily and quickly available to the law enforcement officer involved in day-to-day operations, but also to provide the crime statistics and information essential to effective police planning and crime prevention.

INTERNATIONAL POLICE SYSTEMS

On the international level, storage and retrieval of police information is made possible by the International Criminal Police Organization, better known by its cable address: Interpol.

Although its supreme authority, the General Assembly, meets annually in a different capital city, Interpol's headquarters is really its General Secretariat, located in Paris and staffed by officers of the French police. The Forgery and Counterfeits section is located in The Hague.

Interpol's principal functions are the recording, analysis, and dissemination of information contributed by the police of member nations. Its interests cover three main categories: criminals who operate in more than one country; criminals who remain in one country, but whose crimes affect other countries; and criminals who commit a crime in one country, then flee to another to escape the consequences of their action.

Interpol's criminal records office contains information regarding the identities, aliases (also known as AKA), associates, and methods of working (modus operandi, or MO) of international criminals. This information is sent to the police of interested member countries by radio or confidential circular.

Interpol issues five types of confidential circulars (notices):

1) A request that a particular criminal be detained for extradition (red or *wanted*).
2) Information regarding the MO of a criminal who may currently be staying in a particular country (green or *warning*).
3) Information regarding a missing person or one under suspicion (blue or *suspicion*).
4) Descriptions of unidentified bodies (*black*).
5) Information regarding stolen property (especially jewelry or works of art) believed to have been smuggled out of the country in which the crime was committed.

The police of each member country (there are presently 114) communicate with Interpol through a local clearinghouse known as the National Central Bureau (NCB). The NCB for the United Kingdom is Metropolitan Police headquarters, London. For the United States it is the Treasury Department, Washington. For Canada it is Royal Canadian Mounted Police (RCMP) headquarters in Ottawa.

The Secretary General of Interpol, J. Nepote, adds this commentary: "In each country, a police department, usually the headquarters of the national criminal police, is appointed by the government to handle all criminal cases with international ramifications within the framework of the organization. This department—or Interpol National Central Bureau—is, at the national level, a coordinating and centralizing body for dealing with international police matters.

"There is, at the General Secretariat, a Records Department, the task of which is to collect and classify as much information as possible about international criminals and offenses. The question of using an international computer at the Secretariat to process criminal data is still only at the exploratory stage, although at the national level some countries are using computers to deal with both management and records problems.

"Fifty-one National Central Bureaus are connected to the Interpol radio network. The national stations are grouped according to geographical zone—there are seven zones in all and there is a regional station for each zone. The regional station is responsible for maintaining contact with all the national stations in its zone and with the Central Station at the General Secretariat."

Criminal Files

The ICPO-Interpol criminal records system essentially provides multiple access points to two main files: case files (DA or *dossier d'affaires*), and individual files (DI or *dossier individual*).

In 1970 there were 2,573 case records. They are kept in folders. Each dossier has a *synthesis* folder which contains summaries of each stage of the investigation, cross linked by DI numbers to the individual records of all persons involved. There may be several sub-folders to hold various documents connected with the case, each having a face sheet itemizing the documents it contains. There may also be a notice sub-folder holding copies of ICPO circulars regarding stolen property issued in connection with the case.

Both the DA and DI records are numbered sequentially and chronologically within the year in which they are opened. For example, the 121st case opened in 1975 would be numbered DA121/75.

In 1970 there were 19,186 individual dossiers (DI). Each has a synthesis folder whose face sheet lists the following information:
- Surname
- Given names
- Date of birth
- Place of birth
- Details of parentage
- Aliases, nicknames and diminutives

- Marital status
- Occupation
- Contacts (with their DI numbers)
- Address history
- Vehicles used
- Identification documents (passport, etc.)
- Travel history
- Summary of cases in which involved (with DA number)
- What currently wanted for
- Criminal history.

There is also a notice folder containing Interpol circulars regarding this person: wanted (red), warning (green), suspicion or missing person (blue), unidentified bodies (black). The folder has an envelope to hold the fingerprint card and photographs.

There are also 191,900 reference folders. These are created in the following circumstances:

1. To hold records of minor offenders.
2. To hold files concerning cases being handled by a few NCB's with no involvement on the part of the General Secretariat of Interpol.
3. Case files which as yet contain insufficient documentation for General Secretariat intervention.
4. Correspondence concerning several NCB's that deal with matters of general information or statistical matters.

These are sequentially and chronologically numbered without reference to year.

Group A: General Records Section

The DA and DI Files come under the general records section of Interpol, Group A. File access and control is achieved by use of indices and registers.

The *name index* affords access primarily to the individual files. It exists in two forms: the name index proper and the phonetic index. The former contains both master cards (FM for *fiche mere*) and alias cards (FA for *fiche alias*) with the following information: role if not criminal (victim, etc.); surname; given names; date and place of birth; AKA if this is a master card; VFM (*voir fiche mere*) if this is an alias card; DI number; and PM (*pour memoire*), listing numbers of other cases and individuals with whom the subject is connected.

Three kinds of persons are listed in the name index (there are 1,119,886 names):

1) Criminals: offenders, accessories, accomplices, receivers.
2) Other persons involved in crime: plaintiffs, complainants, victims, witnesses.
3) Missing persons, including adults, juveniles, and persons who have lost their memory.

The *phonetic index* is the same as the name index proper except that the name or AKA is rendered in its French phonetic spelling. (For another solution to the misspelled name problem, see the Remington Soundex code reproduced in the appendix.)

The *general special information index* affords access to the case files. It is classified under 124 headings. Numbers 1-38 concern such things as vehicles, firearms, boats, aircraft , stolen property, unidentified bodies, documents, firms and business premises, with entries filed by serial number when such exists, otherwise by date of occurrence. Headings 39-115 concern crimes and offenses, and numbers 116-124 concern special events and new offenses like marijuana farms (118).

An index card gives a description of the item or event, date, place, serial number if any, and DA number.

The registers are bound volumes in which is recorded the fact of creation of a dossier. There are registers for the case (DA), individual (DI), and reference files. There are also four kinds of secondary register:

- Daily changes to index cards;
- OV (*objets voles*), or stolen property register;
- Unidentified bodies register;
- Register of requests for information about people or cases.

Group B: Special Identification

Group B is the special identification group. It has charge of five files.
1) The *10-print fingerprint card index*, at time of inquiry containing 80,913 records.
2) The *single fingerprint file*, containing 3,570 records, especially of burglars.
3) The *photograph index*, containing 6,441 records. The photographs are classified according to the Bertillon *portrait parlé*, or likeness in words. Each photograph is classified according to three groups or ratios:
Group 1—line of forehead and nose/angle of chin,
Group 2—bridge of nose/base of nose,
Group 3—angle of antitragus (the conical projection behind the opening of the ear)/shape of lobe.

The observations that make up these ratios are recorded in the form of whole numbers assigned to classes, not measurements. Photographs are also classified according to category of offender:
- Murder, armed robbery, aggravated theft
- Ordinary theft and receiving
- Pickpockets and hotel thieves
- Fraud
- Forgery
- Drug traffic

Records are filed according to the offense category, the sum of the Bertillon numerators, and the sum of the Bertillon denominators.

4) The *descriptive or colored tab index*, containing 1,450 cards. Its purpose is to make it easy to locate a person's record when all that is known about him are items regarding his appearance and MO. There are 290 items that can be coded into colored tab patterns. If five or six particulars are recorded by witnesses—say, that an offender was a *man* who committed *armed robbery* in a *health resort, fair-haired, very tall,* and *wearing spectacles*—it would be easy to identify the offender were there a card on him in the descriptive index. The cards are linked to DI's.

5) The *punched-card index,* containing 15,934 cards. These are visual coordinate index (VCI) cards with spaces for 2,000 punches. Each card represents a characteristic; each punch location represents a DI number. In a search for a *man* of *Belgian* nationality, who committed *armed robbery* in *Chile* in *1959,* cards would be pulled entitled

1959, THEFT, ARMED ROBBERY, CHILE, BELGIAN

When the stacked cards were held up to the light, the hole where light shone through would correspond to the file number of the individual sought.

NATIONAL POLICE INFORMATION SYSTEMS

Before discussing national police information systems, it is well to note three principal points of difference between U.S. and Canadian law enforcement.

In the United States, practically every federal department has its own enforcement arm. Some have several such branches. In Canada, all federal law enforcement is the responsibility of the RCMP. This paramilitary body also polices Canada's two territories and provides police services under contract to eight of Canada's ten provinces.

In the United States the Department of Justice has the powers of enforcement, prosecution, and punishment of federal offenders. In Canada, federal Department of Justice drafts legislation and prosecutes offenders. The Solicitor-General's Department has responsibility for the RCMP, the Canadian Penitentiaries Service (CPS), and the National Parole Board (NPB).

Finally, in the U.S. there are fifty state penal codes, in addition to the U.S. Federal code. In Canada there is only one criminal code.

National Crime Information Center

The U.S. Federal Bureau of Investigation (FBI) operates the computerized National Crime Information Center (NCIC). The communications network linking NCIC to federal and state law enforcement agencies is shown in Figure 4-1.

As of August 1, 1974, there were 5,009,909 active records in NCIC, broken down as follows:

Wanted Persons	149,430
Stolen Vehicles	886,232
Stolen License Plates	288,181
Stolen Articles	966,478
Stolen Guns	748,878
Stolen Securities	1,540,930
Stolen Boats	10,104
Criminal Histories	419,670

To illustrate the volume of activity of the NCIC, on July 17, 1974, 187,037 transactions were processed, or 2.16 transactions per second over a 24-hour period. In the same month (July, 1974), NCIC network transactions totaled 4,876,286, or an average of 157,299 daily. Operating performance figures in hours for that month show

. Unrestricted operational time	703.5
. Restricted operational time	29.2
. Scheduled downtime	3.3
. Unscheduled downtime	8.0
. Hours in the month	744.0

Restricted operational time indicates NCIC was accepting only certain types of messages because of concurrent file maintenance operations. Scheduled downtime means NCIC was not operational because of preplanned testing and servicing of the equipment.

Two recent NCIC "hits" illustrate the day-to-day value of the system. In Massachusetts two state troopers stopped a motorist for a minor traffic violation. The suspect appeared to be evasive, and the officers requested a *wanted persons*

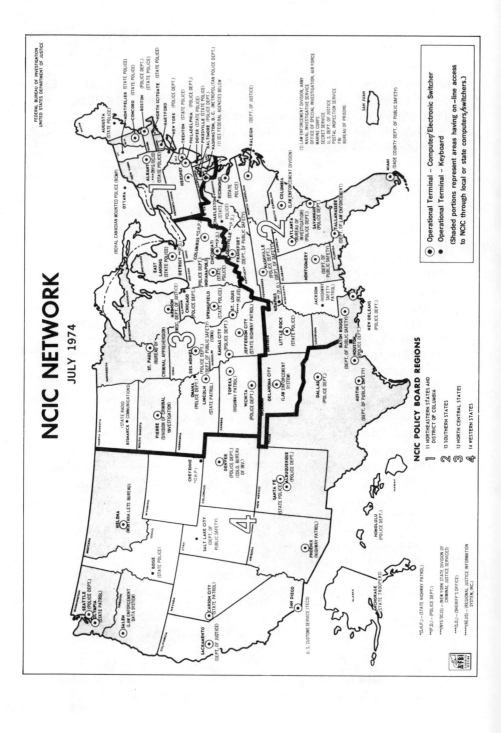

check through the Massachusetts connection to NCIC. (It is called LEAPS–Law Enforcement Agencies Processing System.) As a result, information was obtained that the suspect was wanted on a two-year-old murder warrant.

In another example, in Santa Barbara, California, a police officer observed an individual riding a 10-speed bicycle which appeared to have been recently repainted and bore no city license tag. Upon stopping the cyclist, the officer further observed that the bicycle serial number had been scratched away. The suspect was advised of the California Penal Code section pertaining to removal of serial numbers from bicycles and was arrested pursuant to that section. When the suspect furnished an out-of-state address, the officer requested a *wanted persons* check. Such a record for this suspect was found in the NCIC, placed there by a county sheriff's office of a southern state. Contact with the officer recording the information confirmed that the state would extradite the suspect on a no-bail warrant for grand larceny.

Clarence M. Kelley, Director of the Federal Bureau of Investigation, describes the National Crime Information Center as follows: "The NCIC was established as a service to the criminal justice community. Local, state and Federal law enforcement agencies enter data in and inquire of the system. The officer who has NCIC relations responsibility is usually assigned to either the identification or communications branch of the particular agency and has been designated to serve in this position by the head of the agency. Their ranks range from Commissioner, Superintendent, Director, Commanding Officer or Chief, to Lieutenant or Sergeant."

The FBI Director lists the following eight files maintained by NCIC:

1) The *vehicles file* includes unrecovered stolen vehicles, vehicles wanted in conjunction with felonies or serious misdemeanors, and vehicle parts such as unrecovered engines and transmissions which are serially numbered. The minimum information necessary for entry of a stolen vehicle is the Vehicle Identification Number (VIN) or license plate data, description of the vehicle, date stolen, the identity and case number of the agency holding the theft report. Other points of identifying information which can be handled in the system and which are considered useful are the model, style, color and year of the vehicle. Inquiries are based upon VIN or license plate data.

2) The *license plate file* includes unrecovered stolen/missing license plates provided all plates issued are missing. Minimum information necessary is the license plate data, date stolen, and the identity and case number of the

agency holding the theft report. Inquiries are based upon license plate data.

3) The *gun file* includes serially numbered guns stolen or lost. A weapon which has been recovered with ownership undetermined may be entered as a "recovered" weapon. All stolen gun entries must contain serial number, make, caliber, type, date of theft and the identity and case number of the agency holding the theft report. Inquiries are based upon the serial number of the gun.

4) The *article file* contains data concerning serially numbered stolen property, including power tools and appliances. Minimum information necessary is the serial number, type article, brand name, date stolen, and the identity and case number of the agency holding the theft report. Other important data handled in the system is the model of the article. Inquiries are based upon the serial number.

5) The *wanted person file* includes data concerning individuals for whom Federal warrants are outstanding or for whom a warrant has been issued by a jurisdiction for a felony or serious misdemeanor. The offense must be an extraditable one. All wanted person entries must contain the name and descriptive data relating to the individual and at least one numerical identifier such as date of birth, type of offense, date of the warrant, and the identity and case number of the agency holding the warrant. Other important information handled in the system includes data such as place of birth, height, weight, complexion, scars, marks and tattoos, NCIC fingerprint classification, aliases, and description of any vehicle known to be in possession of the wanted person. Inquiries may be based upon the individual's name and at least one numerical identifier associated with the subject.

6) The *securities file* contains serially numbered securities, including stocks and bonds and travelers checks and money orders, which have been stolen, embezzled or counterfeited. Personal notes or personal checks do not qualify for entry in the NCIC files. All entries must contain type of security, serial number, denomination, issuer, owner, date of theft, and the identity and case number of the agency holding the theft report. Other important data handled in the system are the security date and issuer of the security. Inquiries are based on type, denomination, serial number, and name of owner printed on the security, if available.

7) The *boat file* contains information concerning unrecovered stolen boats valued at $500 or more which have a permanent identifying serial number

affixed. All boat entries must contain the registration/document data, hull serial number, identity of the boat manufacturer, and the identity and case number of the agency holding the theft report. Other important data handled in the system includes description of outer hull material, type propulsion, overall length and color of the boat. Inquiries may be made using registration/document data or the hull serial number.

8) The *computerized Criminal History (CCH) file* contains arrest, court, and custody/supervision data relating to individuals arrested for serious crimes. Entries must contain descriptive data concerning the individual and must be based upon fingerprint identification. Inquiry arguments for the CCH file closely parallel those of the Wanted Person file.

All of the above files records are subject to entry, modification, and deletion functions, as well as inquiries. Positive responses to the first seven file groups average 1200 per day.

NCIC does not have an intelligence file nor does it store data relating to jewelry or garments.

SEARCH

An organization called SEARCH (System for Electronic Analysis and Retrieval of Criminal Histories) suggests some new directions in law enforcement information systems. SEARCH came into being in 1969 as a project funded by the Law Enforcement Assistance Administration (LEAA). It was envisaged as a multistate effort designed to create a prototype computerized criminal justice information system for the exchange of criminal histories among different jurisdictions and to develop a prototype statistical program based on data drawn from individuals proceeding through the criminal justice system. More recently, in 1974, SEARCH was incorporated in California as a non-profit corporation known as Search Group, Inc., with headquarters in Sacramento.

In the words of FBI Director Kelley, "The stated mission of the new Group is (1) to develop and test technological advances which may have multistate utilization, (2) to assist LEAA in implementing programs, (3) to establish liaison between LEAA and the governors, and (4) to create a pool of expertise to assist state and Federal government agencies in the criminal justice area."

In 1972 Project SEARCH conducted a successful experiment in which fingerprints were transmitted from coast to coast by a communications satellite, demonstrating the utility of satellite communications for criminal justice needs.

Another glimpse into the future impact of new technology on the exchange of criminal justice information was offered by Donald E. Santarelli, then Administrator of the LEAA, in a speech on May 2, 1974, at the Project SEARCH International Symposium on Criminal Justice Information and Statistics Systems. Mr. Santarelli proposed that Congress create a private, nonprofit corporation he dubbed the "Comsat of Criminal Justice" to administer and operate a national criminal justice telecommunications system to transmit data over long distances by satellite.

Perhaps anticipating fears over the potential concentration of power in centralized criminal information systems, Mr. Santarelli emphasized the desirability of placing the operation of the satellite and attendant support systems in the hands of the states and localities, with the Federal government represented but not in a dominant role. In an argument that applies to NCIC as well as to the proposed telecommunications satellite, he pointed out that "The overwhelming majority of criminal justice data resides at the local level. The great bulk of law enforcement communications today—and tomorrow—are and will be local, state to state, and between locals and states."

Canadian Police Information Center

The Royal Canadian Mounted Police has the responsibility for policing 23 percent of Canada, on a population basis. It divides its files into administrative and operational files, the latter dealing with criminal matters and with security and intelligence (S&I).

Its criminal record file is derived from the Fingerprint Section (FPS) of the Identification Branch. In its manual form the file contains one million records. Each consists of a fingerprint card, submitted on persons charged with an indictable offense (felony), cross linked to photographs, if submitted, and a charge sheet. The charge sheet carries the date and place of each conviction, charges and disposition, and name and rank of the officer contributing the information.

Records of pardoned criminals are held in escrow and not released to anyone. Records are not made in the case of summary convictions (misdemeanors) or juvenile convictions.

The governing principle is whether or not a subject's fingerprints are taken. (Fingerprints taken by the military or for civil reasons are excepted; these do not become part of any operational file.) Should a subject's conviction be subsequently overturned, his record will be expunged if he requests return of his fingerprints. In other cases records are kept until a criminal dies, a fact that must be confirmed by fingerprints submitted by a police agency.

The Canadian Police Information Center (CPIC) began operations in 1972. It employs 300 persons, mostly sworn civilian members of the Force. The CPIC computer is linked by common carrier lines (telecommunications of Canadian National/Canadian Pacific Communications) with the ten RCMP headquarters in each province. Minicomputers used to concentrate messages are installed at Vancouver, Edmonton, Regina, Winnipeg, Toronto, Montreal and Halifax.

All terminals can both send and receive data. Users are potentially able to gain access to all system files through their terminals. Data contributed to the system is accumulated on magnetic tape and validated against the system before being filed. Criminal record information, however, is an exception. This information is controlled by ident only, inasmuch as criminal record information must be accompanied by a fingerprint card.

The system communicates with 250 police forces. These are Police Act forces only—municipal or provincial police, and the RCMP. Since Canada has two national languages, CPIC files are supplied in either English or French.

An advisory committee determines policy with respect to rights of access, confidentiality and security. This is a cooperative police network and each member determines the allocation of terminals within its command.

The system contains entries concerning:

1) Outstanding warrants (wanted persons)
2) Stolen motor vehicles, license plates, boats, aircraft, etc.
3) Stolen property, especially firearms and stock certificates.

There are three basic kinds of warrants: warrant of arrest, bench warrant (issued because of non-appearance in court), and warrant of committal (issued because of non-payment of a fine). Warrants of arrest can be general or local; the latter are issued when an agency doesn't want to spend the money to bring a culprit back from a distant point. Warrants entered on CPIC must be revalidated by the supplying agency every thirty days.

Member police agencies are allowed to bank data with CPIC for their exclusive use. This privilege is exercised in the case of summary offense matters and local warrants. It is planned to extend CPIC by computerizing the S&I files.

In 1971 Assistant Commissioner A.C. Potter, Director of CPIC, provided additional insight into the Center's policies and activities.

Q. What records information can a member police force get from CPIC?

A. Member police forces may ask information regarding the record of a single individual at a time. They can't ask for an entire category.

Q. What is the level of access at the various terminals?

A. Right now the conversation has been that all terminals are equal in respect of the amount of access one can gain from the field. I should imagine some 400-plus terminals placed on line.

Q. What is your protection against wiretapping?

A. Communications lines leased from the common carrier are private dedicated lines. No additional safeguards are being proposed at this time to protect against wiretapping. Investigation in this regard, however, is continuing.

Q. What safeguards are there against introduction of spurious terminals?

A. The computer will recognize only legitimate terminals. Unauthorized terminals being introduced into the network would immediately be detected.

Q. Are there any restrictions on terminal users creating ad hoc files of teleprinter outputs?

A. Under the present manual system, police forces throughout Canada maintain their own comprehensive record systems. With the implementation of CPIC, the reverse to the question raised undoubtedly will occur. There will be no reason to build up local filing systems as it will be more expedient and advantageous to utilize the CPIC data bank.

Q. Will all your one million criminal records eventually be put on CPIC?

A. The present file of individuals with criminal records has accumulated during the past sixty years. No decision has been taken as to how many of these records will be computerized.

New Scotland Yard

Central files maintained by New Scotland Yard in Great Britain include individual case records, the Nominal Index, Wanted/Missing Persons Index, and Criminal Record Office File.

Individual Records

Individual records are kept in respect of all persons who are convicted of crime. There are currently some 3-1/4 million such records, of which nearly 2 million are held on microfilm.

Nominal Index

The Nominal Index, which includes aliases, currently totals about 4 million names. This index is at present being converted to computer working and is scheduled to be completed (including reconciliation) by about the end of 1975.

The information shown on the nominal index slip is that which will enable a searcher to identify a person, viz., name, date of birth, place of birth, height, deformities, abnormalities, marks and scars, date and place of first conviction, *modus operandi* if recorded, and CRO number, but no details of the criminal record, which is located on the Criminal Record Office file and is only supplied on request, after search and identification.

Wanted/Missing Persons Index

Preparation work is already being undertaken in connection with the computerization of New Scotland Yard's Wanted/Missing Persons Index, which consists of approximately 80,000 persons. It is also proposed to build into the computer an index of disqualified drivers and persons who are given suspended sentences. It is also the intention to process stolen checks.

Criminal Record Office File (CRO)

A Criminal Record Office file contains a *descriptive form* which includes full personal description—aliases, deformities, peculiarities, marks, scars, etc.—details of convictions, sentences, *modus operandi*, etc., name in which convicted, and the latest available photograph. It also contains an *antecedent history sheet* which, in addition to the subject's personal background—date and place of birth, schooling, employments and domestic circumstances—will show details of any absconding from detention, removals to hospitals and changes of circumstances of detainees. In addition there is a *result form* for each of the convictions on the descriptive form, with list of cases taken into consideration when the subject was convicted, if applicable.

Information from a CRO file is available to police upon request, either by allowing officers to have sight of the file or sending them the comprehensive descriptive form.

STATE POLICE INFORMATION SYSTEMS

The New York State Information and Intelligence System (NYSIIS) is probably one of the most extensive computerized regional systems, and as such provides a useful profile of such a system. Potentially capable of containing over seven million records and servicing 3,600 terminals, NYSIIS is larger than many national police information systems.

The system contains manual as well as computer records. Graphical and narrative material is held in manual form.

Effective September 1, 1972, NYSIIS was absorbed into the newly created

New York State Division of Criminal Justice Services. DCJS is responsible for the maintenance and operation of the following files, which, to a major extent, are now fully computerized:
1) Fingerprint files
2) Name files
3) Summary case history files (rap sheets)
4) Wanted and missing persons files.

Fingerprint File

The fingerprints of approximately 4.3 million records are now contained in this file. These include both criminal and non-criminal records. In the latter category would be the fingerprints of applicants for positions or licenses for which fingerprinting is required by law.

Although the part of the master fingerprint file containing cards of persons born prior to 1903 is still searched manually, the remainder of the master file is searched by computer. DCJS statistics indicate that approximately 80 percent of all searching activity is now against the computerized portion of the file.

Approximately 500,000 sets of fingerprints per year are received by law from police agencies, penal institutions and governmental agencies involved in employment or licensing activities. No fingerprints are received by DCJS from non-governmental agencies, nor is information furnished from the files to such agencies. Approximately 50 percent of all incoming fingerprint cards are identified with a prior card on file.

Approximately 220,000 arrest fingerprint cards are received each year in DCJS over a Statewide Facsimile Network, making it possible to classify and search such fingerprints and transmit any prior criminal record information back to the arresting agency by facsimile within a matter of hours. This rapid response program is deemed to have definite advantages in assisting the courts in procedures involving bail and temporary release.

Name File

The name files now contain approximately 5.7 million name and alias cards pertaining to individuals for whom there is on file one or more sets of fingerprints.

Computerization of the manual name files was started some years ago, and at the present time the computerized file contains around 1.5 million names. It is anticipated that this computerized file will expand rapidly, since all names on incoming identification inquiries that are not already part of the file are being added on a daily basis.

Name searches are conducted by DCJS personnel only for authorized governmental agencies. Total name searches now approximate one million annually.

Summary Case History File

These computerized files contain a chronological listing of the arrest and incarceration fingerprints that are on file. Copies of the computerized Summary Case Histories are forwarded to authorized governmental agencies who submit fingerprint cards to DCJS. In addition to the chronological listing of fingerprint cards, the Summary Case History also includes identifying information such as name, date of birth, FBI number, etc.

Wanted and Missing Persons File

This is a totally computerized file which at the time of writing contained information on approximately 24,000 persons. This information is received from authorized governmental agencies (primarily police agencies) and includes name, sex, year of birth, plus data as to the crime for which wanted, etc. The validity and currency of the file are checked periodically throughout the year to confirm wanted or missing status.

Inquiries (challenges) may be made on-line against the file through the Statewide Police Teletype Network. It was estimated by DCJS that approximately 780,000 such inquiries would be made during 1973. No official statistics are available concerning the actual number of valid "hits" made against the Wanted/Missing Persons File. It is impossible in many instances to determine the eventual outcome in those cases where the file indicates that a tentative identification has been made in response to a particular challenge. It is estimated, however, that the actual number of valid hits during the course of a year comes to approximately 5,000.

MUNICIPAL SYSTEMS

The great bulk of police work is done at the local level. It follows that the greatest concentration of records is generated in local and municipal police and sheriff's department information systems, with wide variances in the content and handling of such records. They may vary from the single file cabinet in a township police or sheriff's station to the vast computerized or semi-automated records systems in major cities like Los Angeles, New York or Toronto.

It should be remembered that much law enforcement activity is generated by events and people other than known crimes or criminals sought under wants or warrants. Law enforcement officers responding to *any* situation can result in some form of police action, whether the initiating event is a vehicle check, a minor traffic violation or the commission of a felony, with a resultant inquiry against existing files or the creation of a new record.

Common Files

The heart of any police records system, large or small, is the *master card index*, often called a name index. This is usually a card index, alphabetically arranged by subject names, listing all people contacted by police in day-to-day operations, including suspect, victim and witnesses involved in any report of a crime, but also including missing persons, traffic violators, people with gun permits, and locally licensed individuals.

A file card in a name index should include:
• Name of subject
• Date of birth
• Physical description
• Reason for contact
• Offense or circumstance
• Case number
• Charge or booking number if subject is arrested.

Other commonly held files in municipal police systems may include (1) accident and incident report files, (2) identification and criminal history files, (3) arrest files, and (4) recovered or stolen vehicle files.

A Large Metropolitan Records System

An approach to the common elements in police records systems was observed in studying the system employed in a major city of over two million population. This records system, only partially automated, includes a Central Index and a Complainant and Victim File.

CENTRAL INDEX. The key element in accessing the police records of this system is the Central Index. It consists of one million 3x5 cards housed in eight manually operated elevator tub files. It is sequenced alphabetically by subject name. Each entry consists of name, address, color-coded file reference, and a brief personal description. Entries are made on the basis of phone calls from district commands and later substantiated by comparison with the official report.

The following kinds of entries are found in the Central Index:
1) Wanted persons
2) Missing persons
3) Persons having criminal records (felonies)
4) Persons having summary conviction records (misdemeanors)
5) Operator's license suspensions
6) Interdicted persons (those prohibited from buying liquor)
7) Persons on probation
8) Parolees
9) Juvenile contacts
10) Arrest reports

When, in the course of an investigation of an occurrence, a warrant is issued for a suspect, a warrant card goes into the Index. When the suspect is apprehended, the warrant card is pulled and an arrest card entered. If the suspect is not convicted, the arrest card stays in the index for a year; at that time it is removed, held in a vault for another year, and subsequently destroyed. If the suspect is convicted, the arrest card comes out and either a summary or criminal card goes in, keyed to his record, which is held in another file.

Follow-up cards are also inserted after conviction. If the subject is placed on probation, a probation card goes into the file and remains there during the period of probation. If he is confined and subsequently paroled, a parole card will then go into the Index and remain there during the period of parole. Should he escape from custody, another warrant card would be filed. If he is eventually pardoned for his offense, his record would be expunged and the criminal card removed from the Central Index.

COMPLAINANT AND VICTIM FILE. This file constitutes an index to occurrence reports. It contains 200,000 tabs, each 3x1-1/4 inches. They are color coded to denote the kind of occurrence and filed alphabetically by the last name of the complainant and the victim.

Ten kinds of occurrence reports are used:
1) General occurrence report, used in cases of crime and mental illness; specifically crimes of assault, robbery, burglary and larceny.
2) Supplementary reports on occurrences already reported.
3) Fraudulent check offenses.
4) Bicycle and tricycle occurrences.
5) Motor vehicle occurrences.
6) Impounded or held vehicle reports.
7) Missing persons reports.

8) Lost and found reports.

9) Homicide or sudden death reports.

10) Records of arrest.

Accident reports are filed by a mira-coding system which affords access by names of persons involved, victims, and the location and date of the accident.

THE CRIMINAL JUSTICE PROCESS

Although there are minor differences among the states of the United States, as well as with other countries, the criminal justice process is similar for all jurisdictions whose legal systems are derived from the English common law. It is beyond the scope of this book to examine in detail the complete criminal justice process. However, it should be noted that each step produces its own family of records. As the U.S. Department of Commerce observed in a 1970 study of the compilation and use of criminal court data, "There is no single dossier to tell the whole story of a defendant's passage through the Criminal Justice System; different kinds of data reside in different buildings, generated and controlled by different administrators. The whole story then is an amalgam of these various parts, and . . . each treats the defendant from its own point of view alone. . . ."[3]

These steps include:

1) *Arrest*, with or without a warrant.

2) *Preliminary hearing* before the nearest judge or magistrate, unless waived; may result in the accused being discharged for lack of evidence or bound over for trial.

3) *Coroner's inquest*, in the case of homicide or unexplained death; the coroner's report is an advisory finding.

4) *Grand Jury* proceedings, which may result in an indictment (or True Bill) or a finding of No Bill; in some jurisdictions lesser offenses, particularly misdemeanors, may be prosecuted on the basis of an "Information," filed by the prosecuting attorney on the basis of a police investigation without a Grand Jury indictment.

5) *Arraignment*, at which charges are read and a *Plea* entered.

6) *Trial, Sentencing,* and *Appeals.*

7) *Probation*, where a convicted person is released under supervision for a prescribed period, rather than being sentenced to an institution. Probation records thus come into being.

8) *Confinement*, which results in the creation of prison records.

9) *Parole,* where the convicted person is released under supervision prior to the completion of his sentence, for the unexpired period or some other

prescribed term. Parole records are kept by the assigned Parole Officer and the Parole Board.

ELEMENTS OF PERSONAL IDENTIFICATION

The principal point of identification for an individual is the person's name and identity numbers. A system proposed by Technical Committee (TC) 97 of the International Standards Organization (ISO) is described in an Appendix. It is called the Standard Identifier for Individuals (SII). Also described are the identity numbers in use in the U.S., Canada, France, Sweden and Denmark. Record-keeping organizations customarily issue their own file numbers as well.

Other names are also important; for example, maiden names of women and names used during former marriages. Nicknames are commonplace, and an alias or AKA does not always signify an intent to deceive. Some persons may be known by more than one name; American Indians, for instance, often have both anglicized and tribal names.

Other commonly used elements of identification include *vital data,* such as date of birth (DOB), place of birth (POB), date of death, and agency reporting it, and citizenship, including date and place of naturalization. Technical Committee 97 of the ISO has proposed a standard numeric form of reporting dates. There is also a standard numeric code for reporting named places in the United States. These systems are set forth in the Appendix.

Residence history for identification purposes should include the location, date and method of acquisition, other occupants, telephone number, and periods used (summer, winter, weekends, etc.) for all residences currently used by the subject. For prior residences it is necessary only to note date moved in, date moved out, and location.

Identification by Physical Description

There are twenty commonly used points of personal physical description.

1) *Ethnic data* includes race, apparent national origin, and ethnic group.
2) *Sex:* The Japanese TC-97 has suggested six classifications: 0, unknown; 1, male; 2, female; 3, transexual; 4, bisexual; 5, asexual.
3) *Height* may be divided into four categories:
   - Less than 5 ft.
   - 5 ft. to 5 ft. 6 inches
   - 5 ft. 6 inches to 5 ft. 10 inches
   - over 5 ft. 10 inches

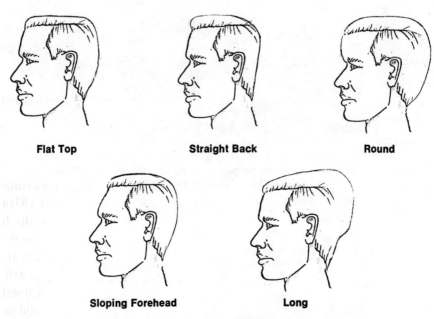

Flat Top   Straight Back   Round

Sloping Forehead   Long

Figure 4-2.   **Common Head Shapes**

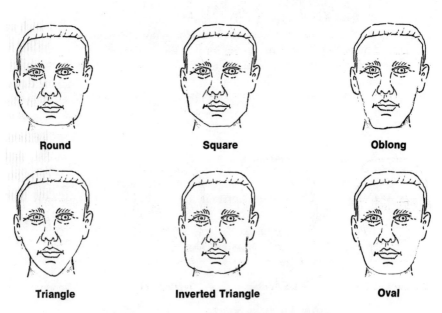

Round   Square   Oblong

Triangle   Inverted Triangle   Oval

Figure 4-3.   **Common Face Shapes**

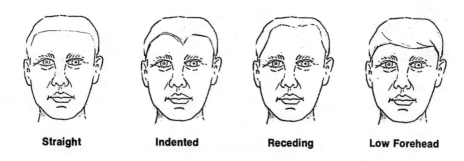

Figure 4-4.   Common Hairlines

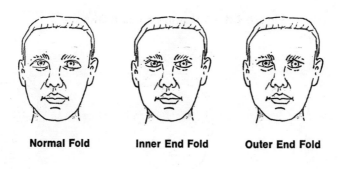

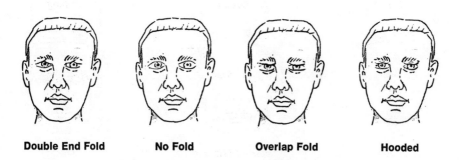

Figure 4-5.   Common Types of Eyelid

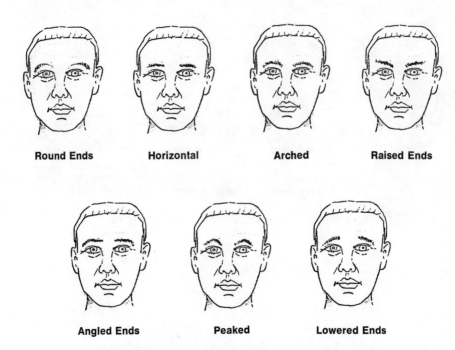

Figure 4-6.   Common Types of Eyebrow

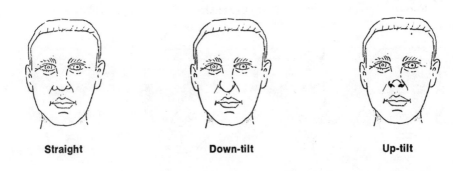

Figure 4-7.   Common Types of Nose (Full-face)

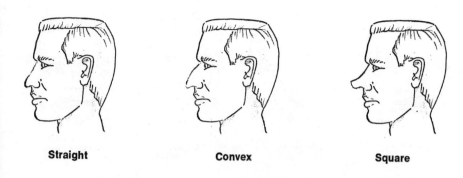

Straight   **Convex**   **Square**

Figure 4-8.   Common Types of Nose (Profile)

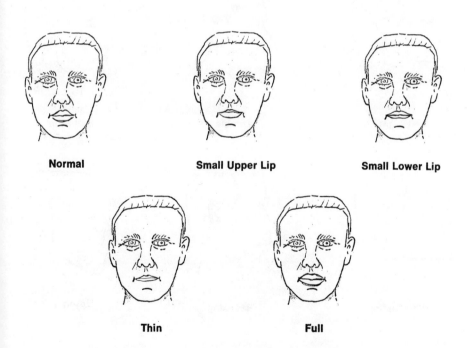

Normal   **Small Upper Lip**   **Small Lower Lip**

Thin   **Full**

Figure 4-9.   Common Types of Lips

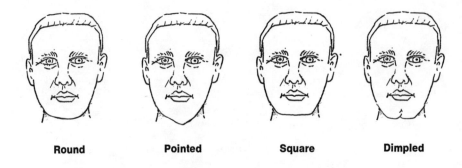

| Round | Pointed | Square | Dimpled |

Figure 4-10. Common Types of Chin (Full-face)

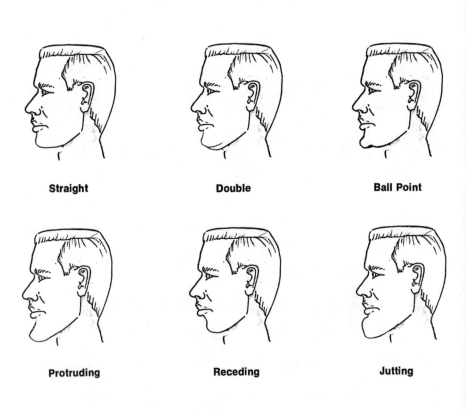

| Straight | Double | Ball Point |

| Protruding | Receding | Jutting |

Figure 4-11. Common Types of Chin (Profile)

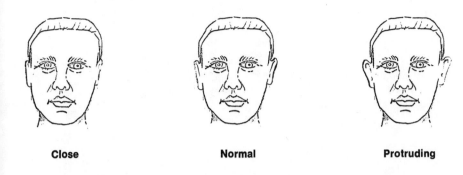

Close   Normal   Protruding

Figure 4-12.   Common Types of Ears (Full-face)

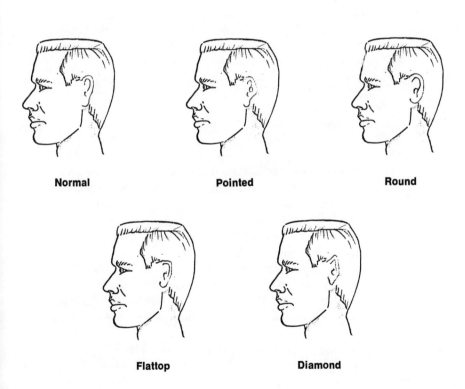

Normal   Pointed   Round

Flattop   Diamond

Figure 4-13.   Common Types of Ears (Profile)

4) *Weight* may also be divided into four categories:
- Less than 100 lbs.
- 100 to 140 lbs.
- 141 to 180 lbs.
- Over 180 lbs.

5) *Build*—heavy, medium or light.

6) *Head Shape:* Five common head shapes in profile are illustrated in Figure 4–2.

7) *Face Shape:* Six common face shapes in full-face are shown in Figure 4–3. Also note if the face is deformed or distorted.

8) *Complexion:* Note both color (albino, light-fair, ruddy, sallow, dark-swarthy, light black, chocolate brown, black) and texture.

9) *Hair:* There are five points of identification:
- Color: blond, red, brown, black, partially gray, gray, dyed.
- Texture: fine, straight or wavy, coarse, kinky.
- Style: bald, partially bald, short, long, toupee.
- Dressing: well-dressed, unkempt, bushy.
- Hairline: four common types are illustrated in Figure 4–4.

10) *Facial Hair:* points of identification include mustaches, beards (including type) and sideburns.

11) *Eyes* have six common points of identification:
- Color: blue, gray, green, hazel, brown, black.
- Type: normal, deep-set, bulging, crossed.
- Defects commonly affecting both eyes, such as squinting, blinking, bloodshot, glasses worn occasionally or continually, noticeably nearsighted, blind.
- Defects commonly affecting one eye, such as cast, granuloma, missing eye, patch, artificial, closed.
- Eyelids: Seven common types are illustrated in full-face view in Figure 4–5. Also note bags or crow's feet under eyes.

12) *Eyebrows* may be trimmed, bushy, continuous, plucked or shaven, or of a particular shape. Seven common types are illustrated in full-face view in Figure 4–6.

13) *Nose:* Three common types are illustrated in full-face view in Figure 4–7; three types are shown in profile in Figure 4-8. Note also if the nose has been broken.

14) *Mouth:* There are three points of identification:
- Lips: Five common types are shown in Figure 4–9. Note also if the subject has a harelip.

- Shape of teeth (protruding, spaced, broken, etc.)
- Condition of teeth, including stained, good, false, missing or visible gold, etc. (Note that a dental chart may be the only key to identifying a badly burned or decomposed body.)

15) *Chin:* Four common types are shown full-face in Figure 4-10; six common types are illustrated in profile in Figure 4-11.

16) *Ears* may be large or small, scarred, cauliflower or amputated. Note whether earlobes are present, naturally missing or amputated. Note whether subject is hard of hearing in one or both ears, and whether or not he uses a hearing aid. Three common types of ears are shown in full-face view in Figure 4-12; five common types are shown in profile in Figure 4-13.

17) *Scars,* birth marks, pockmarks, needle tracks, warts, moles, tattoos, partial paralysis or immobility, amputations, naturally foreshortened or withered members, all provide distinctive identification. Figure 4-14 provides an atlas for the location of scars, marks and amputations. In the case of amputation or foreshortening, note whether or not the loss is compensated by a prosthesis, built-up shoe, etc.

18) *Deformities* include such as round or sloping shoulders, right or left shoulder low, slack abdomen, lordosis back, chicken breast, hunchback, use of cane or crutch.

19) *Common blood types* are O, A, B or AB. These are additionally differentiated by the Rhesus factor: positive (+) or negative (-). The Japanese TC-97 committee of ISO has been tasked with developing a uniform system for reporting blood types but has as yet reported no success.

20) *Physical defects* that may require periodic visits to a hospital clinic or medical practitioner include diabetes, epilepsy, cardiac problems, asthma, renal dialysis, methadone maintenance.

Identification by Behavior

There are ten behavioral characteristics commonly used as an aid in identifying a subject:

- *Speech patterns,* including quality (soft, gruff, effeminate, etc.), national or regional accent, speech defects such as a lisp or stuttering, muteness, speed and characteristic pitch.
- *Walk,* including characteristic gait or limp.
- *Handedness:* left, right or ambidextrous.
- *Habits,* such as nailbiting, biting the lip or mouth, gum chewing, body or

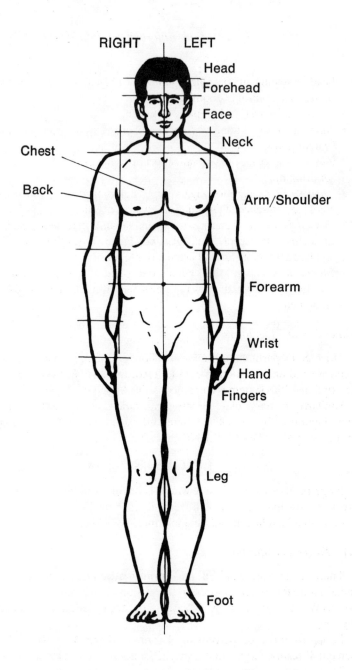

Figure 4-14. Location of Scars and Marks

head scratching, uncontrolled flatulence or belching, finger drumming, hair or mustache twisting, doodling, etc.

- *Nervous disorders,* such as palsy or twitch.
- *Narcotics use,* including whether lawful or unlawful, drugs used and history of treatments.
- *Alcohol use,* including amount, effect on behavior, customary social setting for drinking.
- *Tobacco use:* cigarettes, cigars, pipe including distinctive brands; chain smoking; presence of tar stains on fingers or teeth.
- *Sexual behavior:* heterosexual, homosexual, bisexual, juvenile, sado-masochism. Preferences may also indicate the type of premises the subject will frequent. Note level of activity (high, normal, low).
- *Mental disorders:* hospital or clinic, date of admission, patient identification number, tentative diagnosis, type of treatment, date of discharge or elopement.

Other Personal Identifiers

The U.S. Department of Labor's Dictionary of Occupational Titles provides a concise and unambiguous means for recording a subject's *occupation.* A brief description of this system is contained in the Appendix.

Similarly, the name of a business organization can be specified concisely and unambiguously by use of the Standard Identifier for Organizations (SIO) proposed by ISO/TC-97. (See Appendix.)

FINGERPRINTS

Fingerprints are the only sure way to confirm the identity of a subject. There are two principal aspects of fingerprint identification: classification by the patterns of all ten fingers; and single print classification.

Ten-Finger Classification

There are five principal full fingerprint patterns: arch (A), tented arch (T), radial loop (R)—points to thumb, ulnar loop (U)—points to little finger, and whorl (W). (See Figure 4–15.) In cases of double loops, look only at the ascending loop.

Loops comprise 65 percent of all prints, whorls 30 percent, all others 5 percent. Racially, Latins run to whorls, Scandinavians and Eskimos to arches.

There are 1,024 *primary* Henry classifications. They are derived by coding each hand according to location of each whorl pattern, summing the result and adding one:

little finger, 16
ring finger, 8
middle finger, 4
index finger, 2
thumb, 1

The *primary* classification is shown as a fraction: right hand code number over left hand code number. The primary classification for no whorls is 1/1; for ten whorls it is 32/32.

The *secondary* Henry classification subdivides fingerprint patterns into more than one million classes. It is obtained by coding the patterns of the two index fingers using only the capital letters—A, T, R and U: and by coding the patterns of the remaining fingers using only the small letters—a, t and r.

A set of prints having all ulnar loops (the single most common class) would have the primary and secondary classifications 1U/1U. A set of prints having ulnar loops on both index fingers and arches on all other fingers would have the classification 1aU3a/1aU3a.

Further subclassification within the primary and secondary groups may be made by counting the number of ridges from the core to the nearest delta (see Figure 4–15) or by measuring the core-delta distance.

The perpendicular distance from the core to the crease (first metacarpus) can also be used for classification, as can the crease length (the unobstructed length of a line tangent to the top of the crease), and the angle between the core-delta line and the core-crease line.

A computer-assisted system for classifying fingerprints and searching files has been under extensive evaluation and testing at the FBI Identification Division. The system is called FINDER. It was planned to compile a pilot fingerprint data base by the end of 1973.

The New York State DCJS is currently transmitting fingerprints for analysis by facsimile. It uses twenty-six facsimile stations, of which five are in New York City.

Single Fingerprint Classification

Classifying single fingerprints affords the opportunity to make identification of suspects from latent prints lifted at the scene of a crime. It can also substitute for identification cards, passwords and keys as a personnel access control measure. Such a system is used by the Federal Reserve Bank of New York to control access to its transaction computer bank.

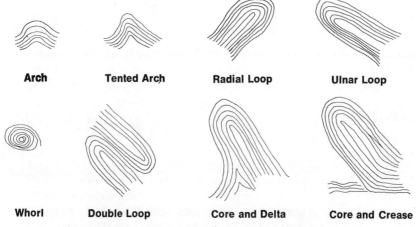

Arch   Tented Arch   Radial Loop   Ulnar Loop

Whorl   Double Loop   Core and Delta   Core and Crease

Figure 4-15. Fingerprint Classification Patterns

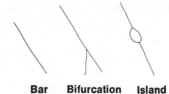

Bar   Bifurcation   Island

Figure 4-16. Single Print Characteristics

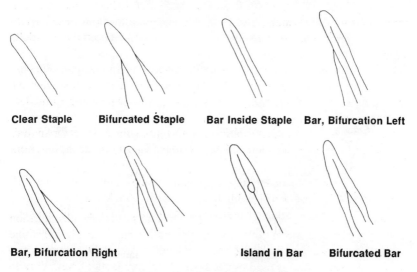

Clear Staple   Bifurcated Staple   Bar Inside Staple   Bar, Bifurcation Left

Bar, Bifurcation Right   Island in Bar   Bifurcated Bar

Figure 4-17. Common Core Loops

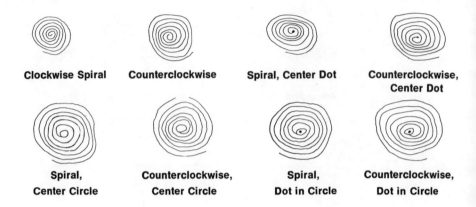

Figure 4-18.   Common Core Whorls

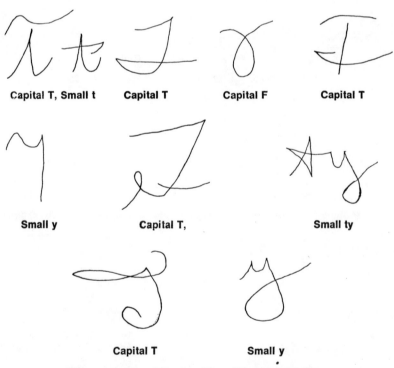

Figure 4-19.   Handwriting Characteristics

Police departments are building up single fingerprint files on certain types of criminals, especially auto thieves and break-and-enter men. Single fingerprint classification in connection with loops and whorls are by far the most numerous classes.

Loops: A staple is a recurring ridge; a loop pattern is made up of several concentric staples. The area enclosed by the innermost staple is called a *core.* Cores and staples may be distinguished by *characteristics* or minutia. Three kinds of characteristic—bars, bifurcations, and islands—are illustrated in Figure 4-16.

The coding for a loop pattern is given by recording the type of core and the type of the two innermost staples. Eight loop core types (A to H) are shown in Figure 4-17. A mutilated fingertip is classified as an L core.

Whorls: A whorl is a spiral and is classified according to whether it is clockwise or counter-clockwise. Core characteristics include (a) dots, (b) circles, (c) dots within circles, and (d) nothing. Eight whorl core types are shown in Figure 4-18.

HANDWRITING

There are twelve characteristics to look for in a subject's handwriting that are useful for identification purposes:
- Skill and ability.
- Odd, that is, non-Palmer systems.
- Line quality: shaky, angular or smooth.
- Pen pressure.
- Pickup stroke on letters.
- Connecting strokes between letters: smooth, angled or broken.
- Ending strokes on letters: blunt, horizontal or sweeping upward curve.
- Embellishments: the beginning strokes of capitals, finish strokes on "y" and finish strokes of words.
- Sweeping curved strokes or angles.
- Spacing between letters, wide or close.
- Alignment: height of letter above the base writing line.
- Proportion: for example, a tail on the "y".

The capital and small "t", the capital "F", and the small "y" frequently exhibit distinctive handwriting characteristics. The phrase "Twenty-Five Dollars" written several times according to the subject's habituation can be useful for comparison.

Figure 4-19 illustrates eight common handwriting characteristics.

IDENTIFICATION OF PROPERTY

Property identification is concerned mainly with motor vehicles, firearms, bicycles, jewelry, tools and appliances, garments (especially furs), and questioned documents. Commonly accepted elements of identification for these categories include the following:

Motor Vehicles

Key elements in identifying stolen vehicles are registration data—license number, year and state, and name and address of owner—and such descriptive data as serial number, motor number, year, make, type and color of car. Other useful information includes type of transmission, brakes and steering, optional equipment such as air conditioning, radio or tape deck, and the description and value of personal property left in the vehicle at the time it was stolen.

Firearms

Firearms are identified on the basis of registration, including certificate number and reason for issuance, and descriptive data: serial number, type (single action revolver, double action revolver, semi-automatic, fully automatic), make, color, barrel length, number of shots (magazine only). Microphotographs of rifling marks on a sample projectile and ejector marks on the cartridge case may be useful.

Bicycles

Note registration data, including tag number, year, city and state; and such descriptive data as serial number, make, model, style, intended sex of user, frame size and color, attachments and accessories such as gears, carrier, light, bell or horn, type of brakes.

Jewelry

Voluntary inscription with the owner's driver's license number or SSN/SIN number is especially valuable in identifying stolen jewelry. Description should include name of piece, intended sex of user, value, material, initials or monograms, inscriptions, jeweler's or maker's marks, design, color, shape, size and number of items, kind and weight of stone, serial number or watch movement number for watches.

Tools and Appliances

Useful identifying data includes serial number, name of item, value, material, name-plate data, chassis and sub-assembly nameplate data, plant-account data and how inscribed, design, color, shape, size, maker, model, year, number of items.

Apparel

Note name of garment, intended sex of user, value, material, initials or monograms, laundry or dry-cleaning marks, design, color, shape, size, maker and label, number of items, number and quality of skins in the case of furs.

Questioned Documents (Bad Checks)

Necessary for identification are a specimen check with endorsement indicating the hand used, facsimiles of actual checks passed, kind of check, bank and branch or corporation, names used in signature and endorsement.

The main points in identifying a bad check are the methods used in setting forth the date, written dollar amount, the "and" following the written dollar amount, the "cents" portion of the written dollar amount, and the "cents" portion of the numeric dollar amount.

OCCURRENCE INVESTIGATIONS

Police occurrence investigations generate a wealth of recorded information. The specific content of those records will vary according to the event, be it a crime or a case of mental illness, a homicide or a missing person report. It is of value in this study, however, to note the basic content of any police occurrence report, as well as the content of a record of arrest.

Occurrence Reports

The basic facts that must be included in any police record of an occurrence include:

1) Identification of all police officers involved by name, rank, shield number, organization and command, including the role played by each, such as (A) first at scene, source of initial information, or receiver of complaint; (B) author of report or investigating officer; (C) receiver of report; (D) supervisor checking report; (E) notifier of other persons or agencies; (F) recipient of persons or property, or custodian at time of release.

2) Time, date and place of occurrence (including police command area, date and time of report, type of premises involved, initial occurrence and any subsequent occurrences (including interviews).

3) Value of any property stolen, lost or damaged, whether it was insured, and the name, address, telephone number of the insurance company or adjuster, and their file number.

4) Name, age, address, telephone number, occupation (or type of business), business address and telephone number, and relationship to victim of all parties involved, interviewed, or notified, including the complainant.

5) Date and time of issue of any warrants or wanted or missing notices for individuals, type of document, authority, serial number, radius (in U.S., whether will extradite), and the time, date, and message number of all advisories to other agencies.

6) Description of all suspects, wanted or missing persons in complete detail, setting forth their involvement in the occurrence. If suspects cannot be identified, this must be so stated.

7) Names of all victims, type of business if a firm, occupation if an individual, sex, age, nationality, marital status, and address.

8) Description of all occurrences in detail (MO).

9) Description of all vehicles involved in the occurrence.

10) Source of initial information: station personnel, persons at the scene, telephone, telegram, letter, telex or radio, including date, time and originator.

11) Record of outcome, including action taken (and if no action, why).

Record of Arrest

A record of arrest includes the following information:
- Prisoner's surname, given names, and AKA.
- Address.
- Sex, age, DOB, place of birth.
- Occupation, SSN/SIN.
- Operator's license number, vehicle registration.
- Arresting officer, booking officer.
- Location of arrest.
- Apparent injuries to prisoner and hospital to which taken.
- Property and cash taken from prisoner, including his signature when cash is taken and returned.
- Telephone calls made (to lawyer or immediate relative), including numbers dialed and prisoner's signature.

- Charges, warrants, etc., name and address of complainant and victim of the offense, and its place and date.
- Names of persons jointly charged with the prisoner.
- Cost of meals furnished.
- If held for another police department, name of place to which transferred, department, date and time transferred, signature of officer receiving the prisoner.
- Date and time bailed or cell number.
- In the case of a juvenile, the name of his school, grade, notification of parent or guardian, court date and name of officer taking the juvenile.

INTELLIGENCE INVESTIGATIONS

Police intelligence investigation differs from occurrence investigation in that the latter deals with cold fact concerning an actual incident or crime, while the former is concerned with potential crime and must of necessity take into account informed speculation and reasonably grounded suspicion.

The Hoover Commission in 1955 defined police intelligence as "all the things which should be known in advance of initiating a course of action." It is basically an information gathering process, anticipating the need for action or decision.

Such information is usually divided into three categories:

1) *Strategic intelligence,* which is long range in nature.
2) *Counterintelligence,* which is concerned with protecting the police agency against penetration or subversion by its enemies.
3) *Line intelligence,* which is information necessary for day-to-day police planning and operations.

Intelligence information tends to deal with (1) individuals, (2) organized crime, (3) criminal operations, (4) youth gangs, and (5) subversive organizations.

Individuals

A criminal intelligence file on an individual contains most of the general headings found in any background investigation, but with a particular emphasis toward potential criminal activity. Among the areas of special attention are:

- Business and employment history, including union membership and activity, work habits, visible sources of income as related to observed standard of living, licenses held.
- Family history, including attention to relatives with whom a close personal relationship exists even though blood ties may be somewhat distant.
- Educational history, including assessment of the subject's intelligence level;

languages spoken, read or understood; and attendance at any subversive schools.

- Military history, with particular attention to occupation specialty and proficiency with weapons or explosives.
- Marital history, past and present, current relationship with spouse, and any known extramarital associations.
- Social history, including religion; business, professional, service, veterans, or fraternal organizations of which he is a member.
- Criminal history, covering not only known criminal activities and crime specialties, degree of expertise, details of known or suspected crimes, and MO, but also any known associations with other criminals or with criminal or subversive organizations. Such a file will also include details concerning geographical area of activities, addresses of hangouts, membership and role in criminal organizations, association with homicides, authority to possess firearms and reasonable belief that the subject may unlawfully possess firearms, visitors and contacts while in prison, legal counsel, vehicles owned or used and their garage locations, and other data of potential importance.

Organized Crime

In one sense all crime is organized; of interest here is *syndicated* crime, particularly, in the United States, the highly organized and tightly controlled group known as the Mafia, or *La Cosa Nostra.*

Wherever found, such syndicated criminal groups have common characteristics. They have a number of members who engage in similar criminal activities for profit and rely on these activities for their primary source of income. They attempt to dominate one or more categories of crime and anticipate a continuous, indefinite period of operations. They are dedicated to punish any member or outsider who informs on or otherwise poses a threat to the group. (The famed *omerta,* or "conspiracy of silence," of La Cosa Nostra binds each member to silence under pain of death.)

Such criminal groups are commonly implicated in narcotics, gambling, labor and business racketeering, loan sharking, receiving stolen property, hijacking, prostitution, alcohol, tax evasion and counterfeiting. In order to exist profitably, organized crime is also associated with widespread political and judicial corruption.

Intelligence information relating to organized crime will cover criminal activities of the group, MO, geographical areas in which active, addresses of business activities which are fronts or hangouts, personnel of the group and their roles in the organization, homicides associated with the group, associations or conflicts with other organizations, references to other police files, and any other facts or suspicions.

Criminal Operations

Criminal groups more loosely organized than syndicated crime groups may also be a subject for police intelligence investigation. Such groups are less stable in their structure and organization, and are sometimes organized solely for the commission of a particular crime. They commonly participate in such crimes as burglary, arson, armed robbery, prostitution, swindles, and shoplifting, among others.

Youth Gangs

Police intelligence files in many cities are maintained on active gangs with an average age of 21 or less who engage in group fighting or other anti-social activities. These files include information on criminal and other anti-social activities, geographical areas in which active, meeting places or headquarters, involvement with narcotics arrests, social agency contacts, names of core members including AKA, age group, number of members and ethnic composition.

Although currently controversial, pre-delinquent records also exist in some large cities. They record not necessarily delinquent conduct, but factors indicating probable or possible trouble areas.

Subversive Organizations

Law enforcement agencies, especially on the national level but also including some regional or larger city police agencies, maintain intelligence files on known organizations that pose a threat to public peace and order. These may include "hate" groups and organizations that conspire to alter the political or economic structure of their own or other friendly nations by force or violence.

The violent activities of dedicated revolutionary groups or "armies" in recent years, including hijacking, assassination, kidnaping and extortion, have become a subject of increasing concern for police agencies at local, national and international levels.

Intelligence investigation of subversive groups seeks to develop information concerning:

- Objectives, including policy statements or manifestos.
- Criminal and other activities, including geographical areas.
- Organizational structure.
- Publications.

- References to data held by other agencies.
- Names, addresses and AKA of leaders and members.
- Financing, including dollar level and sources.
- Contacts with other individuals or groups, public officials, foreign embassies and agencies.

POLICE RECORDS ACCESS

Every law enforcement agency has restrictions on the release of information both within the agency and to outside agencies. In most cases these are locally initiated restrictions, imposed by the law enforcement commander in question, with the exception of specific legal restrictions imposed by outside organizations, such as state or court restrictions on the dissemination of juvenile crime records, which in many jurisdictions are permanently sealed.

The governing principle in controlling police information on file is a demonstrated need to know. A spokesman for the metropolitan police department studied in this chapter, for instance, the head of its Records and Inquiry Bureau, stressed that law enforcement agencies alone were authorized to obtain records from the system, and then not every police officer. A record is released only upon demonstration that it has a bearing upon an investigation in progress. In such cases a typewritten copy of the record is prepared for release; the file itself is retained. In the case of stolen property, a record is kept of all vehicles reported stolen by license number and of other property by description. These records are on computer, and information is available to victims and their insurance companies.

In general, such restrictions seek to safeguard the privacy of the person with a police record. They also seek to protect police personnel, intelligence information itself, and information sources. Controls tend to become tighter as the information becomes more sensitive or secure, and as the size of the police agency increases.

Computerized Crime Data Problems

It may reasonably be stated that most police agencies similarly restrict the release of information to those persons, agencies and organizations with a need for the information. However, the proliferation of computerized crime data banks, particularly the FBI's national crime computer (NCIC), has caused a rising concern for the rights of privacy of the individual and the dangers of abuses in the dissemination of criminal information. Instances have been cited in which criminal records were used by a wide variety of government, civilian and private groups. The state of Massachusetts, with its active Commission of Privacy and Personal Data, has led others in its concern for this problem. In refusing to join the National Crime Information Center, Massachusetts Governor Francis W. Sargent asserted that the state's own investigations revealed that more than 75 agencies (ranging from mayors to credit and insurance companies) had had access to criminal records.

Such criticisms led to the introduction of a dozen bills in the U.S. Congress in 1974, all seeking to impose varying degrees of control on the exchange or dissemination of criminal records. Included were a bill sponsored by the Justice Department and even stricter legislation introduced by Senator Sam J. Ervin. The thrust of most of this legislation would be to insure that (a) such criminal data would be accurate, with the subject of a criminal record having the opportunity to challenge its accuracy; (b) it would be kept up-to-date, with particular attention to the inclusion of the disposition of the case in any arrest record; and (c) access to the data should be more scrupulously limited to law enforcement agencies.

In the absence of such legislation, however, control of crime data will reside where it has always been, with the police agencies themselves, whether local, state, national or international.

CONCLUSIONS

Law enforcement officers are keenly aware of their oath to enforce the law without fear or favor and in a dispassionate manner. They are also highly conscious of the adverse effects that a prior criminal history can have on the life chances of an individual who sincerely wishes to avoid future criminal involvement.

It is this dual concern that must govern police information systems, now and in the future. On the one hand, to administer the criminal justice process for maximal gain to society as a whole requires a modern record-keeping system that is accurate, comprehensive and timely, capable of providing the needed information to the proper officers as quickly as possible. At the same time, the record-keeping system must provide for the security, confidentiality and privacy of the information it stores and handles if it is not to become operationally and socially counter-productive.

Chapter 5

IN-FILE REPORTING AGENCIES

"Annual income twenty pounds,
annual expenditure nineteen six,
result happiness.
Annual income twenty pounds,
annual expenditure twenty pounds ought and six,
result misery."

—Charles Dickens, *David Copperfield*

INTRODUCTION

A variety of informational and reporting agencies contribute to loss prevention by warning the potential victims. In general, their information is compiled by collating reports of loss.

In this chapter we will examine the functions of file-based credit-reporting agencies, especially in relation to the large retail market, and two nationwide computer-based services, Credit Data and Credit Index, which supplement the protection afforded by these credit bureaus.

In addition, a modern system for registering liens against personal property

123

will be examined. Although this system does not exchange loss information, it does establish a barrier to fraudulent sale of property subject to prior encumbrances.

Finally, we will examine the protective measures adopted by banks, financial companies, and the insurance industry—all prime targets of the "something for nothing" element.

PROBLEMS OF RETAILERS

Full-line department stores extending credit to customers, employing many people, having large numbers of suppliers, and being interested in market research and other sophisticated marketing techniques, have a close interest in records. At the other end of the scale, the small independents with few employees, no credit facilities, and manual records have only an academic interest.

Retailers are collectors and repositories of many types of information about customers, employees, and suppliers. In addition, they use information supplied by others—credit bureaus, other credit grantors, personnel investigators, and previous employers, for example.

Information about an individual falls into two categories. The first includes generally available and non-objectional information such as address, place of birth, and ownership of home or car. Into the second category falls more privileged information, such as income level, health record, employment record, and credit record. (However, independent research conducted in 1972 by a major credit bureau indicates the individual has little objection if his credit record is exposed, provided that he has actually applied for a new line of credit.)

Types of Retail Information

The types of information that are accumulated within a retail organization include the following:

1) Information obtained when a customer opens an account may include his address, age, family responsibilities, employers, income level (usually within brackets), whether he has a telephone, length of time he has worked for his current employer, value of his capital assets, extent of his obligations to others, and his life insurance.

2) The record of use of an account, including defaults in payment, is the ledger record of the customer's dealings with the retailer and indicates the nature of purchases made. The record includes information regarding the

customer's paying and buying habits, particularly in relation to delayed payments.

3) Marketing information can be built up by the retailer from material in his files relating to credit for use by customers. Credit customers can be broken down by geographical area, age, income level and other classifications to build selective mailing lists for advertising and distribution of samples. Additional information can be derived from responses to mail solicitation. A retailer can also use the raw material in his customer account files to develop profiles of customer characteristics by groupings.

4) Retailers keep extensive records on current or prospective employees. To the basic information on the employment application is added information derived from the individual's employment record. Some retail employers retain files on former as well as current employees.

5) Supplier records include commercial credit information.

Information under all these headings is stored by retailers either on a manual basis or in computers owned or leased by themselves, or provided by computer service bureaus.

Outside Sources of Information

Credit bureaus are commonly used by retailers as a source of information about the credit worthiness of customers or potential customers. In some cases, either because no credit bureaus operate in the area, or for other reasons, credit experience may be exchanged directly among credit grantors.

Credit bureau material is coded and released only to members of the bureau who have agreed to abide by its rules of confidentiality. In most cases, bureau members receive either verbal or written summaries of the subject's file.

In the more informal exchange of information, formal assurances of confidentiality have not been established, but discretion governs the transmission of information. Retailers obtain information on the identity of prospective customers from market research companies and directory companies, and newspaper information relating to executive moves and birth notices.

Retailers obtain references from previous employers and, for particular positions, may obtain security-related information from investigation companies, credit information from credit bureaus and, with the permission of the employee, health information from medical record sources.

IN-FILE CREDIT BUREAUS

The file-type credit-reporting agency is also known as a credit bureau or file bureau. Many large credit bureaus have been set up by the credit grantors themselves.

Sources of Information

The credit bureau relies on credit grantors to provide it with information. When a person applies for credit or a loan, an application is filled out and the credit grantor and bureau invariably exchange information. This includes the applicant's address and employment status. The exchange of information warns the credit bureau of an individual who is applying in numerous areas for credit or loans.

The credit grantor also provides the bureau with information as to balances outstanding at any time, manner of payment, whether there are bad debt or collection problems with the borrower.

Credit bureaus also gather information that is on the public record, such as registered chattel mortgages, court records for consumer debt including division court judgments, county and Supreme Court judgments, foreclosures, bankruptcy, press clippings of criminal convictions, change of name, and non-responsibility notices.

The president of one large credit bureau reports that its members are continually encouraged to report all derogatory information such as bad debts, overloaded accounts and serious delinquencies. Although members do not automatically report all new credit transactions, the bureau learns of new transactions through actual inquiry.

Positive information is introduced to the bureau's files on a request basis; that is, many clients request that the bureau update trade information as a regular part of its service. Consequently, the bureau updates an average of three trade lines per application on fifty percent of all inquiries. (In this context a trade line represents the experience of one subscriber with a particular consumer at the time the entire file is updated.) This means there is a regular stream of positive information going into the file.

The information stored and disseminated by credit bureaus consists of economic and statistical data that are objective by their nature. The information made available through a typical file service agency goes back primarily to its contributors, mostly credit card companies, and retailers. To a lesser extent, landlords request information pertaining to a prospective tenant's credit.

The credit bureau report is only a component of the judgment factor used by the credit grantor. Its file content is not always complete, because some credit grantors do not clear all new accounts through the bureau.

One large bureau reports that about 85 percent of items posted to its files originate from its members. An additional method of obtaining information, direct contact with the subject, is used mainly by investigative reporting agencies, rarely by in-file bureaus. This is done almost always by telephone, with the credit bureau identifying itself and asking the subject to assist them in updating their file on him.

Origins of the Credit Bureau

In ancient times, credit was arranged between acquaintances. The credit grantor based his decision on personal knowledge of the credit seeker and the proposed transaction. However, the granting of credit was accompanied by considerable problems, and there were harsh punishments for debtors who could not repay, as Shakespeare dramatized so eloquently in *The Merchant of Venice*. The important point is that the parties knew each other and their business histories.

As population and trade increased, it became difficult to extend credit on the basis of personal knowledge. Credit grantors simply couldn't know each individual. As a result, credit was extended to applicants who were not acquaintances, but who could show that they owned property. Next, credit was extended to applicants who were not property owners, but whose credit could be guaranteed by property owners.

Demand for credit continued to expand, and credit grantors found they didn't have the staff or the time to gather sufficient information on which to evaluate applications. They needed an independent, reliable and objective third party to collect this information. The result was the credit bureau.

Since early credit bureaus were formed by groups of merchants, they provided credit information by cooperative means, establishing offices to which members reported the status of their accounts, as well as applications for credit. In some communities, individual businessmen established privately owned bureaus. Both types exist today.

The Associated Credit Bureaus

As the number of bureaus grew and as the mobility of the public increased, credit bureaus introduced a system of inter-city reporting. Subsequently, state and provincial associations were established and, in 1939, the Associated Credit Bureaus was incorporated as a non-profit organization. Today the association has over 2,000 member bureaus in all 50 states and 10 provinces, employing approximately 30,000 persons. Its international office is in Houston, Texas. All member bureaus are bonded and licensed under the laws of the state or province in which they operate.

Outstanding consumer credit has grown to $90 billion. Credit bureaus provide more than 50 million brief and factual credit summaries a year, most of them by telephone, to more than 400,000 subscribers. If the subscriber wishes, a written report will be forwarded.

A credit bureau is a clearing house for information, most of which is supplied by the accounts receivable departments of clients. This information is available only to subscribers and is on a confidential basis.

Service contracts are required which certify that inquiries will be made only for credit granting and other business transactions such as evaluating present and prospective credit risks. To safeguard against unwarranted disclosure, credit bureaus refuse service to any prospective subscriber who will not enter into such a contract. Service is discontinued to any subscriber who fails to honor its provisions.

To become a member of the Associated Credit Bureaus, a bureau must first be a member of a state or provincial association. That association will assist a new bureau in its infancy, but will not consider it for membership until it has been in operation for at least six months and is serving the majority of credit grantors in its area.

If the prospective member then shows evidence of financial stability, satisfactory references and ability to service the needs of the community, it is admitted on probation. Full membership is granted when the board of directors of the state or provincial association is satisfied that the bureau will competently serve local and national clients.

Subscribers to the bureaus are credit grantors. They include such businesses as automotive, finance, banks, department and variety stores, home furnishings, building contractors, oil and national credit card companies, real estate firms, and hotels and motels. They pay an annual fee plus a charge for each credit report requested.

To obtain information, a subscriber must identify himself by a code number assigned on contract agreement. File information is never available to non-subscribers. The only exception is the consumer himself. If he visits the office and provides proper identification, many bureaus will reveal everything in his file.

Of the 50 million credit reports given to ACB subscribers in 1969, approximately 80 percent were completely favorable. Another 17 percent were marginal—people who pay their bills, but with varying degrees of slowness. Only 3 percent were unfavorable.

Only 0.22 percent of all reports (7.33 percent of unfavorable reports) resulted in consumer complaints. Of these, 0.14 percent were due to a misunderstanding of the business function of a credit bureau (usually the mistaken belief that the bureau actually approves or disapproves the granting of credit). Mistaken identity accounted for .01 percent of disputed reports (about 5,000). Other factual errors gave rise to another .01 percent.

File Content

Files contain factual material only. No reference is made to race, religion, political affiliation or personality. Specific content of a record includes:

Name (and AKA, if any)
Age
Place of residence
Previous places of residence
Marital status
Family
Place of employment
Previous places of employment
Estimated income
Paying habits
Outstanding credit obligations.

The file record contains ledger entries contributed by the credit offices of member firms. A typical entry includes:

1) Code number of the member supplying the entry.
2) Member's account number designating the subject's account.
3) Date account was opened.
4) Date of last sale at the time the entry was submitted.
5) Highest credit extended.
6) Amount currently owing.
7) Amount past due.

8) Manner of payment.
9) Revision to the entry, if any.
10) Special items.

Manner of payment is coded in the form

A	$NN	N
a	b	c

a = type of account

O, open 30-day charge account
R, revolving account
I, installment account

b = monthly payment required

c = experience with the account.

The experience (c) rating indicating the usual manner of payment is a numerical designation, ranging from 0 (too new to rate; approved but not used) up to 9 (bad debt; debt placed for collection; skip).

An alphabetical code is used to classify various kinds of businesses, from A (Automotive) to Z (Miscellaneous).

An entry is also made each time a member requests information from the bureau regarding the subject. Such an entry includes date, code number of member requesting data, and type of inquiry.

Bureaus record judgments or writs having to do with consumer debt, non-responsibility notices, registered chattel mortgages, conditional sales contracts and convictions for criminal offenses. They also report bankruptcies for 14 years (7 in Ontario by provincial regulations). They report accounts placed for collection, accounts charged to profit and loss, judgments, and court convictions for seven years. Adverse information that cannot be verified at the source is deleted.

Bureaus offering a personnel reporting service do not incorporate such specialized information in credit reports nor make it available to subscribers inquiring about a consumer's credit record.

A typical subject docket used by in-file credit bureaus consists of a folded 5" by 7" jacket which includes an envelope section for holding newspaper clippings, etc. The identifying information and inquiry record are on the front when the docket is folded with the ledger information on the rear. A "special items" section is folded inside. Imagine several hundred thousand of these dockets filed alphabetically in a power-driven elevator tub file, and you can visualize the heart of a local in-file credit reporting agency.

CREDIT DATA, A NATION-WIDE SYSTEM

Credit Data is a subdivision of TRW Inc., based in Redondo Beach, California. All its information is computerized and accessible by remote terminals located in San Diego, Los Angeles, San Francisco/Oakland, Sacramento, Chicago, Detroit, Toledo, Buffalo/Niagara Falls, Syracuse, and New York City. Data may also be obtained by subscribers by mail and telephone.

Credit Data processes 50,000 inquiries daily. About half of these are made directly to the computer by credit grantors with teletypewriter terminals. Answers can be returned within three minutes. File information is released only to credit grantors and certain government agencies as an aid in evaluating credit worthiness and for other business purposes.

As of 1971, Credit Data had an estimated 40 million records on file and were adding new entries at the rate of 50,000 a week. Unlike some credit bureaus (including Credit Index, which we will examine next), Credit Data compiles *all* the credit transactions of its subscribers, including positive as well as negative data. This necessitates handling a lot of information, most of which is innocuous. However, as Credit Data sees it, computers can handle this mass of information with no problem; by compiling credit data on such an exhaustive basis, clues can be found that may predict delinquency in time to prevent loss.

(Other credit bureaus also store positive data. More than 50 percent of requests received from subscribers by the Toronto Credit Bureau, for example, require updating; 74.6 percent of all trade lines are updated favorably and this information is, therefore, positive.)

All Credit Data clients are required to submit monthly reports to Credit Data on the status of all customer accounts. Large creditors with computerized billing, such as department stores, make tapes for Credit Data as part of their regular billing cycle. As a result, about 90 percent of all information in Credit Data reports is positive, indicating prompt payment on the part of the subject.

However, by filing new information each month, Credit Data gets more timely data on delinquent payments than commercial credit bureaus do, because most creditors wait ninety days or more before reporting an overdue account to a local credit bureau. By bringing together all facts regarding a subject's buying habits, Credit Data can generate additional useful information for credit grantors. For example, they can assess point scores to items that are accurate predictors of future credit worthiness. This procedure could permit assignment of numerical credit ratings.

Credit worthiness ratings in the files of local credit bureaus are subjective in nature and assigned by the credit offices of member firms. The adoption of common language by credit bureaus in Canada and the United States has made ratings much more objective.

Credit Data reports are printed by computer on color-coded profile forms with positive information in the blue section, unevaluated data in the white section, and derogatory information in the red section. The records on file contain only financial information. They do not include newspaper clippings of criminal actions or divorces, nor the results of personal investigations. However, Credit Data does report the filing of civil suits in financial matters even though it cannot get the disposition of the suit.

Unlike other credit bureaus, Credit Data has a positive control over misuse of its data by subscribers. The firm checks periodically to see that the sum of rejections and new accounts for each subscriber agrees approximately with the number of inquiries made. A surplus of inquiries might indicate that reports were being used for non-credit-granting purposes. In addition, Credit Data changes client code numbers periodically to prevent former employees from making use of these numbers to get unauthorized reports.

THE CREDIT INDEX

The Credit Index is a computerized data service offered by the Hooper-Holmes Bureau, Inc. Its headquarters are in Morristown, New Jersey. The Index began operations in 1967; three and a half years later its master file had grown to ten million items.

Credit Index collects only derogatory information. This reduces the mass of information that must be handled to one tenth that of Credit Data's. Credit Index stresses that the subjects named in their files cause most of the loss experienced by creditors. Their files represent over half a billion dollars in delinquent accounts reported by subscribers. The file contains the names of known credit card abusers and demonstrates the distinct cross-over between a credit issuing company's delinquents and those of other companies in the same field.

Of this total of items and dollars, a large percentage has been reported by credit card issuing companies such as airlines, auto rental companies, financial organizations, petroleum companies, and general credit card companies: two million items, representing $300 million. Credit card delinquencies amount to 63% by dollar value and only 20% by item count!

The master file is national in scope. The largest number of items on file is from California. New York ranks second, followed by Texas. The total number of items reported in these three states represents over 25% of the master file. These three states also represent 25% of the population of the United States.

In almost all cases Credit Index is able to process a large group of applications and return them to the credit evaluator within 72 hours. Through the use of communications devices, this processing time may be cut to as little as five hours. The volume capability of the Index allows it to handle anywhere from a few dozen to millions of inquiries.

Besides the clearing of applications for credit, the Credit Index has instituted credit card control programs. The delinquent account search program matches a subscriber's sixty-day past due accounts to identify, at this relatively early state of delinquency, those card holders whose unsatisfactory performance with other Index subscribers, and particularly other credit card companies, indicates the need for more immediate action to limit the continuing abuse of their credit privileges.

The average exact name match percentage on these searches has been 8%; but more importantly, over 80% of these matches showed simultaneous or previous abuse within the credit card industry.

Other credit control programs include duplicate account search, designed to search a subscriber's file and cull out multiple card accounts. In this program the system searches for address matches.

At re-issue time, a subscriber may match his re-issue accounts against the master file to identify inactive accounts that are delinquent with other credit grantors, and thus forestall re-issue to probable credit card abusers.

The Index is equipped to number applications serially as they are received. The computer has been programmed to print-out in a second run all matches in serial number. In this way a group of applications, after being processed, will be returned in serial number order together with the print-out showing matches also in serial number order, thereby aiding the credit evaluator in tying the two together.

CENTRAL REGISTRY OF LIENS

In 1967, the Ontario (Canada) Personal Property and Security Registration Act required that a registration system be established under the aegis of the provincial attorney general. This system is intended to provide rapid searches of registered security agreements for the business community. It encompasses a central file and 48 branch offices throughout the province.

The main purpose of the PPSR Act is to provide a central registry which businesses and individuals can query to clear titles to property being bought and sold. The most serious single problem was the fraudulent sale of automobiles subject to lien. Prior to the PPSR system, a potential buyer might have had to search manual files of 48 district offices to be sure the seller had clear title to the car he was trying to sell. (These existing property registration offices are still used as branch media.)

There are 600,000 records on file. Eighty percent of the debtors are individuals; the remaining 20 percent are corporate firms. Over 75 percent of the registrations are for vehicles. Each record has a variable length up to 1,000 characters, averaging 200 characters in length. Consideration has been given to linking motor vehicle lien information to automobile registration.

There are general classifications for collateral and allowances for more specific identification and description. In the case of vehicles, the year, make, body style and serial numbers are recorded. Serial numbers may be registered for other items as well.

The source documents for the PPSR system are the security agreement, which provides the legal basis for the lien, and the financing statement, which is the actual input to the system. They are submitted by county clerks and district court clerks to branch offices of the PPSR system at the time of registration of the security agreement. These agreements consist of chattel mortgages, conditional sales contracts, and assignment of book debts. Once the security agreement is registered, one copy is retained by the secured party and one by the branch office.

There are three copies of the financing statement. One is returned to the secured party after registration, one is retained in the court clerk's office, and the original is submitted to the central office in Toronto for input to the electronic system.

The secured party is responsible for the accuracy of the original documents, as the PPSR system is legally responsible only for transcription and transmission errors.

The financing statement and account control forms are mailed from the 48 branch offices to the central office. The forms are checked off against the control forms, divided, and sent by couriers to service centers operated by National Computer Optics and IBM. They use optical character recognition (OCR) equipment which reads the typewritten entries and stores data on magnetic tape directly to avoid typing or transcription errors.

After the data have been entered onto them, the tapes are sent to the Transport and Justice Computer Center and the forms are returned to the central office. They are retained indefinitely as documents of legal record. The procedures for amending and updating the financing statements are the same as for placing them on file.

Liens against property purchased in other provinces or in the United States may be registered; however, users of the central registry have to call from within Ontario, although it is possible for a non-Ontario firm to establish direct service.

Use of the PPSR system is optional. A creditor need not file a security agreement, nor is he required to amend a change in any financing statement that is processed. A lien could conceivably be retained on the registry even though the debt had been paid and the title was clear.

The registration number of the financing statement is determined by the year, month, day, hour, minute, branch office number, and order of registration. A 16-digit unique identifier is created from this sequence of numbers. The debtors are identified by name, address, sex, and date of birth (the last item is optional). The secured party is identified by name and address.

Anybody can phone from a branch office and have a search done on an individual name for a fee of fifty cents. The user can receive a record of all liens for that individual, as long as he can provide the data (name, address, birth date, sex) necessary to identify the individual. Established businesses have direct call privileges, with Bell Telephone collecting fees.

PROBLEMS OF BANKERS

There are nearly 70,000 banks in North America, and their assets amount to over $500 billion. The principal services offered by banks are the traditional ones of deposit gathering and loans. Banks offer many other financial services, ranging from safekeeping, services to finance and facilitate trade, such as letters of credit and documentary collections, to more recent services such as consumer loans and credit cards.

The business of banking is based upon trust and confidence. Confidentiality is second nature with bankers. Information held by a bank on any customer may be provided by the customer, obtained from an outside source, or gathered by the bank as a result of its experience with a customer.

Account and Loan Applications

In a deposit relationship, a bank must be able to show that it acted in good faith and without negligence. As a depositor, a client frequently receives services, such as check cashing and accepting uncleared checks on deposit, that entail risk to the bank. For this reason, upon opening an account, a customer may be asked for a reference as well as basic personal data.

It is customary for a bank to obtain a reference before opening an account in all cases where the individual is not known. In the case of deposit customers, the reference is usually supplied by the applicant. It may be a person known to the bank, his employer, or evidence that substantiates his identity.

When a person applies to a bank for a loan, he must provide the basic personal data and financial history required to make a full assessment of his credit worthiness. In the case of a borrowing client who is not well known to the bank, a credit report from his previous banker or a commercial credit bureau will be obtained.

Most banks use the services of outside agencies in assessing credit worthiness. The Toronto Credit Bureau, for example, reports that in 1973 its four largest users were chartered banks. Their individual volumes greatly exceeded that of any single department store. On an on-going basis, practically all bank credit card applications are cleared through credit bureaus, as are installment loans.

The following information is taken from an individual applying for a deposit account: name and address; telephone number; occupation and name of employer; identification or reference; signing instructions.

A loan application form can be broken down into three main categories: name and address; employment history; financial data.

The bank also keeps information for accounting and bookkeeping purposes.

Bank Employees

Upon application for employment with a bank, an individual is expected to supply the following information:

1. Name.
2. Present and previous addresses.
3. Personal data: date of birth, height, weight, marital status, date of marriage, number of children, languages spoken, records of serious illness.
4. Preference as to location.
5. Educational background.
6. Employment history.
7. Names of persons to be used as sources of reference.

The applicant also signs the bank's Declaration of Secrecy form, pledging to observe strict secrecy, both during and after the period of employment, regarding the transactions of the bank and the affairs of all bodies and individuals dealing with it. This declaration is reaffirmed annually until resignation or retirement. Each annual signing is accompanied by an explanation of its meaning by the employee's superior officer and includes that officer's signed statement that he has done so.

At all times staff are made aware that customer records are private and confidential. They are reminded that:

1. Conversations of a confidential nature must not be overheard by unauthorized parties.
2. The identity of a caller must be established and it should be confirmed that he is entitled to receive information.
3. Books, records and other documents must not be left available to unauthorized individuals.

All documents of a confidential nature are kept under lock and key with only those officers designated as a "user" having access. For example, personal credit files are restricted to the manager, loaning officers and the senior stenographer. All customer information files and records are stored in vaults overnight. Circular instructions of a confidential nature have a restricted distribution within the bank. This also applies to internal and external correspondence.

Safeguarding Data

The major use of the computer by banks is for check clearing and deposit record-keeping. Over 26 billion checks were processed in the U.S. during 1973.

All checks, deposits and other information are transferred to the Regional Data Center in a locked canvas bag by courier. After processing, vouchers and reports are returned in the same manner. Strict security is maintained at the Data Center, with only authorized personnel having access. Identification cards are worn by staff, and visitors must be accompanied by a senior officer. The computer room and file library are "off limits" to the majority of personnel. Vaults protect files from physical damage, and removal of files requires management authorization.

When Is Information Disclosed?

Information concerning a customer will be disclosed by a bank only:

1. By request of the customer.
2. Under the provisions of a statute.
3. By a process of law.
4. In the course of normal commercial operations.

An example of disclosure by request of the customer would be disclosure of the details of account balance, security holdings and loans, to his auditor for balance sheet purposes.

The state superintendent of banks has the right of access to the affairs of a bank and annually requests certain information regarding loan accounts. The criteria for selection usually involve a dollar amount, loans guaranteed by governments and school districts, loans to corporations owned by these governments, and loans secured by marketable stocks and bonds.

Statutes also cover deposits that are unclaimed for a specified period of time. This information is published in an attempt to locate the depositor or his heirs. In addition, a bank is required to report interest payments for tax purposes, and to comply with government orders for information and production of documents in tax matters.

Other government agencies can approach a bank for information or confirmation in estate investigations, veterans' affairs, welfare agency affairs, Indian affairs, securities commission matters. A bank can be served with a subpoena, summons, search warrant or other order requiring it to testify, produce records for the court, or give access to pertinent records by an officer of the court. A bank is also liable for seizure of customer assets and liabilities under writs of execution, garnishment and judgment.

In conducting the affairs of any customer, a bank will build an opinion as to the customer's character and credit worthiness. A bank will provide "opinion or reference" on a customer as a courtesy to enhance customer service, and for credit information purposes.

When a customer moves to another area, comments regarding his previous banking experience are usually forwarded to a selected local banker to help in relocation of the customer's affairs. Likewise, when a customer goes on a business or pleasure trip, the bank may provide letters of introduction to other banks, referring to his previous banking experience.

An informal letter of credit is virtually the same as a letter of introduction, with the addition of the check-cashing privilege up to a certain amount.

A bank will provide to a credit bureau, upon request, a credit reference with regard to personal installment loans not secured by liquid security or government guarantee. The report covers a five-point rating:

1. Opening date
2. Highest credit
3. Balance
4. Terms
5. Manner paid.

Certain firms are permitted to inquire directly from banks and receive a brief credit report, omitting amounts of borrowings or deposit balances. A written credit reference on an individual will be forwarded to another bank upon request. In practice, bankers' reports for nominal amounts tend to be general and based on experience.

Information reports encompass all requests for credit information taken by telephone and across the counter. The majority of cases refer to queries regarding checks to be negotiated or certified.

In the U.S., information clearing houses have been established on a regional level through which bankers can exchange information regarding credit worthiness of individuals and actual or anticipated attempts to defraud. Such a system is unnecessary in Canada, since there are only nine chartered banks, each of which has its own extensive network of branches.

PROBLEMS OF FINANCE COMPANIES

Finance companies in Canada have established a formalized intercompany reporting organization called the Lenders' Exchange. It was originally set up to protect loan companies from customers who borrowed money from several companies simultaneously, and from borrowers who did not repay their loans. The Exchange also protects some customers from borrowing more money than they could reasonably expect to repay. Its operations are financed by dues of the member companies. These include virtually every consumer loan company.

The Exchange maintains a complete list of all member companies' customers, the starting date of all loans outstanding, and the total amount of the loan. The information is held by customer name, and all information on a customer with loans at more than one company is kept together. The data is on current loans only. No subjective information is included. If a customer is a bad risk, however, it is obvious from the starting date of the loan(s) outstanding.

The Exchange receives information only from its members and disseminates it only to those companies. When a loan is made at a consumer loan company, the name of the customer, some identifying information such as address or occupation, and the amount of the loan and its starting date, are sent to the Exchange. When a loan is repaid, this information is also sent to the Exchange and the information on the repaid loan is removed from the customer file.

To obtain information on an individual, a company telephones the Exchange (the number is unlisted), identifies itself and specifies the individual on whom it requires information.

It is not mandatory for a member company to use the Exchange before making a loan, but it is mandatory to enter all loans made. It is against the rules of the association of finance companies operating the Exchange to make loans to an individual with loans at three companies, and a fine is levied for infractions of this rule. (A consumer may have two open loans on different securities and be an endorser on one other loan. This is called the 2-1/2 loan plan.)

Some companies have upper limits on the amount of a loan to an individual.

They use the information in the Exchange to determine whether a person is eligible for another loan.

The first Lenders' Exchange in Canada was opened in Windsor, Ontario, in 1958 as a pilot project. It proved to be so successful that there are now Lenders' Exchanges operating in 10 Canadian cities under the auspices of the Canadian Consumer Loan Association. To illustrate the level of activity, the Toronto Lenders' Exchange, which commenced operation in January, 1961, currently has an average number of customer cards on file between 235,000 and 240,000. A survey covering six months of 1973 revealed a monthly average of 18,000-plus clearances going through the Exchange.

A much larger counterpart of the Lenders' Exchange in the United States is the National Consumer Finance Association, headquartered in Washington, D.C.

The ACTION System

Some consumer loan companies are now protecting themselves by using a computerized system for recording loans. The ACTION system (advanced computerized terminal integrated on-line network) is available through ITT Data Services. It provides loan accounting and management reports. The significant data stored and processed by the system relative to a borrower include:

1. Name and address.
2. Spouse's name.
3. Year of birth.
4. Amount of loan.
5. Payment schedule.
6. Outstanding balance.
7. Delinquency status and loan charges (rate of interest and insurance fee).

All data is entered by and available only to the subscriber. Although the system is accessed by remote terminal, each terminal points only to the specific records of the subscriber's finance office serviced by that terminal.

The name, address and year of birth are derived from the loan application completed by the borrower. The application itself is retained in the subscriber's own finance office and may contain information which is not included in the automated file, such as employment information, salary, other outstanding loans, or length of residency at indicated address.

A high credit code which indicates the limit of the credit that will be extended by the subscriber is entered and used only by the subscriber's finance office.

Management reports prepared by the system only infrequently carry the names of individual borrowers and even less frequently carry the limited personal profile information which is contained in the system.

A subscriber's decision to make a loan to an individual is made independently of the system. It may be based on credit information obtained by the subscriber from a local credit bureau or a lender's exchange.

A receipt for payment showing amount paid, allocations to interest and principal, and current balance is prepared by the system for the borrower.

PROBLEMS OF INSURANCE COMPANIES

The protective measures used by insurance companies depend upon the kind of insurance they underwrite. Life insurance companies, for example, use the files of the Medical Information Bureau to protect themselves against applicants who fraudulently conceal medical conditions that might lead an insurer to decline their applications or require a higher premium payment to compensate for the greater risk involved.

Insurance companies who write health and accident policies and a variety of related forms of insurance consult the Casualty Index to discover whether their applicants may be indulging in fraudulent practices.

Fire and theft underwriters rely on information furnished by the Fire Underwriters Investigation Bureau to protect them from dishonest applicants and claimants. The FUIB has an investigative function as well as one of furnishing information. That is another of the frequent functional cross-overs that exist in the security profession.

Life Insurance Companies

Life insurance allows groups of people to join together to share the cost of predictable hazards. If this cost were not intelligently allocated and fairly shared, people would not avail themselves of the process. The basic question to be decided when an individual applies for life insurance is how much he should pay to contribute his fair share. If he does not do so, other policyholders will have to contribute more than their fair share.

The persons responsible for selection of risks must allocate the cost of insurance equitably among policyholders. They must see that no applicant succeeds in transferring the cost of an additional hazard to other policyholders. They must be able to assess the acceptability of any risk. Where there is an extra, but acceptable risk, they must see that the individual assumes his fair contribution.

To accomplish this, the underwriter makes use of mortality tables, investment and expense assumptions. But he must have more upon which to base his decision. Consequently, life insurance companies need to collect and use information about individuals which the subjects may not like to have disseminated. This includes:

1. Identification information: full name, date of birth, place of birth, marital status, occupation, residence.
2. Financial information: amount of income, amount of insurance, assets, debts.
3. Medical information: medical history, family history, build and physical condition.

Any one item, taken by itself, is only an indicator and not decisive in an underwriting judgment. Some items may appear to have little relevance, but experience has shown that trivial items may become important when they reinforce other aspects of risk.

A life insurance policy rests on good faith and is based on full disclosure. After a policy has been in effect for two years, the effect of the incontestible clause is that only provable fraud remains as a protection. Thus the person who successfully conceals facts at the time of application achieves legal shelter for his deceit. The companies therefore act under an obligation to their policyholders and to the public to guard against any failure to disclose information or misrepresentation of facts, whether inadvertent or intentional.

Insurers are conscious that an individual's right of privacy *does not encompass a right to profit by withholding information or by deception.*

As one top executive of a major life insurance company says, "Most of the information which would lead an insurance company to decline an application comes from the individual himself. But the standard in life insurance, more than in any other kind of business, is that not everyone is honest. That could apply both to the person who is trying to enter into a contract with you and also to other sources of information. Our business is to make sure we have good information."

In all this two conflicting underwriting objectives may be seen. On the one hand, companies wish to provide life insurance to the greatest possible number of persons. On the other hand, they believe that, because people differ in health, occupations and habits, it would be unfair to the majority if the greater risks facing some people were not taken into account.

The solution has been two-fold. Extra-risk policies with higher premiums than normal are offered to people who cannot qualify for policies at normal premium rates. Secondly, advances in medicine and job safety have substantially increased the number of persons who qualify for life insurance at normal rates, but who would previously have had to pay higher premiums or would have been unable to obtain it at all.

The availability and use of medical information is therefore crucial in life insurance, and for many years an industry system has operated with special attention to the peculiar and privileged nature of this type of information.

THE MEDICAL INFORMATION BUREAU

The Medical Information Bureau (MIB) is an unincorporated, membership association composed of over 700 life insurance companies that do business in all states of the United States and in all provinces of Canada. The bureau's executive offices are in Greenwich, Connecticut. Its information is maintained in an index file that is serviced by Recording and Statistical Division, Sperry Rand Corporation. This servicing agent maintains offices in Boston, Toronto, and Indianapolis, where MIB work is processed.

The Medical Information Bureau was organized in 1902 by an association of life insurance company medical directors as a reference index of medical information on life insurance risks. Each member company furnishes the bureau a brief resume of significant information in its file bearing on the applicant's medical condition and life expectancy. Information on an individual is made available only to member life insurance companies after the applicant has applied for life or health insurance.

Approximately 8,800,000 persons are listed in the Medical Bureau files. Individuals are listed by name, birthplace, and date of birth. All information is in code and only the medical directors and authorized company staff have access to the code books. Annual accountings are required for these code books.

The bureau's principal function is to alert insurers to hazards and impairments discovered by other insurers and not revealed by an applicant. When an insurer declines or rates an applicant because of medical treatment for a serious ailment, the coded resume of significant information is promptly transmitted to the bureau; the action of the company is not. If the applicant later applies to another insurer, but does not disclose this medical history, the other insurer will be alerted when he applies to the bureau for information.

In some cases, even though the policy is issued standard rather than at a special rate, reports are made to the bureau of the results of medical tests that may have future health significance. Also, reports of favorable subsequent medical history are received when there has been prior adverse history noted in the file.

Any type of information relevant to life insurance underwriting may be the basis of a report to the bureau. Over 90 percent of the bureau reports reflect coded medical information. In the case of non-medical information (less than 10 percent), the code symbols are not specific in definition, and merely suggest the need for special investigation by the member.

The sole source of bureau impairment reports is the membership. The bureau receives 1-1/2 million reports each year from its members. Requests for information are received from the members at a volume of 18-1/2 million per year.

If the bureau did not exist, the cost of life insurance would be increased for all, with the honest bearing the added cost of the forgetful and dishonest. The service is of particular value to smaller companies whose sources of information are more limited than those of the larger companies. The bureau's medical data also provides a basis for mortality and longevity studies by life insurance actuaries and medical statisticians.

Members are not permitted to underwrite risks on the basis of information received from the bureau. They may not rate or decline an application on such information. They may underwrite only on the basis of information gathered by their own independent investigation.

When an individual applies for life or health insurance, he is usually aware that some inquiry will be made into his insurability, and this will chiefly concern his health history. In most cases, a specific authorization is signed by the individual, permitting such an inquiry.

It has never seemed in the applicant's best interest to give him specific notice as to an inquiry into his medical history. It has long been the common practice of medical directors to make the results of their medical investigations available, on request, to the applicants' personal physicians.

Qualifications for MIB Membership

The service is made available only to member life insurance companies. To qualify for membership, the insurer must be conducting the life insurance business in the United States or Canada on the level premium, legal reserve plan; it must be in good standing with the insurance supervisory official of its state or province; and it must be of good repute wherever else it does business. Its medical affairs must be administered by a medical director who is a qualified physician. Both he and the company must pledge to maintain the confidential character of the information exchanged.

Upon being admitted to membership, the life insurance company must also pledge to obey the rules of the organization. Service is not made available until these pledges are completed. They must be renewed on the change of medical director, and, in any event, every seven years.

The file used for checking service is computerized. The bureau also maintains in Boston a manual master file used for editing and input purposes.

There are only two methods of communication whereby a member company may secure an MIB record:

1. An inquiry containing identification information may be mailed to the offices of the servicing agent either in Boston, Indianapolis or Toronto. These inquiries are put through the computer master file in Boston, and the coded answers are returned by mail to the inquiring company.

2. If a plan for telecommunications has been approved by the bureau, the home office underwriting departments of the companies may use tele-typewriters to communicate with the computer master file in Boston. The plan must include security provisions for the send-and-receive device in the company's office. Code numbers are used to identify the terminals. The connection is broken by the computer after receipt of inquiry. The sending of answers is subject to data communication "handshake" routines.

A member is not permitted to ask for an MIB report from the bureau unless the member has in its home office a signed preliminary or regular application for insurance, or a signed authorization in connection with an application for insurance.

Information concerning individuals listed in the bureau records is released only to the member companies; valid subpoenas are, of course, obeyed.

CASUALTY INDEX

The Casualty Index was the original service offered by the Hooper-Holmes Bureau, Inc. Located in Morristown, New Jersey, the Casualty Index serves more than 110 subscribers, and over 400 of their branch offices, in all 50 states, Canada, and Puerto Rico.

The Casualty Index files are computerized and contain the names of more than 6-1/2 million individuals, together with their insurance histories. During 1960, Casualty Index subscribers paid 49.1 percent of all the individual health insurance claims paid by insurance companies, or over $350 million out of the total of over $700 million.

The purpose of the Casualty Index is to protect its subscribers against fraudulent insurance practices which might be attempted by either their present or prospective policy holders; and to act as an information center and clearing house, not only for accident and health insurance companies, but also for life insurance companies writing disability contracts.

The Casualty Index maintains a battery of teletypewriters and teleprinters. Its teletypewriters operate on a 'round-the-clock basis, made possible by unat-tended-service features. These teletypewriters send records to subscribers on pre-proofread tapes at the rate of 100 words per minute.

Membership in the Casualty Index makes available two services: application checking and claim checking. The application checking service enables a subscriber to check his applications by teletypewriter, air mail, or a combination of air mail and Western Union telegram. This is a same-day service. Tele-typewriter subscribers can have their records back in from thirty minutes to an hour, or on any other time schedule which suits their needs. In urgent cases, a record can be obtained in five minutes.

The application checking service provides a subscriber with the complete insurance history of the applicant, including accident and sickness claims; physical and moral impairments, and a history of his "shopping for insurance." From his "shopping" history, a company can learn to what companies and on what dates the applicant previously applied for insurance.

The claim service gives each subscriber the opportunity to check his policyholder's claim activities after the policy is issued. It enables him to learn whether other companies are on the claim, whether the policyholder has filed claims with other companies, or whether his claim history is clear.

The Casualty Index subscribers write accident or sickness, franchise in-surance, guaranteed renewable, hospitalization, life policies with disability provisions, major medical, or noncancellable policies.

While membership in the Casualty Index gives its subscribers the privilege of access to a vast reservoir of information, it also places upon them the respon-sibility of faithfully contributing their experience to its files through prompt, daily reporting of claims and impairments. Thus, the type of business which is written and its volume must be such that the interchange of information between the subscriber and the Casualty Index will be mutually reciprocal, beneficial and equitable.

No written contract is required for membership in the Casualty Index. It operates on a gentleman's agreement basis, with a 30-day cancellation privilege by either party. All members pay an annual fee of $500. All branch offices of subscribers are included in the annual fee. A fee of twenty cents is charged for each applicant's name submitted, regardless of whether a record is found or not. An additional twenty cents is charged for each claim on which the Index finds a record.

All teletypewriter charges, including rental of equipment in both the subscriber's office and in the Casualty Index, as well as line charges, are paid by the subscriber.

FIRE INSURANCE

The Fire Underwriters' Investigation Bureau in Canada was organized as a non-profit corporation in 1940 for the purpose of investigating fire losses. Its work later expanded to include theft losses, and information in this category has been collected since 1960. In 1973 the title of the organization was changed to Insurance Crime Prevention Bureaux, with the Fire Underwriters' Investigation Bureau and the Canadian Automobile Theft Bureau being retained as branches.

Although there is no official connection, a counterpart to the ICPB exists in the United States. It has undergone a similar evolution, beginning as the National Board of Fire Underwriters and later becoming the Fraud and Arson Bureau of the American Insurance Association. This Fraud and Arson Bureau was disbanded in 1970. Shortly thereafter, the Insurance Crime Prevention Institute was formed by many of the insurance companies writing casualty insurance in the United States.

The objectives of the Insurance Crime Prevention Bureaux are:

1. To prevent loss of life and property, injury, and damage to property from fire or other causes.
2. To assist in the prevention of criminal offenses that cause loss of life or property, injury, or damage to property; and to collaborate with federal, state or local authorities in the detection, apprehension and prosecution of persons guilty of such offenses.
3. To investigate losses of life and property, injuries, and damage to property and the origins of such losses, and to procure from any source information relating to them.
4. To gather, collate and record statistics and to establish classification of losses of life and property, injuries and damage to property, and the risk of such losses; to make such compilations as may be in the interest of the members of the corporation, beneficial to the public or conducive to the reduction of such losses.
5. To protect and indemnify agents of the corporation from any claims made against them arising out of anything done by them within the scope of their authority.
6. To undertake any measures deemed by the corporation as necessary to protect its members and the public in loss of life and property, injury or damage to property.

The Bureaux stresses the importance of differentiating between them and the adjusters or appraisers in the insurance business. Their clients are the members of the corporation, which includes almost all insurance companies. They make their services of information available only to members. The company is nationwide in the scope of its investigations, and has about 70 employees in Canada, headquartered in Montreal. The Bureaux often collaborates with law enforcement agencies in their work.

The Bureaux issues Loss Investigation Bureau (LIB) cards to members. These cards are a way of indexing special matters in their records, thus facilitating their record-keeping and enhancing the security of their members. The LIB cards supplied to fire and casualty insurance companies enable them to check on the past history of applicants and claimants, especially where some elements of fraud, collusion, or chronic negligence may be involved.

Chapter 6

CREDIT CARD SECURITY

"Is not this a lamentable thing,
that of the skin of an innocent lamb
should be made parchment?
that parchment, being scribbled o'er,
should undo a man?
Some say the bee stings: but I say,
'tis the bee's wax; for I did but seal
once to a thing, and I was never mine
own man since."

—William Shakespeare, *King Henry VI, Part II.*

There are five kinds of credit cards. However, the distinctions between them are becoming increasingly blurred from the user's point of view. They are
1) Bank cards,
2) Oil credit cards,
3) Travel and entertainment cards (T & E),
4) Air travel cards (ATC),
5) Charge account plates.

BANK CARDS

The bank card was originally conceived of as a substitute for ready cash in the wallet or pocketbook. It makes it possible to act when you see a good bargain or to indulge in impulse buying. It has done more to expand the credit economy in which we live than any other single device, and is a fantastic money-making machine for the bank.

How Bank Cards Work

Ideally, the customer should be a depositor in the bank operating the plan. When this is the case, the bank already has a good idea of his credit worthiness and is in a position to make an offset against his account, should he become delinquent in payment of debts incurred through use of the bank card. The customer uses his bank card to make purchases from retail merchants.

In the preferred situation, these retailers are also depositors in the bank sponsoring the plan. The merchant then simply deposits his bank card invoices in the bank. These invoices are discounted by the bank at the rate usually of six percent. That means the merchant's account is credited with $94 for each $100 sale he makes under the bank card plan. Merchants pay $25 for the privilege of joining the plan. This one fee covers all branch locations.

The customer pays for his accumulated purchases in monthly installments made to the plan. An annual interest charge of 18 percent is made on his borrowings. The billing cycle is usually such that interest is added to the unpaid balance of the account before the customer's current monthly payment is credited. The average outstanding account balance is $160.

In addition to the merchant's discount and the customer's interest, the bank also augments its traditional business by servicing the customer's savings or checking account and the merchant's current account.

Details of One Plan

The blue, white and gold decal of the BankAmericard plan is a familiar landmark over most of the globe. The plan is sponsored in the U.S. by the Bank of America. In Canada, the card is called Chargex; participating members are the Royal Bank of Canada, Commerce-Imperial, Toronto-Dominion and Banque Canadien Nationale. In the United Kingdom, Barclay's is the principal sponsor. Other participating banks are in Japan (Sumitomo), Mexico (Bancomer), Colombia (Credibanco), Portugal (Sottomayor), and many other countries throughout the world. There are approximately 36 million cardholders.

The problems and practices of bank cards were examined in interviews with officials of the Royal Bank in Montreal. Operation in the U.S. and other countries is similar.

The Royal Bank is Canada's largest chartered bank, with assets of $9 million and an annual revenue of over $1/2 million. The bank's Chargex cardholder master file consists of 200,000 active records, each 300 characters long. Records are processed daily in the batched mode on magnetic tape at Montreal, Toronto and Vancouver. In Montreal, the file is loaded onto a computer disk; four clerks can query it directly from visual display terminals. At Toronto and Vancouver the clerks must consult a daily print-out of the file.

The inactive file, which contains 400,000 records, is kept in printed form. Reference copies of the entire file are kept for seven years.

A record from a customer's file contains the following entries:
- Name.
- Address.
- Account number

$$\underline{\text{N NNN NNN NNNNN N}}$$
$$\text{a} \quad \text{b} \quad \text{c} \quad \text{d} \quad \text{e}$$

a = "4" designates that this is a bank card.
b = branch number.
c = internal code.
d = customer's identification number.
e = check digit.
- Number of cards on this account.
- Number of plastic cards actually issued.
- Credit limit.
- Area code.
- Source of account (bank branch or participating merchant).
- Details of each sale.

The merchant file, also on computer, contains 40,000 records, each of which consists of 190 characters. A record in the merchant file includes the following entries:
- Name.
- Identification number.
- Branch bank where the merchant deposits his invoices.
- Merchant's Standard Industrial Classification (SIC) code.
- Location.
- Merchant's number in his chain of stores.

- Number of imprinters at this location.
- Type of card for which he nominates holders.
- Discount rate.

When a sale is made, the merchant puts the customer's plastic card into his imprinter. The customer's card contains his name and account number in raised plastic characters. The imprinter contains the merchant's name and location in raised metal characters.

When the three-part sales draft form is run through the imprinter, the customer and merchant data are printed on all copies. Details of the sale are written by hand. One copy of the sales draft is retained by the customer as his receipt. Another copy is retained by the merchant as his record of the sale. The third copy is a computer card and is sent by the merchant to his bank, where it is discounted and credited to his current account.

The Royal Bank uses *account billing*. A brief description of the sale is entered into the customer's file record and printed out on his monthly bill. The bank keeps the invoices for six months, then makes permanent microfilm records of them.

Some charge card plans use what is called *country-club billing*. Here a brief description of the sale is kept by the center and the actual invoices are returned to the customer with his monthly bill.

If a customer calls the bank with a question about an item on his bill, the bank will seek to establish the caller's identity before disclosing any information. The bank will ask the caller his name, address and account number. They will call back to the telephone number listed for the customer's name and address. The bank will only confirm statements made by the customer and will mail a photocopy of the questioned invoices to the customer's address of record.

Authorizations Required

In certain cases, the merchant must call the center for authorization before making a particular sale. These include purchases over the merchant's floor limit (usually $50 but in some cases, such as a jewelry store, as high as $300); when the customer does not have his card with him or presents an expired card; or when the merchant feels suspicion for any other reason.

If the customer presents a foreign card, the center will give him an override limit, allowing him to make purchases above the normal maximum up to a certain sum. If his floor limit is $50, the override may be up to $150. If the amount of the purchase is over the override limit, the center can Telex the center that issued the customer's card for authorization. This could mean a 15-minute delay.

In seeking authorization for a sale, the merchant gives his identifying number and the customer's account number. The authorization clerk checks the customer's record. If the sale is approved, the clerk gives the merchant a randomly assigned authorization number which is recorded and which must appear on the invoice before the bank will credit it to the merchant's account.

In some cases, the authorization clerk will talk on the phone with the customer to clear up problems connected with the sale. The call is never handled with the merchant as an intermediary.

Authorization will be refused if the card has been reported stolen or lost, or if the customer is delinquent in his payments or over his credit limit.

Selection of Risks

The bank card business got started with mass mailings of unsolicited cards to persons nominated by branch bank managers. The Royal Bank processed over a million names until their clientele shook down to its present level.

Today things are different. Some jurisdictions (British Columbia, for example) have banned mailing of unsolicited cards. Now the applicant must pick up a form at his bank or at one of the participating merchants.

The Chargex credit manager checks out the applicant with the local credit bureau. In Montreal it is the Montreal Credit Bureau, a file bureau wholly owned by Retail Credit Canada. Fifty percent of applications are declined. If the application originated at a bank, the manager is informed of the circumstances so he can answer any questions the applicant may ask.

A declined applicant receives a polite letter of refusal. If the applicant comes to the bank or Chargex center and asks why he was rejected, he simply will be told that the bank feels that in his financial position it would be unwise for him to have a card. If he presses for details, he may be told the bank has discovered items that he neglected to mention in his application . . . other financial obligations that make him a poor risk for any further credit.

In most cases, the declined applicant expects to be declined, because he knows he has a poor credit record and has been declined elsewhere.

Cases of mistaken identity do occur, but they are easily solved. Brief questioning of the applicant will make it apparent that he has been confused with someone else of the same name.

Protection from Loss

There are two types of loss with bank credit cards: fraud and collection loss. Collection losses are a small part of the total. When an account reaches the 60 to 75-day stage, Chargex center's collection department sends out the inevitable "your account is delinquent" notices and letters. Then personal telephone contact is made.

If a customer refuses to cooperate, his credit is cut off. If payment is still not made at this point, he is asked to return the card, unless it has expired or is on the verge of expiring. If he does not comply, a card pick-up service may be employed to recover the card.

If all these measures fail, and the outstanding balance is at least $100, Chargex will offset any deposit balance the customer has in his name in any of the Royal Bank branches.

Credit Card Theft

Theft of credit cards can be serious for the bank, because the cardholder's liability is limited to $50 if his card is fraudulently used by another.

Most stolen credit cards are stolen from the mails. Chargex therefore tries by all means available to keep its mailing addresses correct, and frequently changes the manner in which cards are mailed out. They are mailed in small quantities, so that no large stacks of cards accumulate.

One method of credit card theft involves the "slow walker," a person who follows the postman around at the end of the month, picking up family assistance and pension checks . . . and credit cards.

In many major cities, the underworld rents Chargex cards. For a sum of $50 a day (or more), the renter receives a brand-new card, unsigned, in the original wrapper, with the intended cardholder's name and address. The recipient is instructed how to use the card. The renter can use it for about $1,000 in purchases, some of which must be made in specified outlets. At the end of the day, the card is turned in. It is used only once.

Credit card fraud also occurs through collusion, when a merchant knowingly submits sales drafts on a stolen card. For example, the credit center may receive ten drafts, numbered serially, each for $49.95, written on the same stolen card, from the same merchant. When an investigator questions the merchant, he "doesn't remember" the transactions. Obviously, a criminal has bought something worth $200 or $300 and the merchant has taken the other $200 or $300.

Merchants discovered to be participating in collusion are immediately eliminated from the credit card program.

Spotting the Fraud

"Hot-card" notices are issued across the country. In Montreal, for example, there is a "hot-card" list with an average of 250 to 300 cards on it.

When an honest merchant spots a stolen card, he telephones the center. If he retains the card, the center pays him $25 for recovery of the card. The merchant may supply critical information to the center to enable it to track down stolen card users.

Another tactic which may be used in an effort to capture fraudulent card users is to bring pawnbrokers into the program and give them a zero floor limit. This means that every time a customer presents a Chargex card in making a purchase, the pawnbroker must telephone the center for authorization. Since many fraudulent card users look for bargains in pawnshops, many fraudulent cards may be detected in this manner.

OIL CREDIT CARDS

An oil credit card is a convenient way to pay for five or six periodic purchases of gas and oil by writing a single check each month. A large part of the sales of petroleum products is made with oil credit cards. However, gas stations now are generally accepting bank cards as well. Moreover, oil credit cards are being used increasingly for the purchase of other than petroleum products.

The fellow who runs the corner gas station is probably an independent businessman. He may own his station or lease it from the oil company that supplies him. When he makes a credit card sale, the credit invoice most likely is used to offset the delivered cost of petroleum products. Sometimes a customer will charge tires, batteries, and accessories or the price of mechanical repairs. In this case, the oil company is really factoring its dealer's accounts.

The credit card operations of two oil companies were studied. One was Shell Canada, an autonomous member of the giant Royal Dutch/Shell group. Shell supplies a wide range of petroleum products ranging from crude oil and distillate fuels to plastics and pesticides. The other was Supertest, which in 1971 was a small Canadian-owned company, marketing petroleum products in Southwestern Ontario. Supertest has since then been bought out by British Petroleum, a major vertically integrated petroleum company, 51 percent of whose stock is owned by the British government.

Shell Canada has 1.5 million credit card customers. At any given time, approximately 25 cards are being wildly abused. Annually, 1500 cards (or 1 percent) are lost, stolen or overused on a monthly basis. Both classes of cards are listed in a Stop Credit bulletin issued to dealers. Cash incentives are used to encourage dealers to retain and return stop-credit cards. Cards with expiratory dates have not yet been used by this Shell company because of administrative difficulties.

Every two days a list is sent to local credit bureaus which contains the names and addresses of exceptionally slow-paying customers.

The company receives 1,600 bad checks a month. Bad-check episodes are recorded in the company file at the time they are turned over to the credit office for collection.

Information Supplied on Applications

The company relies on local in-file credit bureaus to verify the paying record of credit card applicants. Employment data may be verified by a call to the applicant's employer. The decision to accept or decline an application is based largely on the credit report.

The application form is the basic input document for the file of credit card customers. In completing the form, the applicant supplies the following information:

- Name.
- Address.
- Whether married.
- Whether over 18.
- Length of time at present address. (If less than one year, previous address also.)
- Whether or not home is heated with Shell oil.
- Employer.
- Occupation.
- Length of service.
- Business and home phones.
- If single, name and address of a close relative.
- Finance company.
- Other charge accounts.
- Operator's license number.
- Number of cards desired.
- Intended type of usage. (Automobile, boat, aircraft.)
- Language of correspondence (English or French).
- Authorized signature.
- Date of application.

Records on File

Credit applications are kept in hard copy files. They are retained for two years. Print-outs from computer files are used for collection and customer service purposes.

A master register of customers on file, both active and inactive, is printed twice a year. Old copies are destroyed after each reprinting. A customer service record of purchases and payments is produced twice monthly and retained for six months. Correspondence files are also kept. The computerized files of customers are historical as to purchase and payment information. These files are maintained for as long as the account is active, plus two years.

In 1967, the company began to microfilm its records. The microfilm records are retained for seven years regardless of whether the accounts are active or inactive.

Credit Information Service

National Data Corporation provides a credit card information service to certain oil companies, including Supertest, Gulf, and Texaco. The computer file is located in Atlanta, Georgia. The file can be accessed from remote terminals in Toronto, Canada; Camden, New Jersey; Chicago, Illinois; Reno, Nevada; and Atlanta, Georgia.

The files are aggregated according to the oil company that contributes them. Each record contains the number of a credit card and instructions in coded form telling what the card issuer wants done with respect to honoring that card.

The oil companies banking these data provide NDC with a list of people who have permission to query the file. These people, usually dealers, identify themselves by code numbers. When a dealer is presented with a credit card in payment for a purchase which exceeds the floor limit (usually $15), he is obliged to call a specified NDC center for authorization to make the sale. The dealer identifies himself by his code number and the name of the oil company whose products he handles; and gives the number of the customer's credit card.

The terminal operator queries the computer file. If no direct response is indicated, she gives the dealer a randomly assigned number that the dealer enters on the sales draft to indicate that the sale has been authorized.

If the computer record contains a code number corresponding to a directed response, the operator gives that information to the dealer. If, as a result of such a directed response, the sale cannot be made on credit, the customer is so informed, in whatever verbiage the oil company has instructed its dealer to use for the particular situation.

Supertest has an arrangement with National Data in Atlanta, whereby NDC will store information on a certain number of customers whose accounts are delinquent. They also store warnings of one kind or another with respect to certain customers' current histories. There may be a limit, for example, on the number or value of purchases that an individual customer can make within a specified period of time. This minimizes losses from customers who decide to take the oil company for a ride . . . running up large bills in various locations. When the service station operator calls Atlanta for authorization, he may receive a message that says, "Refuse the sale," "Hold for head office," or similar instructions.

Customers are requested to report stolen cards immediately. This information is stored in the computer as well.

TRAVEL AND ENTERTAINMENT CARDS

The T & E card was originally meant for people who travel and entertain a lot, but don't want to carry a lot of cash. It provides a modicum of credit, but the cardholder, often a businessman or salesman on an expense account, is generally expected to settle up promptly when he is reimbursed for his expenses by his company.

Traditionally, the T & E cardholder would use it for airplane tickets, hotel accommodations, meals in the better restaurants. Ever serving the free-spending traveler, the card companies have signed up florists, jewelers, and all manner of shops and stores. The fact that T & E card companies charge a $15 annual membership fee to cardholders tends to discourage the marginal middle-income consumer who often gets into trouble on account of his bank card.

Because Paris cab drivers don't carry credit card imprinters around with them, it has always been possible to get cash (usually up to some limit, say $200) with a T & E card. This fact itself creates a special security problem in respect to these cards.

The pattern of operation is much the same as with other types of cards:

1) An applicant is checked through his local in-file credit bureau and also with Credit Index, because the T & E crowd is much more mobile than the users of bank cards or oil credit cards.

2) Conversely, the cardholder who can't keep up his payments or otherwise abuses his credit privileges will find himself listed both with his local credit bureau and with Credit Index. (See Chapter 5.)

3) Each major T & E card company runs its own authorization network with

roughly the same rituals of access and service as the banks employ for their cards.

American Express Company

The leader in the field of travel and entertainment cards is American Express Company, whose Amex checks have long served the same purpose for the occasional traveler.

The American Express Card Division, with more than 3.5 million cardmembers and over 100,000 establishments which accept the card worldwide, is heavily dependent upon the use of sophisticated data processing equipment.

Greatly concerned with the confidentiality and security of records and computer equipment, the company has taken numerous steps to maintain security, including the use of computer passwords, identification codes, limited access, and on-the-spot security agents.

The files on cardmembers relate solely to their credit history and past experience with Amex and, except for the initial application which lists home addresses, employment, and references, no personal information about these persons is maintained. Cardholders may, by writing to the company, review, correct, or rebut information which they believe to be inaccurate.

American Express does not release information regarding its cardmembers' credit experience. However, an exception is made in instances where persons who have American Express accounts apply for other types of credit and give American Express as a reference. In such cases, they will advise in a limited fashion whether their experience with the cardmember has been satisfactory.

Amex will also supply this type of information in response to court order, judicial subpoena, or other legal process. In certain cases, such as government subpoena, the investigation may be confidential and unknown to the cardmember.

The information in the cardholder file is computerized and can be accessed from any one of the three operation centers in the United States tied into the company's main computers. These centers are presently located in New York City; Miami, Florida; and Phoenix, Arizona. Access to the receiving sets at these operation centers is limited to those with a "need-to-know." There is no direct phone or mail access to the credit history information on the cardmembers.

As part of the authorization system, restaurants, hotels, and other establishments may call the authorization center in New York to obtain permission for the acceptance of certain charges. However, whether or not American Express allows these charges to be made to its cardmembers' accounts, no information is given during these transactions as to the status of cardmembers' accounts. An establishment requesting approval will merely get a "yes" or a "no," but no reasons.

The Diners Club

Another leading T & E card is the Diners Club card. The Diners Club maintains two basic files: the Master Cardholder file, which is computerized, and the Cardholder Application File.

The computer on which the Master Cardholder File is held is located in Denver, Colorado, and can be accessed from remote terminals in Diners Club regional offices in New York, Miami, Los Angeles and Denver.

In addition to the cardholder's name, address and account number, this file also contains the usual type of monetary data required for billing cardholder charges:

- Amount owing from prior months.
- Payments.
- Credits.
- Charges.

It contains non-monetary data such as:

- Status of the account.
- Warning codes, e.g., lost card, pending adjustment, etc.
- Number of credit cards issued on the account.
- Code which will cause the account to be billed in U.S. or Canadian currency.

The Cardholder Application File contains the original application for a Diners Club credit card on approved accounts. It is manual and cannot be accessed from terminals. Information contained in an application is typical of that in most consumer credit applications, i.e., employment data, references, etc.

Rejected applications are separately stored and retained for two years.

Carte Blanche

Carte Blanche is a subsidiary of the Avco Corporation of Los Angeles, which also owns Avco Finance, a consumer loan company. The accounts representing people or firms who are cardholders are maintained on magnetic tape, microfilm strip, microfilm roll, and microfilm aperture card. Foreign accounts are not grouped, but rather are integrated in the files among U.S. accounts. They are identified through the use of a unique account number.

The member master file is maintained on magnetic tape. It contains:

- Name.
- Address.
- Account number.
- Collection history.
- Payment history.
- Purchase history.
- Type of account.
- Cross-reference information.
- Current amount owed.
- Delinquent amount owed.
- Last billing amount.

A listing of cardholder names and addresses is maintained in last name alphabetical order on magnetic tape. A list rental file on magnetic tape contains cardholder names and addresses in zip code order.

The cardholder application file is kept on aperture cards. An aperture card is a punched card with an insert of microfilm. The keypunched portion contains information for sorting and identification. In this case, the microfilm insert is a photograph of the member's original application for credit. It shows:

- Name.
- Address.
- Employer.
- Previous employer.
- Annual earnings.
- Telephone number.
- Credit references.
- Signature.

Information maintained is released to other credit-extending companies upon their written request, provided their customer has given Carte Blanche as a credit reference.

Credit bureaus receive write-off information as part of a contractual agreement.

Although information is computerized, it is not now being released in any fashion other than by telephone or mail. No information maintained by Carte Blanche is accessible by remote terminal.

AIR TRAVEL CARDS

An air travel card provides a convenient way of deferring payment for air fare. It is especially useful for people who travel frequently in business, but don't necessarily entertain—investigators, journalists and engineers, for example.

You can quickly learn the value of an ATC when a man you're following in New York takes a cab to La Guardia and steps on board the Washington shuttle, leaving you on the ground with your pocket full of subway tokens.

The on-line ATC allows the holder to step up to any airline ticket counter and be on his way in a matter of minutes. There are basically two kinds of cards: personal and industry. In the former case, procedures are much like those for T & E cards. In the latter case, the firm is billed, thus simplifying the filing of expense accounts.

American Airlines

The application for American Airlines' Personal Credit Card is evaluated on the basis of an in-file report supplied by the local credit bureau. They look in particular for any past derogatory situations such as nonpayment of bills, or lawsuits. This information is used solely for reaching a decision on the issuance of an on-line airline credit card.

If the decision is negative, a letter is sent to the applicant stating one of two positions:

1) That the decision was based on information supplied from the local credit bureau. The bureau's address and telephone number are given.
2) That the customer has been turned down as a matter of company policy—because of age, income, inability to verify employment, or the absence of any credit references.

For accounts that have been approved, the airline establishes the necessary address information in its computer system. They do not, however, attempt to establish a credit line or antecedent information based on either the credit report or credit application. The only computer record other than address and receivables information is a statistical record of the number of purchases and times delinquent.

If the account becomes seriously delinquent and the customary dunning and telephone calls have failed to produce a satisfactory reason for the delinquent situation, the account will be cancelled and the balance placed with a local collection agency for further action.

Air Canada

Air Canada is Canada's national air carrier and one of the world's ten largest commercial airlines. Its revenue originates mainly from passenger service ($387 million in 1970); the rest (about $90 million) from freight service, mail and charter. In 1970, Air Canada provided service to 7-1/2 million passengers over 6,700 passenger miles, with an average passenger load factor of 57 percent.

Air Canada's credit cards are honored by Canadian National Railways and by a chain of hotels run by the state-owned rail carrier. Air Canada has two kinds of credit cards:

1) Industry cards are held mostly by organizations. In 1971 there were 40,000 such cards representing over 5,500 accounts.

2) Individual Air Canada-CN credit cards, issued on individual request. There were 142,000 active cards in 1971.

There is both a hard copy and a computerized file for individual credit card holders. The computerized file is solely a billing file and contains only name and address as personal information. The hard copy file contains the credit card application. It is kept in locked cabinets at the credit office, where it is accessible only to credit office employees.

The credit card application asks for the name of the applicant's bank. A check is usually made with the bank and, if necessary, a further check is made with the Retail Credit Corporation. If the application is declined, very few reasons are given to the applicant.

No information is released on the credit card holder file, except as follows:

1) There is some exchange of customer rating with Canadian Pacific. The information exchanged is not specific; the rating is reported either as "good" or "bad." (Canadian Pacific is a private corporation in the air-rail-hotel business which supplements and, in some cases, competes with Air Canada/CN.)

2) A list of "bad cards" is distributed regularly to all organizations honoring the AC-CN cards.

Passenger records are kept as residual parts of the ticket form and in the computerized reservation system. A computerized passenger record contains:

- Name.
- Itineraries (Air Canada and others).
- Point of Contact (telephone number or address).
- Ticketing information.
- Other information when applicable (hotel or car reservation, special arrangement).

The information originates at the reservation office. A passenger record is kept in the file until the last itinerary is completed, then held on magnetic tape for three months.

The passenger file is used mostly to produce passenger lists for departures.

The passenger ticket file is kept six months and is regularly consulted by the police or the RCMP.

CHARGE ACCOUNT CARDS

The department store charge account is a direct descendent of the earliest form of consumer credit: the local merchant who put it on the cuff. The charge account is strictly a local convenience. It does not open doors nationally or internationally. However, a customer who discharges his obligations to local merchants in a responsible manner can earn a favorable credit rating with the local in-file credit bureau, which can help him acquire most of the more widely recognized vehicles for consumer credit.

Basically, the charge card is just a means for identifying the customer. Many years ago, department stores used to distribute coins for this purpose. The author can recall, as a very small boy in Philadelphia, being severely punished when caught playing "store" with neighborhood children using a handful of odd-shaped coins snitched from his mother's dresser. The coins were engraved with the names of "John Wanamaker," "Strawbridge & Clothier," "Sears & Roebuck," "Abraham-Straus," etc.

Charge account procedures were studied at Robert Simpson Co., a predominantly English department store chain, which is also associated with Sears Roebuck Company of the United States in the operation of a mail order business as well as thirty-three Simpson-Sears stores[4]; and at Dupuis Freres Ltee., a French-owned department store in Montreal, Canada. Their procedures are typical of those generally encountered in all of North America.

Simpson's Credit Procedures

Simpson's stores make available to customers charge accounts payable in 30 days and installment accounts payable over terms up to 36 months. Customers using installment accounts are allowed to add purchases up to an approved credit maximum, and in addition to required monthly payments, to pay their account in whole or in part at any time. The percentage of total annual sales made on an installment basis has ranged from about 24 to 27 percent in the last five years.

The installment accounts of the retail stores are sold to Simpson's Acceptance Company, a wholly owned subsidiary of the parent firm, at a price which provides the Acceptance Company with gross income at least equal to the full amount of the service charges which customers have agreed to pay.

All account-customer files are kept in manual form at the accounts department of the head office of the chain. The file consists of an account application form and a record of recent purchases and payments. There is no long-term accumulation of paid-up purchases.

Any customer may specify who has the right to use his credit account, where the monthly statement is to be sent, and who may ask information about it. Information such as payments made and the outstanding balance are available through the customer service office upon identification of the questioner. It is possible but unlikely that such account information could be obtained over the telephone with minimal self-identification of the questioner.

As long as an account is in effect, the company will not give a customer's credit evaluation to a credit reference company. Only the existence of the account will be confirmed. No information is given out on former accounts. However, in cases where fraud is recognized, the company will make any and all information available to any agency which will assist in apprehending the offender or minimizing the company's loss.

Dupuis Freres Ltee.'s Credit Procedures

Dupuis Freres is a Montreal department store serving a mostly French Canadian clientele. It has 1,100 regular full-time employees, plus a varying number of part-time employees during the holiday shopping season.

The credit card owner file contains 50,000 records. A credit card owner record is a hard copy record kept at the credit office. The portion necessary for billing is computerized. The manual record contains information mostly supplied by the credit department:

- Name.
- Address.
- Telephone number.
- Birth date.
- Occupation.
- Bank.
- Credit references.
- Personal references.
- Other accounts.
- Debts.

If the customer is single, an important factor is whether or not he lives with his parents. If he does, he is considered to be a better risk.

Additional information is added to the record if verification is necessary. The higher the credit requested, the more verification is required. Usually two verifications are made:

1) Employment check with the applicant's employer.

2) Credit check by a telephone call to the Montreal Credit Bureau.

Credit applications are refused at the rate of approximately 20 to 40 percent. The higher rate occurs during holiday seasons. When an application is refused, the applicant is told why: applicant's instability, age or antecedents such as a poor credit rating or court judgments. If an applicant believes that the cause for refusal is either erroneous or unjustified, he may come to the credit office for a verbal interview. In case of errors, corrective action is taken.

If a credit card holder gives his Dupuis account as credit reference, Dupuis will supply the following information:

- Credit limit.
- Actual credit balance.
- Monthly payment.
- Paying habits.

No other information is released. Records are considered confidential and kept in locked cabinets at the credit office, where they are accessible to the credit office employees (37 persons). Only five employees are authorized to release credit information. Inactive records are kept for six or seven years, then destroyed.

Dupuis has an internal security service that keeps a file on shoplifters. There are several thousand names in this file. Its use is internal; however, information is exchanged with other department stores at times.

An interview with Jean Trudel, vice-president for finance and control of Dupuis Freres Ltee., suggests that problems, procedures and practices are just about universal in the credit field.

Q. What information do you give to another employer regarding one of your former employees?

A. When our experience was favorable, we give details. When it was unfavorable, we omit the details and restrict ourselves to saying that the employee was engaged from such and such date to such and such date in our company.

Q. What does the file of a customer who has an account with you contain?

A. Name. Address. Telephone. Birthdate. Age. Occupation. Bank account. Credit or personal references. Where he lives. Whether he has other accounts. We find out from the Montreal Credit Bureau whether he is under the Lacombe Law.[5] References are given over the telephone. They tell us whether he has other accounts, makes loans. If the individual has an instability of employment or residence, the investigation ends there.

Q. Do you also get a verification from the employer?

A. When you are able to get it. Generally, all the credit questions that are made pass through the Montreal Credit Bureau. There are three situations. One in which no verification is made. Another which is verified by telephone with the Montreal Credit Bureau. A third in which you pursue the investigation according to the details.

Q. What sources have caused you types of errors?

A. Bad interpretation of names. There is frequently a difference between the name given by the person who calls to get credit and the one by which he is known to the bureau.

Q. What is the rate of refusal?

A. Between 20% and 40% according to the season. There are always more demands during holiday times.

Q. What are the causes of revocation of cards?

A. When, according to our judgment, he has surpassed the limit he has been granted according to his position, what he has on hand, etc.

Q. Do you try to retrieve the card?

A. As often as possible. It's very important.

Q. Do you utilize the services of people who specialize in the retrieval of cards?

A. They are sometimes of use to us.

Q. Do you keep the list of purchases of your clients in your files?

A. We have them on microfilm. The information is revealed to no one, except the law.

Q. Do you have a system for cards that have been lost or stolen?

A. As soon as someone has lost his card, he calls us and it is registered. On our acceptance cards it is marked that the card was stolen.

Q. Do you have files on the people who steal?

A. There is no exchange, but the other stores are informed. If another store checks with us about an individual we give him the information. We have a security service. It is left up to the chief of security to take the necessary steps with the police or to use simple remonstrances. This depends on the gravity and whether it has been repeated elsewhere. These files number about one thousand.

SUMMARY

The proliferating use of credit cards has become an integral part of the credit economy of industrial nations, spanning borders and cultures. This expansion has worked hand-in-glove with the rapid development of computerized data systems, which simplify the process of credit information storage and approval of credit.

Similar patterns have been observed throughout the credit card business, covering bank and oil company cards, travel and entertainment or air travel cards, and store charge account cards.

Relatively small amounts of information are kept on file, beyond an initial application which lists name and address, employment data and credit references; and a current record of the applicant's credit purchases and recent payment history. The most commonly used sources of information for credit card approval other than the applicant himself are the local in-file credit bureau and the individual's employer.

There is an increasing dependence upon central computer systems to enable store clerks, remote dealers or merchants to obtain almost instant authorization for a purchase, either by telephone call or direct signal, within a store or across the country.

Perhaps reflecting general concerns about the privacy of personal information, there is also much greater restrictiveness than in the past over the release of information regarding a person's credit experience, except in cases of fraud or theft (a serious problem with credit cards, since the holder's liability is generally limited), or where the cardholder has given permission for such release.

Chapter 7

MOTOR VEHICLE AND OTHER GOVERNMENT RECORDS

"WHEEL-LESS CHARIOTS 2
HIQQUIO 2

Two chariots inlaid with ivory,
[fully] assembled, painted crimson,[1]
equipped with reins, with leather
cheek-straps [?] [and] horn bits [?] ."

—*Knossos Tablet* Sd 1401, 1400 B.C. (?)
Deciphered by Michael Ventris, 1954

On April 25, 1974, during the course of a special news report on the ABC television network entitled "The Paper Prison," a nation of viewers was told that there are in the U.S. Government some 910 data banks containing approximately 1,520,000,000 records. A report by the Senate Judiciary Committee's subcommittee on constitutional rights confirmed that there are at least 750 such federal information systems—and, even more startling, that no one knows what data is in all of them about whom. Taken together, such systems constitute the largest store of personalized information in the world . . . and they are growing.

Government data banks, at both the national and state level, span a wildly

169

diversified range of information, much of it restricted to the use of the particular agency collecting it, some of it accessible to other authorized government or law enforcement agencies for information exchange, and some of it public information accessible to anyone, in the latter case more often as generalized statistical data than as personal records.

On January 1, 1975, President Gerald Ford signed into law the new Privacy Act, designed to curb misuse of federal records. Acknowledging that the new law fails to provide adequate protection for the individual against unnecessary disclosures of personal information, the President nevertheless commented that the law "strikes a reasonable balance between the right of the individual to be left alone and the interest of society in open government, national defense, foreign policy, law enforcement, and a high quality and trustworthy federal work force."

The Privacy Act requires that the individual give consent before government agencies may disclose personal records to outsiders. However, it permits access to those records by law enforcement and statistical agencies, and by appropriate congressional committees.

Under this legislation, individuals may examine their own records and challenge their accuracy. An individual may also bring a civil suit where he believes that an agency has infringed upon his civil rights, and criminal penalties and fines are provided for willful violation of the statute. It should be noted, however, that law enforcement agencies (including the CIA) are exempt from many of the law's prohibitions.

In this chapter we will examine in some detail one of the largest government data banks at the state level (provincial level in Canada), the record systems of motor vehicle departments, which are, as we discovered in Chapter 2, *the most prolific source of personal information in their activity in dissemination.* Included are the driver and vehicle records of the state of California and the province of Manitoba in Canada, with a summary glance at similar records in Great Britain.

The chapter concludes with a brief look at military records, and at two of the largest national record systems, the Internal Revenue Service and the Bureau of the Census, which are of great general interest but less immediate concern for the security officer or investigator because of the relative inaccessibility of the personal data on record.

CALIFORNIA DEPARTMENT OF MOTOR VEHICLES

The California Department of Motor Vehicles was selected for this study because of its size and the degree of automation in its records processing.

The department is responsible for driver licensing, financial responsibility of drivers and owners, vehicle and boat registration and the issuance of license plates, and occupational licensing and investigations in compliance with the Motor Vehicle Code.

The department maintains 147 field offices and a major headquarters office in Sacramento. The staff needed for the many examining, licensing, registering and information services consists of some 7,000 people.

Total vehicle registrations for 1973 were 15,739,000 on-highway vehicles, and 127,000 off-highway vehicles. Drivers' licenses outstanding for the same year were 12,775,000. Boat registrations totaled 475,000. During a recent twelve-month period the department responded to 8.5 million requests for driver record information (from both law enforcement and private agencies), and 11 million requests for vehicle and boat registration data (law enforcement and private).

In the decades since World War II, California's DMV has faced the same problems besetting all motor vehicle bureaus, only more so. These include steady rises in population, number of drivers and vehicles on the road, along with rapid increases in file sizes and in the number of requests for information from both the drivers' license and vehicle registration files. As a result the DMV has had to turn to modern EDP technology to handle the enormous problems of information storage and dissemination.

Automated Management Information System (AMIS)

The DMV has converted its drivers' license and vehicle registration records to a real-time computer system. This Automated Management Information System (AMIS) consists of a real-time, on-line, random access, multi-computer complex. Its operation has been described in a DMV report:

"Under AMIS processing, inquiries to the master files are entered into the system from local and remote locations as the need for information arises. Responses are returned in a matter of seconds via messages transmitted over telephone lines.

This real-time computer complex will process and store most of the urgent and routine transactions as they occur, providing fast response to most inquiries by either projecting the desired information on video display devices or in other forms desired, such as printed reports, punched cards, punch paper tape, or magnetic tape.

AMIS currently provides real-time access to over 34,500,000 individual driver or vehicle registration records twenty-four hours a day, 365 days per year. This data base represents one of the largest 'people' and property files in the country today."

The figures quoted were for 1971; the data base is, of course, much larger today.

The heart of the department's EDP facilities consists of four major computer systems, all UNIVAC third generation "Series 70" hardware. One of the four systems is a Series 70/45, equipped with 131,000 bytes of main memory. It serves primarily as the communications processor for AMIS. A 70/6 system processes a variety of work including the Automated Name Index. Its data base is stored on 26 high-speed, random access discs, each disc pack storing approximately 1,350,000 name records. The 70/6 system is equipped with 262,144 bytes of main memory.

The two workhorses of the AMIS complex are the twin Series 70/55 computers, one for the Master Drivers' License file, the other for the Master Vehicle Registration file. Core storage capacity for each of these two machines is 524,288 bytes. Connected to each 70/55 is a series of fourteen tape drives, each capable of passing 60,000 bytes per second to the processor through a tape controller, a sort of traffic policeman that regulates which tape drive will pass its information to the processor and which will receive information from the processor.

The master files of each DMV division are stored in UNIVAC Mass Storage Units, each with a capability of storing approximately 3 million or more records. The combined mass storage units can store up to 57 million records. Over 40 million are currently on file.

Who Uses AMIS?

Most of the information in DMV files is considered to be public record data. In addition to providing information to its own field offices and law enforcement agencies, the DMV sells vehicle registration and drivers' license record information, with the exception of information relating to a person's physical or mental condition, for a small fee (75¢, for example, for a vehicle registration report by license plate number or vehicle identification number).

Some of the major users of AMIS are:

• California DMV Field Offices (23 have direct inquiry capability).
• The Los Angeles Police Department (L.A.P.D.).
• California Highway Patrol and its field offices, the Alameda Police Infor-

mation Network (P.I.N.), and most California city police departments and county sheriffs' offices, all through the California Law Enforcement Telecommunications System (CLETS).
• The National Auto Theft Bureau.

Drivers' License and History File

The drivers' license and history files are maintained by the Division of Drivers' Licenses. The files contain magnetic images of the information on every driver's license issued in the state. Attached to this information, whenever applicable, is the driving history of each licensee, including the date and type of every Vehicle Code violation and the legal disposition of each offense. If a driver was cited for speeding, the section of the Vehicle Code violation is shown, along with the date of the citation, the license number of the vehicle the person was driving, when he went to court and the court's docket number, whether he forfeited bail (paid a fine in lieu of trial), and so on.

The most important applications into the Drivers' License File are these:

1) Law enforcement agencies and courts use drivers' license records in the identification, apprehension, and disposition of possible offenders of the law.
2) The DMV's own Driver Improvement Analysts use AMIS in obtaining up-to-date driver record information for hearings.
3) The DMV's Research and Statistics unit provides reports based on file samplings to various and governmental safety agencies.
4) Automobile insurance companies are AMIS's largest users of low priority driver information, obtained on a fee basis. The information enables insurance companies to make more accurate decisions regarding risk, coverage, etc.

Vehicle Registration File

The Registration master file has a magnetic image of the data contained on the registration certificate of every vehicle or vessel registered in the state, including information relating to both the vehicle's description and its owner. Vehicle description data includes the license plate number, vehicle identification number, DMV codes for body type (sedan, station wagon, etc.), manufacturer, year of make, year first sold, etc. Ownership information is broken into two groups: registered owner and legal owner (usually a lending agency when the car or vessel has been financed).

Stored within the registration file is the Vehicle Identification Number file, acting as a cross reference index to the registration file. The manufacturer's Vehicle Identification Number (VIN) for each vehicle is stored in this file and is used to gain information on a vehicle or its owner when the VIN is known but the license number is not. A VIN inquiry can thus be made in place of the standard license number inquiry.

Requests into the Registration File are made in much the same way as those against the Drivers' License File. These include the following:

1) Law enforcement agencies and courts use the Registration files to determine legal or registered ownership of a vehicle for such reasons as locating the owners of abandoned vehicles, providing full descriptions of stolen vehicles, determining whether or not homemade or highly modified vehicles meet certain safety requirements, etc.

2) DMV Field Offices use the Registration master file to determine the status of records in the case of lost registration certificates, questionable ownership, etc.

3) Law enforcement agencies additionally use this file through low priority inquiry to determine the name and address of owners who have been cited, or who have failed to pay fines and fees or report to court.

Automated Name Index (ANI)

Previously, in order to access an automated record, the driver's license or vehicle registration number or VIN had to be known and recorded. The ability to access both master files using only the name and specific additional identifiers has been provided by the Automated Name Index.

Under this computerized system, one common name index is used to cross-reference both the driver and vehicle files. An AMIS user no longer needs to know the driver's license number or vehicle license number in order to make an inquiry; the person's name is enough. The ANI provides the user with the named person's driver's license number and any vehicles or vessels registered in that person's name, after which a normal inquiry can be made. If the name, address and date of birth are known, the response from the ANI system is almost instantaneous. With name and address, it is almost as fast. Where the name alone is known, and that name is a common one (John Smith or Mary Jones), the system will count the number of John Smiths and Mary Joneses. If 16 or more responses are indicated for a single ANI inquiry, the user will be informed of the total number of records meeting the input criteria. More specific data will require another inquiry.

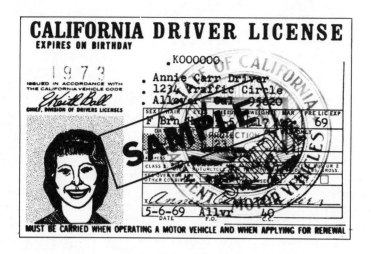

REPLY TO INQUIRY MADE TO SAMPLE DRIVER'S LICENSE

DATE:03/30/71*TIME:08:02*
DL/NO:K000000*B/D:06-03-45*NAME:DRIVER ANNIE CARR*ADDR: 1234
TRAFFIC CIRCLE
ALLOVER 95620*EFF:05-20-69*
STATUS
LIC/ISS:05-06-69* LIC/MLD:05-20-69* EXP/BD:73*CLASS:3 *END/CERT:NONE*
LEGAL HISTORY
NONE .
ABSTRACTS-ADULT
VIOL/DATE:01-02-71*CONV/DATE:01-29-71*SEC?VIOL:22350   VC*
DOCKET:*899998*DISP:B*COURT:57680*VEH/LIC:SAM026*
FTA:NONE
ACCIDENTS:NONE
END

Figure 7-1: Response from the Drivers License Master File
(Courtesy California Department of Motor Vehicles)

REPLY TO INQUIRY MADE ON SAMPLE REGISTRATION

DATE: 02/01/71*TIME:08:00
REG:71*LIC#SAM026*YRMD:70*MAKE:FORD*BTM:SD*VIN#:OR30F106599
R/O:ROE RICHARD/MARY*2415 1ST AVE*CITY:SACRAMENTO   C.C.:34
ZIP#:95818
SOLD:10/03/69*ISSD:01/01/71*LOCD:4
L/O:U O M E LN CO*2570 24TH ST*CITY:SACRAMENTO
TYPE:11*CYL:08*SMOG:3*VEH:11*BODY:O*CLAS:AC*FEE:0054
END

Figure 7-2: Response from Vehicle Registration Master File
(Courtesy California Department of Motor Vehicles)

Urgent Inquiries

The California DMV's master files may be accessed directly by a variety of remote terminals or telecommunications networks. Inquiries may originate from Video Data Interrogators (VDI), Keyboard Send and Receive Devices (KSR), or Automatic Send and Receive Devices (ASR). Each inquiry from a remote unit is transmitted over telephone lines to the Sacramento main office. Inquiries from the headquarters terminal are routed through special telephone cabling to the appropriate computer system.

The first stop in the computer complex is the communications processor. It validates the message, determining whether it pertains to drivers' license or vehicle registration information, and whether it is an urgent or non-urgent request. If the message is an urgent inquiry, it is then routed to either the Drivers' License master file or the Vehicle Registration file. The computer stores the message, calls the appropriate program into memory, extracts or reads the information requested from the data file, formats it as required, and transmits the response back to the communications processor. The communications processor in turn sends the response to the originating remote terminal or specific telecommunications network. All of this occurs without noticeable interruption in the current processing on the computer. A typical reply to an inquiry into the Driver's License File is shown in Figure 7-1; a reply on an inquiry for Vehicle Registration information is shown in Figure 7-2.

The process is completely computerized, requiring no manual intervention for normal operation. In the event of a momentary delay caused by a high incidence of urgent requests, the processor simply queues the requests until the messages can be processed in turn.

The described type of operation, in which all of the computer systems are operating, is known as the "simplex" mode. A back-up system has also been devised for AMIS. When one processor is down for any length of time, the other processor goes in backup to the one that is down. If, for instance, the Registration computer system is shut down, its master files are "switched over" to the drivers' license computer for processing, and vice versa. This is known as the "dual" mode of operation. In this manner, each master file is always available to AMIS users. The capability of one processor to handle another's master file is relatively unique. California's DMV is one of the few agencies in the United States having this capability.

Non-Urgent Inquiries

Instead of being routed directly to the appropriate master file, "non-urgent" inquiries are stored on tape located on tape drives connected to the communications processor. The tape is periodically physically removed and taken to the appropriate master file processors. There the requests are stripped from the tape and fed into the computer for processing. Information retrieved from the master files is listed on appropriate forms by an on-line high-speed printer. The listed forms are then delivered or mailed to the inquirer.

Non-urgent inquiries may also be received in the form of punched cards. These are read into the processor, which retrieves the requested data and records it on tape. The tape is then punched out by means of a tape-to-punch utility program, so that the requester receives the information back in punched card format. Law enforcement agencies generally employ the punched card method. Various insurance companies employ the method by which the non-urgent reply is listed on forms and delivered or mailed back to them.

The Future of AMIS

The California DMV believes that AMIS has streamlined the department's internal practices, advanced the state's law enforcement capabilities, and helped to some degree to alleviate the crowded state of California's court calendars.

For the future, faster, smaller and more reliable equipment is envisaged. AMIS or one of its "offspring" may eventually reach all the way to the individual law enforcement officer, in the form of a remote video device in his patrol car. Drivers' licenses may be issued, complete with photographs enclosed in laminated plastic, within minutes after an applicant has passed his examination. Each new transaction will be recorded on the master file within minutes after it occurs, providing all users with absolutely up-to-date data.

MANITOBA (CANADA) MOTOR VEHICLES BRANCH

For another example of the type of information gathering conducted by a registrar of motor vehicles, the Manitoba (Canada) Motor Vehicles Branch was studied. It provides information for the province's government operated automobile insurance plan (AUTOPAC).

The law setting up AUTOPAC specified that the services of investigatory credit-reporting agencies were not to be used to screen applicants for automobile insurance. At the same time the law provides that "The Administrator of the AUTOPAC plan may gather whatever information he requires to discharge his duties, the provisions of Manitoba's Privacy of Personal Information Act notwithstanding."

AUTOPAC consists of three parts:

1) No-fault insurance that pays the cost of medical expenses and direct loss to victims of accidents. If a driver accumulates demerits (points) as a result of traffic violations, the cost of his insurance rises. If he acquires the maximum number of points, his license is suspended. No-fault insurance must be bought when a driver obtains or renews his license.

2) The registered owner of a motor vehicle must purchase AUTOPAC public liability insurance at the time he registers or re-registers his vehicle. Registration is for one year, and a face amount of $50,000 is mandatory. (Higher limits are available. An owner can also go to a private insurance company for higher coverage, in which case he may be subject to the customary Retail Credit Company investigation.)

3) The registered owner of a motor vehicle must also purchase collision insurance, minimum $250 deductible. $100 and $50 deductible coverage is available at higher premiums. A surcharge for public liability and collision insurance is levied against owners of vehicles who have been involved in accidents.

Drivers' License Files

The drivers' license file consists of 440,000 records. The file is stored on a computer but printed copies and copies on microfilm also exist. All drivers who hold licenses, or have held them within the last five years, have records on file.

Microfilm records are kept on any person convicted of a driving offense within the last ten years. Documentary records are kept of notices of suspension, accident reports, medical and optometric reports on drivers.

A driver's license record includes such data as name, address, date of birth, sex, license number, convictions and demerit points, reports of accidents and MVB actions, conditions or restrictions, insurance coverage, driving test information, medical data where pertinent, and vehicles owned by the driver.

The following inputs are received to the drivers' license file:

• Application (with birth certificate and recent photos).
• Results of driver's test or retests.
• Court convictions.
• Medical transactions.
• Complaints about drivers.

The following information from the drivers' license file is available from the Motor Vehicles Branch to the recipients specified:

1) *MVB Main Office:* Computer-driven displays are used to check applications for drivers' licenses, review complaints relative to the assessment of penalty points, produce transcripts, complete reports of convictions, and collate reports of accidents and convictions. The computer is used to match up various possible permutations of the driver's name so that Jonathan L. Doe can't avoid assessment of demerit points by giving his name in court as J. Livingstone Doe.

   By definition, a *transcript* is a copy of the driver's record, except for the section "Action by MVB." To be admissible in court, a transcript must be signed by the registrar of motor vehicles and the deputy minister of transport, of which the MVB is a branch.

2) *The Royal Canadian Mounted Police* have five computer-driven displays. They can get the driver's record with two exceptions: juvenile convictions (under 18) and actions by MVB. The RCMP also gets a microfilm copy of the file.

3) *City police* in Winnipeg, St. James and St. Boniface have microfilm copies. Other police phone or write for specific information.

4) *Insurance companies* can get transcripts.

5) *Credit bureaus* can get verification of the validity of the license and the driver's name and address.

6) *Employers* can get a transcript if the driver has given his written consent.

7) *Other state and provincial MVB's* can get transcripts on request. When an out-of-province driver is convicted of an offense, a record of the conviction is sent to his home state or province.

8) *Examining physicians* receive transcripts when their medical opinion of a driver is requested.

9) *Attornies* can get copies of their clients' transcripts.

Vehicle Files

The vehicle file is also stored on computer. It contains 420,000 records, each 160 characters long. It is updated weekly. A microfilm copy of the file is made available to the police.

A vehicle record includes such data as the name, license number, address and date of birth of the owner; age, make, style, color, model and serial number of the vehicle; insurance; number of cylinders; use (business or pleasure) and area of operation (business vehicles).

Information from the vehicle file is available to the public for a small fee. It costs 50¢ to get the owner's name and address if a vehicle license plate number is known. It costs 50¢ to obtain the plate numbers of vehicles owned by an individual if his name and address are known.

BRITAIN'S DRIVER AND VEHICLE FILES

In his admirable study of *Private Lives and Public Surveillance*, James B. Rule has examined in depth some of the same personal information systems studied here, though in general with a different focus. His chapter on vehicle and driver files in Great Britain[6] makes clear that motor vehicle and driver records in Britain are remarkably similar to those in the U.S. and Canada, suggesting that the internal dynamics and purposes of such information systems dictate similar record-keeping practices.

There are two main files: driver files and vehicle files. Data contained in the former is much the same as in other systems. The vehicle files, however, are more historical in nature, providing an accumulative record of ownership from the time a vehicle is first sold until it eventually finds its way to the scrap heap at the end of the road.

In the past there has also been more decentralization of records in Britain than in the other systems studied here, with local records offices maintaining "blacklist" files on drivers who have been denied licenses for medical reasons or by court decree, as well as a permanent record of every vehicle originally registered in that local office. However, as elsewhere, vehicle and driver records in Britain are in the process of moving into the age of the data bank, with records being incorporated into a centralized, computerized installation at Swansea, under the direction of the Department of the Environment.

Typically, Britain's driver and vehicle files are most frequently accessed by law enforcement agencies in connection with driver or vehicle identifications and criminal investigations. However, the information in these files is commonly available, as in the United States and Canada, to a wide variety of other government and private agencies, including insurance companies, lawyers and other individuals, sometimes with the payment of a small fee.

With the transition to a centralized data system, scheduled to be complete by 1976, it would appear that the content and dissemination of information in driver and vehicle files in Britain will become increasingly similar to such systems in the United States and Canada.

OTHER GOVERNMENT RECORD SYSTEMS

Among the largest data banks at the national level are the files of the Internal Revenue Service, which, in addition to business and individual income tax records for every taxpayer, also include over 220,000 intelligence files; the records collected on a decennial basis by the Bureau of the Census; Social Security records; Selective Service records, which include approximately 15 million persons on file; some 30 million files on veterans and their families maintained by the Veterans Administration; and the FBI's crime files. (At the end of the 1973 fiscal year, the investigative and administrative files of the FBI numbered over 6.4 million; the general index for these files contained over 57.4 million cards.)

Internal Revenue Service

It has been said that behind every successful man there stands a tax collector. Over the years the government collects, in paper form, all the facts about each citizen's personal income, assets and business affairs. Most people regard such information as extremely personal and private; as a result a strong tradition of confidentiality has made income tax records among the most inaccessible to outsiders. As Hal Herbert, Canada's Assistant Deputy Minister of National Revenue/Taxation, which closely parallels the operations of America's IRS, observed to the writer, "We have found that people are more concerned about the integrity of their financial affairs than they are about anything else."

The computer has brought a new sense of urgency to questions about incursions into such confidential information as personal tax records. For the Internal Revenue Service, however, the computerization of tax records has not resulted in any changes in the kind of data in its files or in the availability of that information to other agencies. Its principal impact has been in making possible more efficient *use* of the information it collects. With modern computers it is easier and much faster to extract salient figures from returns; to cross-check individual income reports against, for instance, corporate payroll reports; to analyze the accuracy and validity of individual returns against statistical probabilities as well as against previous returns by the same individual. Data can be stored on magnetic tapes and converted to microfilm, making it much more accessible to the IRS itself. The data, however, is the same as that previously contained on the paper returns, and the same constraints governing release of information from the files apply.

That these restrictions are not always sufficient to allay the fears of taxpayers regarding the confidentiality of their tax records was demonstrated in some of the excesses generally included under the "Watergate" umbrella. The IRS drew some criticism for its role in the events involving attempts to use the IRS's taxpayer files against political "enemies." In justification, it should be noted that two former IRS commissioners tried to block access to the information, even though they were only partly successful.

In the aftermath of Watergate, legislation was proposed in September, 1974, by the Treasury Department itself to provide tighter restrictions on the release of information from individual income tax records. In letters to the House and Senate, Treasury Secretary William E. Simon said that the new legislation would ensure "the maximum confidentiality of tax returns and tax return information consistent with effective tax administration and legitimate needs of other federal agencies to obtain tax information for law enforcement and statistical purposes and of states for purposes of their own tax administration."

Simon's proposals quite clearly define the areas in which tax information from the files of the Internal Revenue Service are available to other agencies or individuals. These include:

1) The President, who has access to individual tax records and can also designate White House staff members who may see returns. Under the new legislation, however, he will no longer be able to determine on his own which other federal agencies may see returns.
2) Law enforcement agencies, particularly for the prosecution of tax fraud and related crimes.
3) Other federal agencies for statistical purposes.
4) The tax-writing committees of Congress, and other committees by Congressional resolution.
5) The various state governments, who receive federal tax returns of their residents for purposes of their own tax law enforcement.
6) The taxpayer himself, requesting to see his own returns.

Even these limitations seem broader than many who are concerned about the privacy of personal records would like to see. However, the more specific restrictions on access to tax returns embodied in new legislation, coupled with the unfavorable national reaction to the revelations of attempted abuses of the IRS by high government officials, has in fact had the effect of reaffirming and reinforcing the confidentiality of individual tax records for the future.

Census Bureaus

Every democratic country has a census bureau. In the United States it is the Bureau of the Census. In Canada it is Statistics Canada.

The organic law of countries in which people rule themselves through their elected representatives requires that the entire population be counted usually every ten years. This is done so that the congressional districts or ridings can be reasonably apportioned on a population basis.

Countries have taken advantage of this necessary but costly total enumeration to gather facts measuring the nation's progress in such areas as health, education, and economic standard of living. This accounts for the presence in the decennial census of questions about how many bathtubs the family has and the like.

Since many persons consider such questions to be invasions of their privacy, and since each person is legally compelled to answer questions, the various national census bureaus have gone to great lengths to insure the confidentiality of data they collect. Census employees and enumerators take oaths of secrecy and criminal penalties are established for breaking them. Any copy of an individual return is privileged and not producible in court.

Not only is the data gathering process hemmed with safeguards of confidentiality, but so are the statistics published by census bureaus. There is always some lower geographical limit below which no statistical breakdown of figures may be published. It may be the block face (all houses on one side of the street between two intersecting streets) or enumeration area (the area covered by one enumerator, typically 125 people). The reason for imposing these limits is that within such an area the special attributes of a particular individual may be sufficiently unique that he could become personally identifiable.

Modern data handling techniques make it possible to define statistical categories made up of persons or firms sharing two or more defined characteristics (such as male dentists, over 45 years old, and living in New York City). Census officials have to make sure that no such group is reported in terms of aggregate statistics unless it contains at least three to five entries or more.

Even then, the information may be withheld if it includes a single person or firm accounting for more than a certain proportion of the group total in respect to some attribute. This proportion is usually 70 to 80 percent. Statisticians speak of cases like these as examples of *small sample disclosure.*

Census officials are aware of another potential leak: *residual disclosure.* This could occur when earnings of a business like, say, flour milling, are being reported on a city, county and state level. It might happen that within a county five out of six flour mills would be located within a certain city of that county. In such a case, one would only have to subtract the city total from the county figure to obtain the earnings of flour mill #6.

These and other considerations lead national census bureaus to omit many figures of potential interest to city planners and the like.

A recent concealment technique is not to eliminate totals for small groups, but rather to *inoculate* them by adding in or subtracting out random errors. When this is done, the average figures taken on a large-area basis, such as a state, will be accurate even though the figures for smaller areas like counties may be grossly inaccurate, and purposefully so.

Use of census data to obtain confidential data regarding individuals or corporations is fraught with danger to the investigator. You can never be sure that a potential disclosure has not been anticipated by census officials and some measures taken to obscure it. Even censual data cannot be accepted in the absence of other confirming evidence.

MILITARY RECORDS

Practically every activity encountered in civilian life is reflected in the military setting and consequently in military records.

Formerly, say 20–30 years ago, there were vast individual differences among the record-keeping practices of different countries; different service arms (Army, Navy, Air Force, Coast Guard, or National Police); and between officers and enlisted people.

Today there is more homogeneity of practice because

• Armed forces of various nations cooperate closely in supernational bodies such as NATO.

• Service arms have been unified to a greater or lesser degree (Canadian soldiers, sailors and airmen all wear the same green uniform; and "colonels" command warships.).

• The increasing importance of the roles played by enlisted specialists has brought about some breakdown of some of the barriers between officers and enlisted people.

There usually exist two copies of each serviceperson's record: one which accompanies him to his duty station and one kept at national defense headquarters. The latter exists in two forms: as a conventional manual jacket, and in computer-sensible format for use in personnel planning.

Records of former servicepeople are held in microform in archival facilities.

A serviceperson's record consists of many parts—sometimes called jackets—several of which have civilian counterparts and a few of which are specific to military establishments.

Health Record

Contains results of physical examinations conducted periodically and in connection with enlistment, promotion or reenlistment; waivers of physical defects discovered but deemed not to be disqualifying; actions taken by Clinical Boards; admissions to sick bays, infirmaries and hospitals; diagnostic procedures and results; medical treatments; descriptions of surgical procedures; diagnoses and discharge summaries. Incidents of disease or trauma are classified as whether existing before entry to service; incurred in the line of duty; due to misconduct; incurred not line of duty; or in action against an armed enemy.

Copies of health records may be obtained by servicepeople, former servicepersons or their survivors.

Copies of health records are acquired usually in order to press claims for veterans' or survivors' benefits. There is a considerable information exchange with the Veterans' Administration.

Pay Record

Includes regular pay and its computation reflecting changes in rank; special pay for hazardous duty or special qualifications; pay increments based upon longevity; allowances for dependency, quarters and rations reflecting the serviceperson's life style during different time periods; allowances for travel of the serviceperson and dependents including shipment of personal goods (with substantiating orders, endorsements and itineraries); allowances for maintenance of uniforms or civilian clothes (e.g., CID/CIC—Criminal Investigation Division—Counter Intelligence Corps, etc.).

Deductions include: income tax withheld; dependency allotments; insurance premiums; savings bonds; fines reflecting disciplinary actions; sick misconduct (SKMD—formerly included venereal disease, now usually includes only sunburn or self-inflicted wounds); damages to government property; prior overpayment; lost time such as absent over leave (AOL) or absent without leave (AWOL), or non-performance of duty on account of imprisonment (NPDI).

Special payments include readjustment allowances, reenlistment bonuses, payment for unused leave, and severance pay (usually awarded in cases of medical disability). A serviceperson or former serviceperson can obtain an abstract of his pay record. These copies are required usually in order to substantiate a request for adjustment of the veteran's property assessment (New York State allowed such adjustments).

Leave Records

A chronological tabulation of annual leave earned, leave taken and whether or not chargeable against annual leave, and addresses while on leave.

Record of Instruction

Concerns attendance at military schools, colleges, special courses and correspondence courses. These records recite the school name and location, subjects taken, hours of instruction, dates, and marks received.

Enlistment Data

The information taken at enlistment corresponds to that taken on any application for federal employment. Emergency data form lists the serviceperson's next of kin (NOK). A qualifications questionnaire completed at this time and results of tests taken provide a basis for subsequent training and assignment.

Correspondence Jacket

This is a collection of all official letters originated by, concerning, or describing the subject, including orders with endorsements, changes in rank or designation, actions by courts of inquiry, courts martial, review boards, and evaluation boards.

A common nonjudicial disciplinary procedure is to send an offender (almost always an officer) a letter which may be one of three kinds: caution, admonition or reprimand. A letter of reprimand has the most serious consequences. All types diminish the recipient's chance of being picked for promotion by a Selection Board.

Qualification Record

The qualification record contains fitness reports (Personnel Evaluation Reports) filed by subject's commanding officer periodically or when the subject is transferred.

A fitness report contains the subject's name, rank, service arm, serial number (now his SS/SIN), unit or station, reporting period, date and the reason for the report.

The report covers duties performed, courses taken, flight experience for aviators, preference for future assignments, next highest level of responsibility for which the subject is in training, whether the subject is qualified, remarks and recommendations by the reporting officer including whether the reporter considers this to be a favorable or unfavorable report.

Both the subject and reporter must sign the report and the subject can appeal an unfavorable report.

The *qualification record* in computerized form (qualifications card) provides the basis for personnel planning in the military establishment.

The data contained in each entry referring to a specific person at a specific time include:

- *Identity:* Name, Rank, Date of Rank, Designator, Branch, Prior Service.
- *Pay:* Date Obligated Service Expires, Date of Next Longevity, Amount of Next Longevity, Dependency Allowance, Additional Payments.
- *Restrictions:* Physical Limitations, Rotation Date, Race, Sex, Languages Spoken, DOB, Place of Acceptance, Residence.
- *Qualifications:* 1st Job Code, Date Qualified, 2nd Job Code, Date Qualified, Occupation Code, Dictionary of Occupational Titles Entry.
- *Present Posting:* Date Received, Duty Status, Military Appropriation Number, Date Attached.
- *Last Posting:* Received from, Authority.
- *Next Posting:* Transferred to, Authority.

Chronological Service Record

This formerly was the principal record maintained on enlisted persons. Each line entry includes: change code, station or unit, rank, job code, months of duty and whether or not overseas, rating for proficiency (out of 4.0), rating for conduct, and leave taken.

Typical change codes include: CR (change of rank), Des (deserted), Dis (discharged), Enl (enlisted), EE (end of enlistment), Ext Enl (extended enlistment), Reenl (Reenlisted), RAD (released from active duty), Ret (retired), AOL, AWOL, SKMC, NPDI, R (received) and T (transferred).

A serviceperson or former serviceperson can obtain a transcript of his chronological service record, in lieu of a lost or missing DD-214 (see below).

Discharges

The credentials most often presented to potential employers, etc., by former servicepersons are discharge certificates and notices of separation (DD-214).

Frequently, veterans frame these important papers and present photostatic copies. This practice may be acceptable if the subject has first registered the original documents with his county clerk. In this case, the documents will bear a page and liber (book) number, the county clerk's signature and raised seal. In case of suspicion, the authenticity of the document can be verified by calling the county clerk.

There are several kinds of discharge certificate:

- *Dishonorable* (yellow)—awarded by a general court martial, usually subsequent to a term of imprisonment. Marks its holder as a felon.
- *Bad Conduct* (blue). Also awarded as a punitive measure. Marks its holder as a miscreant.
- *Undesirable* (white). Issued as an administrative measure. It indicates that its holder has been adjudged unlikely to ever become a satisfactory serviceperson.
- *Clemency*. Means the holder, who formerly held an undesirable discharge, has rehabilitated himself by performing some sort of "alternative" service.
- *General*. Mildest form of less-than-honorable separation. Often given in cases of under-age enlistment.
- *Under Honorable Conditions*. Means that the holder, through no fault of his own, was unable to carry out his responsibilities.
- *Honorable*. Means exactly what it says on its face: "Awarded as a Testimonial of Honest and Faithful Service."

A discharge may carry additional information on its reverse side: place of discharge and authority, serial number, DOB, place of birth, date of entry, highest rank, abstract of service and medals awarded. It may also be stamped to show special payments made in the Department of Defense or the VA.

The DD-214 is a necessary co-factor of the discharge certificate. Neither should be accepted without the other.

Most importantly, the DD-214 confirms the subject's citizenship and describes him. It also recites selective service information, specifies the subject's service specialty and lists the service schools he attended.

In case of doubt concerning the authenticity of a former serviceperson's credentials, request the applicant to obtain a Transcript of Service and have it sent directly to your address.

Dissemination

Who can see whose service record?

Service records are classified CONFIDENTIAL.

The records of spooks simply state that certain of their assignments were

SECRET and give no information regarding them. The Defense Intelligence Agency, National Security Agency, etc., have their own records systems.

There are no detailed rubrics concerning the handling of run-of-the-mill service records. Requests for information are dealt with on a need-to-know basis. In the case of a serviceperson, clearly his commanding officer, a superior in command, or someone acting in their behalf, can pursue any information he needs to carry out his responsibilities.

Inquiries from outside the military establishment would normally be directed to the senior field commander or to the central personnel agency (Chief of Naval Personnel for the Navy) for decision and action. Certainly, inquiries would be directed to the latter in the case of former servicepersons.

Defense contractors would normally work through their contracting officers and police officers through their corresponding opposite numbers in the CID, CIC, ONI (Office of Naval Intelligence) or whatever.

The author is personally aware of only two generally successful procedures for getting information regarding former servicepersons:

- Ask the ex-serviceperson to request a copy of his own records, or, better still, to confirm specific facts about which you may entertain doubt.
- Have the service representatives of veterans' organizations request information on behalf of a member or applicant for membership—these would have to be bonafide veterans' organizations such as the Veterans of Foreign Wars, Disabled American Veterans, the American Legion, or the Royal Canadian Legion.

The services do not usually respond affirmatively to inquiries for copies of records purported to have been made by a veteran's dependents or survivors unless the inquiry is substantiated by complete documentary evidence of the dependency or survivorship relationship and of the veteran's inability to make the request himself (marriage license, death certificate, etc.).

Chapter 8

MEDICAL RECORDS

> ". . . Whatsoever things I see or hear concerning
> the life of men, in my attendance on the sick
> or even apart therefrom, which ought not to
> be noised abroad, I will keep silence thereon,
> counting such things to be as sacred secrets."
>
> —Hippocrates, 460 B.C.

Medical records, like those of a lawyer, are popularly supposed to be confidential, protecting the rights of privacy of the individual. But in the case of medical information much of this presumed confidentiality rests upon little more than the Hippocratic Oath.

In most legal jurisdictions medical privilege is not recognized. A physician can refuse to give evidence in court regarding his patients only at his own peril. And statute law often makes the reporting of certain incidents or treatment mandatory—for example, New York's Battered Child Act, or requirements for reporting gunshot wounds.

Medical records are producible in court and are generally exempt from the Hearsay Rule (that is, they can be accepted at face value without the accompanying testimony of the persons who observed the data, recorded it, transcribed it, etc.).

The medical profession has to be concerned with both the welfare of the patient and the good of the community as a whole. Measures to protect the confidentiality of medical records therefore must seek to achieve an equitable balance among the conflicting interests of the individual, the health service professions, and society. Sometimes—as with other categories of records—these objectives seem to be at cross-purposes.

On the one hand, medical records are a rich source of personally identifiable information concerning or describing individuals. There are acute social and economic pressures to enlist the aid of computers in massive programs for collating and linking individual medical records, in the interest of improved patient care, more effective action against such general medical crises as epidemics, government programs such as national health insurance, the allocation of funds for medical research, and the development of needed medical services and facilities.

On the other hand, the life chances and quality of life of individuals can be adversely affected by disclosure of portions of their medical records to agencies not directly concerned with patient care and treatment.

Primary Source of Medical Information

The patient is the primary source of medical information. Successful treatment generally requires full and complete disclosure by the patient of such facts as:
- Genetic history—the possibility that a condition or a susceptibility to disease is genetically linked to the patient's parents or grandparents.
- Prior medical history—immunizations, allergic reactions, surgical procedures, results of diagnostic procedures performed earlier and difficult to repeat, prior episodes of disease or trauma that may have pertinent after-effects.
- Recent exposure to infections or contagious diseases.
- Recent ingestion of chemical substances with adverse physiological effects (non-medical use of drugs).
- Details of recent trauma—e.g., self- or consensually inflicted wounds, child battering, gunshot wounds.

For many reasons, this full disclosure is not always complete or reliable. In an emergency situation, the patient may be in no condition to communicate at all. When he can, he may be embarrassed by the facts, or he may be either forgetful or uninformed. And he may deliberately conceal information because he fears that criminal charges may arise from disclosures, or because he is afraid that personal opportunities or social relationships may be damaged by that disclosure.

Social Uses of Medical Information

Medical data may be said to originate primarily for the good of the individual patient concerned. But for the good of the community, some information must sometimes be extracted from these records. In some instances this information need not be specifically linked to an identifiable individual, as in the case of data used in medical research or in the instruction of medical professionals. Other information must of necessity be related to particular individuals when it is needed to

- Suppress epidemics (e.g., recent contacts of a patient suffering from venereal disease);
- Prosecute crime (rape, aggravated assault, child abuse, unlawful surgery);
- Repress trafficking in narcotics and dangerous drugs.

Additional uses of information from medical records, subject to more debate concerning the social benefit of disclosure, include the following:

1) Potential employers are interested in selecting candidates who will be capable physically and mentally of performing successfully in the positions they seek.
2) Insurance companies are interested in seeing to it that policyholders pay premiums that reflect their fair share of risk based upon their physical condition.
3) Credit grantors want assurance that a potential debtor will be capable of discharging the obligations he seeks to undertake.

In addition to these circumstances, the interest of the public at large is often involved in the well-being of individuals in positions of public service. Obviously the general welfare could be seriously threatened by a high official suffering from mental illness, an airline pilot susceptible to cardiac arrest, a bus driver who may undergo an epileptic seizure, a ship's pilot with uncorrected defects of vision, among many other examples.

Other Factors

A special problem in the disclosure of medical records is the recognized danger of ignorance about the information. Raw medical data is potentially dangerous in the hands of individuals who lack the professional training and contextual knowledge needed to interpret it properly. Improper interpretation or the introduction of self-serving bias can not only unfairly injure the individual, but in many instances might ultimately be detrimental to the community. And among the persons least likely to interpret medical data correctly is the patient himself.

From the security man's point of view, the problem of security and confidentiality of medical records is perplexing. Nowhere does there currently exist an institutionalized provision for a trained, informed and impartial professional empowered to review an individual's medical record and, at the patient's request, release to prospective employers, regulatory bodies, insurance companies, credit grantors, or welfare agencies the facts of life expectancy or physical capability needed to assess the case. (In some proposals to create such an office, the officer is referred to as a *medical ombudsman*.)

Many large hospitals and health care facilities have their own policies regulating the release of medical information, usually restricting that release to authorized police and government agencies, except at the discretion of the Director or similarly responsible official. However, as a general rule the existing medical records system is notoriously inept with regard to security. An unauthorized person seeking information can often get just about anything he wants—and by methods that fall short of burglarizing a psychiatrist's office.

ADVERSE EFFECTS UPON THE INDIVIDUAL

That disclosure of portions of an individual's medical history outside of the patient care-and-treatment context can adversely affect his life chances was dramatically emphasized in August, 1972, when publication of U.S. Senator Thomas Eagleton's history of psychiatric treatment forced his withdrawal as the Vice-Presidential nominee of the Democratic Party.

It was argued that the interests of society were paramount and best served by his resignation from the ticket. Arguments in favor of such countervailing interests can be raised in many similar cases. These interests merit consideration—as do those of the individual.

On the mundane level, one's medical history can affect his life chances in many ways:

1) Employment in certain occupations (e.g., food handling) and by particular employers or agencies.
2) Promotion or retention in certain positions (e.g., handling radioactive material).
3) Admission to educational institutions and to specific courses of study (e.g., physical education, medical schools).
4) Obtaining a license to drive an automobile, pilot a ship or airplane, or to box.

5) Purchasing insurance, which may be a prerequisite to employment or to obtaining capital to start a business.

The quality of life may also be adversely affected in both tangible and intangible ways by medical factors and their disclosure. Intangible effects may include personal self-esteem, reputation in the community, and interpersonal relationships, especially in marriage. More tangible effects include:

1) Determining eligibility of benefits: workmen's compensation, disability pensions (military, veterans, police, railroad), disability allowance, blind institutes, etc.
2) Eligibility to purchase insurance to provide for retirement or benefits to survivors.
3) Imputing culpability or civil liability, as in cases of drunken driving; wounding; child battering; unlawful use of alcohol; non-medical use of drugs; rape and carnal knowledge; and paternity, malpractice and accident liability.
4) Non-medical uses of medical data such as tracing "missing persons" or establishing a physician's tax liability.

PRESENT CLIMATE CONCERNING DISCLOSURE

In-depth information regarding disclosure of personally identifiable information from medical records was developed by the author in 1971 during a study for the Canadian Privacy and Computers Task Force (PCTF).

The principal tool of investigation was a questionnaire mailed to over 2,500 operators of data systems containing personalized information that was already or likely to become computerized. Approximately 400 addressees were in the classification covering "Health or Vital Statistics." These included hospitals and nursing homes, health insurance plans, and public health agencies. Of the total of 1,268 responses, 182 were in the health and vital statistics field.

Of particular concern here are the answers to a question (number 13C7 in the questionnaire) asking respondents to indicate what sources were used in collecting identified information about individuals for storage in their files. The choices were *never used, sometimes used, generally used, always used,* or *does not apply*. Among the source categories listed was "Medical practitioners and hospitals."

Fifty-two percent of respondents said they obtained at least some information from medical sources. A breakdown of responses is shown in Figure 8–1.

Function of Respondent	Sometimes	Generally or Always
	(percent)	(percent)
Health and vital statistics	98	75
Charitable institutions	91	66
Social welfare	91	43
Insurance	91	41
Regulatory agencies	83	33
Law enforcement	78	33
Major industrial employers	70	20
Public utilities	68	39
Educational institutions	62	16
Oil companies	59	35
Service industries	52	23
Private investigators, collection agencies, insurance adjusters, etc.	39	9

Figure 8-1: Use of Personalized Medical Information

The use of medical sources by associations (37 percent), general merchandising houses (31 percent), banks (15 percent), and investment services (12 percent) was on a *sometimes used* basis. General use by respondents in these classes was negligible. Publishers (29 percent) and employment agencies (40 percent) answered entirely in the same *sometimes used* column.

Motor vehicle bureaus and credit reporting agencies reported that medical sources were never used. However, there is evidence (see Chapter 7) that some motor vehicle bureaus do gather medical data. And it has been seen (Chapter 3) that investigatory credit-reporting agencies sometimes acquire data of a medical nature from laymen, as when neighbors of an applicant for life insurance are asked questions concerning his apparent health, weight or habits.

The one Personal Property Security Registration System responding (this agency is also discussed in Chapter 5) stated that personal data was *generally* obtained from medical sources.

PRESSURE FOR MEDICAL INFORMATION

There are six primary sources of pressure for bigger and better medical information services:

1) *Financial and Regulatory:* This may involve health insurance plans, the disciplinary bodies of the health-service professions, or, in cases of fraud by either physician or patient, law enforcement agencies.

2) *Patient Care, Diagnosis and Treatment:* This is the traditional focus of medical records and its improvement is the reason most frequently advanced for creating large data banks of medical histories. To the records maintained by hospitals, diagnostic laboratories, physicians, clinics, and nursing homes, must be added special data banks oriented towards patient care such as Medic-Alert, tissue banks, and donor registries.

Replying to questions submitted by the Privacy and Computers Task Force, The Ontario Medical Association in Canada had this to say regarding care and treatment data banks:

> "If remote, direct access systems are used, adequate safeguards should be devised to ensure that the user has access to only that information to which he is entitled. The greater danger to privacy lies not with the computer or its software. The real danger exists when multiple hard copies of the master file (print-out) are disseminated. People, not computers, breach privacy.
>
> "We feel that electronic data processing can facilitate administrative services and assure privacy while at the same time being used to gather personal information. With proper controls, centralized data banks could actually enhance the privacy of patients' records."[8]

3) *Institutional:* This perspective protects establishments against the infirmities of the individual. It encompasses company medical departments and medical staffs of insurance companies. Chief among institutional data banks are the Medical Information Bureau and the Casualty Index, both discussed in detail in Chapter 5.

4) *Forensic:* This application marshals medical evidence to prove or disprove culpability or civil liability. It includes assessment of disability, identification from spoors, and sanity determinations. Also involved is the question of legal discovery—i.e., the right of the defendant in a criminal trial to have reasonable access to the medical evidence that may be presented against him. While the forensic focus is relatively unimportant in terms of the number of individuals involved, it is high in dramatic impact.

5) *Public Health:* This perspective focuses upon protecting the public from infection, contamination and communicable disease. Control of epidemics necessarily entails collection and dissemination of personally identifiable medical information. Public health officials generally enjoy authority for search and seizure that goes beyond that normally accorded law enforcement officers.

6) *Education and Research:* This has to do with the clinical training and continuing education of health-service professionals. It raises two significant questions with respect to privacy: the first has to do with patients who serve as teaching subjects; the second concerns establishing problem-oriented data banks to acquire new knowledge regarding particular diseases and the effectiveness of various therapies. (Among such problem-oriented data banks are the Professional Activities Studies and Patient Activity Studies in Ann Arbor, Michigan (PAS), and the Obstetrical Statistical Cooperative in Brooklyn, New York.)

As for patient privacy, physicians have found it necessary to acquire detailed facts about the patient's socio-economic background in order to diagnose and treat certain conditions. New technology has extended the facilities for observation in the teaching situation. Closed-circuit television cameras, two-way mirrors, and tape recorders are commonplace. And the increasing diversity of medical specialties means that a patient will be seen by a larger number of residents and interns than in the past.

The educational perspective contributes to much of the U.S.-Canada traffic in personalized medical information. Results of a study of this traffic are shown in Figure 8-2.

LOCUS OF MEDICAL INFORMATION COMPONENTS

	Within One Province	Within Canada	Partially in U.S.
Records	85%	9%	6%
Patients	46%	30%	24%
Information Recipients	30%	44%	26%

CANADA-U.S. TRAFFIC IN MEDICAL DATA

	None	Some	Frequent
Receive Information	48%	44%	8%
Send Information	43%	49%	8%

Figure 8-2: Exchange of Personalized Medical Information (U.S.-Canada)

It might be argued that clinical data in educational and research studies need not be personally identifiable. Researchers, however, insist that unique identification of records is essential for long-term studies. These are becoming increasingly important in medical research.

An alternative to use of personal identifiers may be the use of unique random digit combinations as record identifiers. These identifiers could be linked to patient names on input documents only by a "scramble" tape, which would be kept under conditions of utmost confidentiality.

PROPOSED INFORMATION SYSTEMS

E. R. Gabrieli[9] has proposed a comprehensive medical data bank that would include the following:

1) *Family background data:* head of household, spouse, family home, and family income.
2) *Obstetrical supplement:* prenatal visits, delivery, examination of newborn, post-partum examination, weight gain, and observation of the premature.
3) *Pediatric record:* patient identification; past history (immunization, surgery and trauma, medical illness including childhood diseases, x-rays, and medication); family history (mother, father, siblings, and grandparents); infancy (development, functional inquiry, physical examination); pre-school and pre-adolescent (school development).
4) *Adult:* identification, referral, occupation, social history, past history, family history including children, functional inquiry, physical examination, and the diagnosis and therapy of each medical and surgical incident.

Gabrieli and other proponents of bigger and better medical information systems advance a number of cogent arguments in their behalf. These argued advantages deserve closer attention.

Lower Health Care Costs

Gabrieli points out that in the United States the direct cost of the present archaic system for recording medical data exceeds 18 million dollars—28 percent of the total cost of health services. Fiscal claim processing is seen as representing 25–40 percent of the cost of operating a medical practice or clinic. Such costs would be substantially reduced through the use of medical data banks.

Better Emergency Care

Gabrieli argues the need for personal medical data in emergency situations, citing in particular the needs of diabetics on insulin, hemophiliacs, epileptics, and individuals with penicillin allergy. Present problems of acquiring such data are exacerbated by the increasing mobility of the population of industrial societies—but data transmission is a unique advantage of computerized systems.

The emergency situation, however, points up some of the concerns raised over medical data banks. If a patient in an emergency is unable to provide his code number, giving access to his data, how will the hospital extract this information? And if such access is made possible, what safeguards will insure that it cannot be obtained in non-emergency cases? Will others, such as employers, be able to gain access to the records? Will a record of all accesses be kept and made available to the individual?

The Canadian Medical Association has commented on this problem:

"Medical records are different from other voluntary statements, because in almost every circumstance, a patient seeking medical care would wish that his full medical history be provided to the physician. However, he doesn't want this information freely available to everyone. Some method of controlled access must be provided."[10]

Medical History Information

Quick, accurate past medical history information regarding the patient would have obvious value in treatment. The physician would not have to rely on the sometimes faulty memory or statements of the patient. Gabrieli asserts that, by enabling the physician to focus full attention on the current illness, this should lead to improved diagnosis.

Genetic Background Information

Gabrieli views genetic background as an important part of the clinical file. Every time a disease which may be hereditary is diagnosed, the fact should be recorded on the records of all blood relatives of the patient. Diabetes is cited as an example. In a comprehensive data bank, such cross referencing would be simple.

Family histories of individuals, including births, marriages, procreations and deaths, are now contained in many vital records systems. These records are widely computerized and potentially linkable, and there is substantial experience with the use of computers to compile such family histories. It is only a short and obvious step to linkage of these histories with hospital records.

In the words of the Ontario Medical Association (Canada):

"As linkage between diverse records pertaining to the same individuals is made simpler, it should become increasingly practicable to examine a multiplicity of variables and to give to the study of human well-being a statistical basis that one could not get in any other way."[11]

Sharing of Clinical Experience

A comprehensive medical data bank would make possible the sharing of clinical experience as a way to improve diagnoses. The physician would be able to compare his case with those in the data bank. Such an access to total medical experience is seen as helping to close the gap between existing medical knowledge and bedside medicine, since it will enable the physician to look up diagnostic criteria, treatment, and prognosis from his computer terminal. In addition to improving the accuracy of diagnoses, the process would contribute to the continuing education of the health professional. And, since parts of many clinical judgments may be wrong, the feedback mechanism afforded by the data bank would help the diagnostician to avoid repeating the same error every time he encountered such a condition. (Gabrieli cites as an example a radiologist misinterpreting a certain bone change.)

On the other hand, the fact that a medical diagnosis is essentially a probability statement, as is, of course, the prognosis, points up the danger previously cited of allowing medical information to be made available to laymen whose judgments might adversely affect the life chances of a patient.

Follow-up Advantages

Long-time follow-up is another advantage ascribed to a comprehensive health data network. This requirement implies that individual records within such a data bank must be uniquely identifiable.

It has been pointed out that current health statistics record events rather than people—a serious deficiency in evaluating that information. The linkage of source records and other linkages (such as that between hospital records and death registrations) would eliminate duplicated case counts and make much valuable follow-up information available to the health services. It could provide, for instance, improved statistical knowledge of the successes and failures of current methods of treatment, the risks of readmission to a hospital for the same or related causes, or the risks of death following discharge after surgery.

Social Benefits

Acquisition of information by government is underlined as a social benefit by proponents of a central medical data bank. In the area of social planning, it is suggested that population health data would assist in the planning of transportation agencies, housing authorities, school curricula, courts, welfare and social assistance programs, vocational guidance, and generally the entire urban and rural culture.

The relationships among social and economic environments, work histories, and personal and family histories of disease—all of which influence the nature and risks of disease—are largely inaccessible to study based on single files of records. A medical data bank would make possible the linking of information on social characteristics of people with their health records.

Faster feedback of information through a data bank would improve the self-evaluation and adjustment of the health delivery system itself. It has been shown that turn-around time becomes a problem when such information must be acquired from a periodic census or synthesized from year-end reports from various institutions. Faster feedback is seen as leading to maximal use of the health dollar, real-time ordering of priorities in the light of unmet needs, and optimal allocation of existing priorities.

The Ontario Medical Association (Canada) has observed:
"Although the amount of use to which hospital beds are put is well described in routine tabulations, these fail to indicate how many people are involved, how many of these make repeated use of the facilities, and the extent to which certain sectors of the population place disproportionately heavy loads on the hospital insurance system.

"Such data could point to special needs for preventive measures with a view both to reducing the amount of ill health and to lightening the load on hospital facilities. Linkage within the hospital insurance files would provide data on repeated admissions of the same individuals. Linkage with other personal records that contain socio-economic data could provide measures of the extent to which various sectors of the population require hospital services."[12]

The Problem of Unique Personal Identification

The need for unique identification of each subject in the development of computerized records has been previously discussed (see Chapter 1). Here it should only be reemphasized that, while linkages of medical records may sometimes be carried out satisfactorily using names and other common personal identifying information, the speed and efficiency of such operations is dramatically increased through the use of a common system of unique numerical personal identifiers. The future of the "ultimate medical data bank" depends upon the adoption of such a system of unique identification.

EXISTING DATA BANKS

Examination of existing medical data banks discloses a vast disparity between what now exists and the comprehensive medical data bank envisioned by Gabrieli and others.

The Ontario Health Services Insurance Plan has perhaps the largest existing medical data bank in Canada. It resides in eleven magnetic tape files, three of which deal with hospital insurance. Executives of the Ontario Plan discussed some of the problems specifically relating to the acquisition and handling of data. These included administrative problems and those relating to the structure and quality of data.

Long range administrative problems include:
1) Development of alternative payment plans for physicians;
2) Consideration of the right of a patient to see his record or possibly to erase or modify portions of it;
3) Creation of privacy review boards;
4) Use of accumulated medical data for planning and economic analysis;
5) Establishment of comprehensive social data systems.

Problems concerning data structure and conditioning include:
1) Standardizing upon a unique patient identifier (see above);
2) Elimination of non-specific or garbage diagnosis (e.g., "upper respiratory infection");
3) Devising a meaningful coding format for the more common types of report;
4) Correlation of hospital episodes and office visit information;
5) Interfacing with clinics as opposed to physicians in private practice;
6) Interfacing with problem-oriented practices (as opposed to practices oriented towards physiological systems).

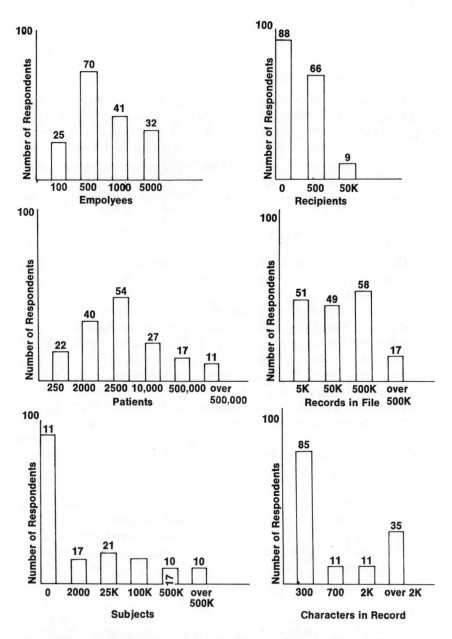

Figure 8-3: Quantitative characteristics of the Response Base, Privacy and Computers Task Force Mail Questionnaire (1971). Health and Vital Statistics Category Only.

Existing Hospital Data Banks

Not much progress has been made towards computerization of patient records. The accompanying graph gives a quantitative description of the response base in terms of the distribution among respondents to the Privacy and Computers Task Force (PCTF) survey of employees, patients, subjects (principally registrants of vital statistics offices or cases filed by public health agencies), information recipients (persons accessing patient files or obtaining registry information), records held on file, and size in characters of each record.

It was found that 42 percent of health service organizations used computers for processing records, but only 16 percent of these users had their own facilities; the rest rented time on machines controlled by other organizations. Less than a quarter reported they had computerized all or most of their patient records.

The most used sources of medical information regarding patients were the patients themselves (used by 98 percent of responding organizations), other health service organizations (96 percent), and the patient's family (94 percent).

Fifty-seven percent of responding organizations sought information from the patient's employer; 52 percent from educational institutions attended by the patient; 50 percent from friends and neighbors; and 49 percent from law enforcement agencies.

Fifteen percent of respondents reported receiving complaints from patients regarding their methods for collecting data.

Security of Hospital Records

There is a high degree of self-satisfaction with the level of security accorded medical records. Less than a quarter of the respondents to the PCTF survey agreed that they need either new or more detailed organizational rules to govern collection and use of personalized data; or additional physical safeguards on collection, storage and distribution of personally identifiable information. A serious question exists as to whether this confidence is justified.

Release of Information

Half of the organizations responding make individually identifiable information available to persons or organizations outside their own in addition to that information made available by such reporting and production of records as might be required pursuant to process of law. One quarter release information to law enforcement agencies on request.

Sixty-nine percent of respondents have a written policy regarding release of medical records; however, questions arise regarding the implementation of such policies. Fourteen percent of the respondents do not monitor the actions of their employees in carrying out organization policy regarding disclosure. Sixty-nine percent do monitor the actions of their employees, but have never found one violating the confidentiality of records in trust. Seventeen percent reported that they do police the actions of their employees, have caught offenders on occasion, and in such cases have taken disciplinary action against them.

Eighteen percent of the organizations responding have received complaints from patients regarding what was perceived as improper disclosure of medical information.

A direct relationship is observed between the misuse of records where it occurs and the size and frequency of use of the file. Little risk is seen for a dormant record containing minimal information. An extensive dossier with a wide circulation within a service agency is much more vulnerable to misuse of the information it contains.

Rights of Patients to Records

A serious problem in the management of medical records arises from the claimed right of patients to see their records. The right of the patient to remove inaccurate or erroneous information from his record is recognized as basic. On the other hand, should a person judged insane, or severely disturbed, have access to his psychiatric records? Should a patient be exposed to information he does not understand and might misconstrue? Should he have access to a physician's personal observations about the patient, which have in the past been regarded as the physician's property and may have been withheld for medical reasons?

Traditionally, the decision of how much information should be released to a patient belonged to the patient's personal physician, who released only that information which in his judgment he felt the patient should learn. But the passing of that information into a medical data bank, and out of the physician's direct control, creates new ambiguities in this area of the patient's right to information on his own record.

The volume of complaints regarding the patient's inability to see his own record has led at least some medical people to believe that in this era, in which the medical profession has become largely demythologized, clouds of suspicion engendered by refusing access to a patient may in some cases be more injurious to the physician-patient relationship, and by extension to the patient's well-being, than the psychological trauma of any facts the patient might discover in his record.

(In this connection it is assumed, of course, that the reasons for denying access to the patient are legitimately concerned with promoting his welfare and not merely contrived to spare the physician the need to explain to the patient facts regarding his condition or to shield the health service professional and organizations from malpractice suits.)

The complexity of the issue is suggested by some questions raised by the Ontario Medical Association (Canada) in terms of a fairly common situation:

"A physician in Ontario may wish to administer to his patient a questionnaire such as the Minnesota Multiphasic Personality Inventory (MMPI). This long questionnaire can then be sent to a laboratory in California where it is interpreted by a computer and a report is returned to the attending physician. The report may suggest that the patient shows definite evidence of suicidal tendencies or of schizophrenia. Many would believe that the patient should not have access to such a report.

"If the patient did have right of access, should he be able to see the records of the physician or of the data center that performed the analysis?

"Should a data center ever divulge information to anyone except the physician who forwarded the material for analysis?

"What would be the situation if the patient were, in fact, sane, had been erroneously labeled schizophrenic because of misinterpretation at the data center, and then denied access to his record on the grounds that he was mentally ill?

"If laws were ever devised to provide in Canada rights of privacy and of information and recourse for the aggrieved, how could such laws be enforced if the data bank is located in another jurisdiction?"[13]

Such questions are more easily asked than answered. They transcend national boundaries and local concerns. They are questions to which the health service community—and society itself—must respond if the social and medical contributions of the ultimate medical data bank are to become a reality.

Chapter 9

STUDENT RECORDS

"The presence of a body of well-instructed
men, who have not to labor for their daily
bread, is important to a degree which
cannot be overestimated; as all high
intellectual work is carried on by them,
and on such work material progress of all
kinds mainly depends, not to mention other
and higher advantages."

—Charles Robert Darwin, *The Descent of Man*

On January 29, 1969, a phalanx of tough riot police, wearing helmets and face shields, stormed up idle escalators towards the ninth floor of Sir George Williams University in Montreal, Canada. The riot squad was headed for the university computer center, where for more than a week some ninety dissident students had barricaded themselves. The rioters had brought the critical data processing functions of the university to a standstill.

In the last, crisis-filled minutes of the occupation, the rampaging students dumped file drawers filled with punched cards, documents and magnetic tapes onto the floor of the center and out of windows. Their actions hopelessly confounded the continuity of university records, registration cards and student transcripts.

209

Then, as the police burst into view in the big plate glass window comprising one wall of the computer center, the desperate rioters set the piles of paper on fire. Before police broke through the student barricades and brought fire hoses into play, fire reduced the university's two million dollar computer to a total ruin.

This was not an isolated incident. During the student unrest of the late 1960's and early 1970's, computers ranked close to Department of Defense related research centers as targets of violence—at Stanford University in Palo Alto, California, for instance, no less than in Montreal.

Why the computer? A number of facts may be relevant. At Sir George Williams University, as on many other campuses, the computer was highly visible and vulnerable. It was expensive. It was seen as essential to the operations of the university. And it may have been viewed by some students as a dehumanizing influence strongly affecting their lives.

From early childhood through their university studies, students are inexorably caught up in a "numbers game" of grades and marks and tests. The data center brings that game to its ultimate dimension, faceless and impersonal, the final report card to view with anxiety and suspicion and even fear.

Are such fears justified? What kind of records do schools and universities keep on students? How accessible is this information, and how widely is it disseminated?

In Chapter 2 it was seen that a great deal of information of a personal nature is, in fact, obtained from universities and other educational institutions. More specifically, it was learned that

- 16 percent of all information exchanged among organizations originates with educational institutions. In contrast, only 5 percent of this information is obtained *by* educational institutions.
- 21 percent of organizations who collect personalized information about individuals get at least some of it from educational institutions.
- Educational institutions rank second among organizations most likely to release personalized information about individuals.
- Educational institutions rank third among organizations most likely to receive complaints from individuals regarding disclosure of such information.

EARLY RECORDS

In the days of the one-room schoolhouse, at the turn of the century, student records tended to be informal. Teachers and principals were able to keep track of individual performance and progress with no difficulty. Even then, however, some kind of "record of progress" was necessary to determine how students were getting on, when they were able to be promoted to the next grade, and which students displayed the aptitude and ability for higher education.

Records, then, as a measure of learning and performance, are inherent in the educational process.

With the explosion of population in the twentieth century, along with rapid extension of educational opportunity to more and more students, such records have tended to become progressively more extensive, more complex, more formal, and more standardized among different schools and school systems, under pressure from an increasingly technological and industrial society that demands trained people of demonstrated competence.

Today, in the age of computerized information systems, schools have been said to maintain the most comprehensive data bank of all. All schools, from the primary grades up, keep detailed and confidential records on every student. In addition to grades, awards and promotions, such records include personal remarks and assessments by school psychologists, teachers, counselors and administrators. Quite often such records may be seen by outsiders more readily than by parents. And the records accumulate and stay with the child throughout public school, even following him when he moves to a different school in a different city, district or state.

The attempt to measure student progress and performance in school systems of enormous size and diversity has also led to an increased emphasis on standardized assessments, through standardized tests that measure aptitude and achievement. These results become a particularly significant part of the record for students going on to vocational schools or colleges and universities. Moreover, statistics drawn from such standardized test programs make it possible to evaluate not only individual performance but also the performance of schools and school systems. From such comparative statistics come, for example, the concern in California in the early 1970's for below-average levels of reading performance among students in the state's primary and secondary public schools, a determination that would be impossible to make without uniform national tests.

Almost all early school records include data concerning:
1) Learning performance, including a cumulative record of grades, test scores, etc.
2) Health and physical disabilities.
3) Background information, including information about parents.

4) Personal assessments and comments (by teachers, counselors, school nurses, psychologists, administrators).

5) Extracurricular activities, hobbies and interests.

The kinds of forms used and information collected, however, vary widely from school to school and district to district. In spite of the pressures for standardized measures of student ability and performance, and the growing involvement of state and Federal government in education, elementary and secondary schools in the United States continue to be largely under local control, acting under policies established by local school boards and administrators. It is therefore impossible to generalize about the kinds of information kept in early student records, the uses made of such records, or the accessibility of the information to outsiders or even to parents.

A single public school records system was studied in some depth. While its records policies will not be universally applicable, they are fairly representative of the problems and practices in a modern school system which has begun to be computerized in its record keeping.

A PUBLIC SCHOOL RECORDS SYSTEM

The North York Board of Education is part of the public school system of Metropolitan Toronto, in Canada. It has under its jurisdiction approximately 105,000 students, 2,100 non-academic staff, and 5,000 academic staff. They are distributed throughout 112 public schools, 25 junior high schools, 18 secondary schools and 2 vocational schools. For 1970 the operating budget was 85 million dollars.

The Board of Education has three areas of operations: administrative services, plant operations, and academic instruction. Our study focused on the student and staff files and the role of the computer processing provided by administrative services.

Student Records

The basic data record is the Ontario School Record I (primary) and II (high school). Physically the record is a stiff manila folder, printed on four sides, which provides a convenient storage medium for substantiating documents and relevant correspondence.

The school principal decides what information is gathered, processing procedures, and the usage of data. The OSR's are stored and maintained in the schools. They follow the students when they are transferred; no copies are retained. The records of graduates are stored. The student records are available to principals, vice-principals, counselors, teachers, nurses, and school psychologists. Generally, the students or their parents have the right to review the record card.

The computing center provides three types of services for the principals: grade reporting, scheduling, and enrollment. The students complete a basic data form, an update form, and course selection forms. The teacher completes the grade report forms. The basic data form contains information on the student, guardians, emergency contacts, and school standing.

Student records are all batch processed with a driver picking up and returning forms to the schools. Key punching is done in the computing center.

Grade reports are issued four times yearly, scheduling reports in the spring, and enrollment reports in the fall. The school personnel are responsible for verifying information. There are no historical EDP files.

Teachers Records

The basic employment application form contains identifying information, educational history, and professional experience. An assessment is recorded on the application form if the applicant is interviewed. Summary 3x5 cards are maintained both by the individual school and the Board's central office, as the individual principal is responsible for hiring.

Once a teacher is hired, he completes an acceptance form, acknowledging terms of employment. Documentation of professional training and experience is subsequently added to the form.

The historical employment file is maintained by the central office and it is updated with experience information, assessments by the principal, and teacher incident reports. Teachers may discuss their records, but are not allowed to see them because of the confidential information they contain.

The elementary school principals maintain summary record cards on their teachers, but not historical files. The cards are returned to the central office when a teacher is reassigned or leaves. No information beyond verification of employment is given out by the central office.

The EDP personnel file has four parts:
• Master Payroll
• Name and address
• Earnings
• Check reconciliation.

The file contains basic data needed for accounting procedures. Each record contains 500 characters, but the four parts are to be consolidated into one file and the record size will be expanded to 750 characters to allow for more fringe benefit data. Monthly payroll lists and accounting reports are issued as necessary. No historical EDP files are maintained.

Non-Academic Staff Records

All support staff files are centralized and contain less extensive information than the teacher files. The processing of hard copy files is similar to that for teacher files. The staff EDP files are the same as for the teachers.

Computing Center

The data processing center, located in the main administration building, houses a medium-sized computer. There are two portable machines used for instruction. Twenty-eight people work in the center; none are bonded.

The center provides services for:
• Student files
• Payroll
• Processing student programs (in teaching computer science)
• Test scoring
• Work-order records
• Inventory records
• Instruction.

Normally, three generations of tapes are maintained. One generation is stored off-site in a cabinet in a secondary school. The center affords minimal effective security from either physical threats or improper access to data.

The Metropolitan Board of Education is concerned about the fact that the borough boards are developing separate computing centers and information retrieval systems. The central board has recommended uniform record-keeping systems and is considering establishing a central information system.

Policies of Confidentiality

The central counseling offices have assumed the responsibility of providing ethical guidelines for handling records in the school systems, particularly student records.

The school counselors themselves function under a code of professional ethics. The counselor, among other duties, enters the school's recommendation on university applications and responds to inquiries from prospective employers. He may also be called the guidance officer. The counselor spends much of his time with students who are in one kind of trouble or another.

With respect to disclosure of information from student records, the Ontario School Counselors Association says:

"Pupil records are kept for accuracy, authenticity, and future reference. Much of the recorded information is confidential. If schools maintain records of pupil information which is personal in nature, or given in confidence, the school must protect the pupil and his family and not permit unwarranted persons to have access to the information."[14]

The following guidelines regarding handling of student records are currently in effect:

- Pupil records are maintained and managed in such a way that unwarranted persons do not have access.
- Teaching staff and school secretaries are instructed yearly in the procedures to be followed in maintaining pupil records and handling requests for information.
- Parents may receive a valid interpretation of the pupil's record, but confidential information given by a pupil is not reported to the parent without the pupil's permission. Such information is not recorded in the pupil's record.
- Except for court orders, investigating agencies are not given information without the written consent of the parent. Cooperation with police officers may be extended with respect to factual data that is not confidential.
- When reporting pupil information to referral agencies, the written consent of the parent is obtained. When a request for information is made by telephone, a return call is made to check on the caller.
- When a pupil transfers to another school, his folder is sent on at the request of the receiving school. *Before forwarding, the folder is carefully edited and non-pertinent information removed.* For transfers to private schools or corrective institutions, a transcript of pertinent information only is forwarded. When more detailed information is requested, parental permission must be obtained.
- Principals have the responsibility for the quality of pupil information gathered, the care with which pupil information is recorded, safeguarding of confidential information, and for ethical practices in interpreting the data.
- When a principal or teacher is given information by a pupil that a criminal act may be committed or that a human life is in danger (e.g., threatened suicide), the responsibility of a citizen takes precedence and appropriate measures are taken.

UNIVERSITY RECORDS

As late as the beginning of the 1960's, the university still viewed itself as standing *in loco parentis*. Rules and regulations over student activities were generally accepted and disciplinary measures enforced for infraction of university rules. Cheating on examinations was a most serious offense and an "honor code" system was often practiced. The university looked after its own, and students involved in minor breaches of the peace were turned over by city police to campus authorities for disciplinary action within the university. Even such episodes of disease and trauma as could be handled without prolonged hospitalization or major surgery were treated in the university infirmery.

Today the role of the university has changed from that of a stern but understanding foster mother *(alma mater)* to that of a dispenser of public knowledge and little more. Rules and regulations have often been either abolished or turned over to student control. In some institutions attendance at lectures is voluntary and not even recorded. Final examinations have been abolished in many courses. Records of disciplinary infractions are minimal and beyond parking tickets practically nonexistent.

In such a climate there is little many post-secondary educational institutions can say about a student beyond the fact that he attended from one date to another, took a certain number of courses, and received certain marks in them. This is all the records show.

Indeed, when the author, in his capacity as graduate chairman of his department, inquired regarding the academic record of a graduate from one French university who was seeking admission to a post-graduate program, he was told, "Monsieur _____ attended the Polytechnique from 1966 until 1970. According to our standards he is a qualified Chemical Engineer. Any further information you require will have to come from the student."

The example is far from unusual. Nevertheless, the educational process at the college or university level requires and generates a remarkable variety of records held in widely varying degrees of confidentiality and security.

The Academic Sieve

Most universities have no articulated policy for handling inquiries of a personal nature. Of thirty-three universities studied, only two have established formal channels and procedures to insure that accurate and proper responses are made.

A telephone call to a university for information may mean any number of things:

- A prospective employer seeking information about a former student.
- A foreign embassy seeking information about the political activities of one of their nationals currently enrolled.
- An insurance company, credit bureau or the telephone company checking on a student requesting credit or service.
- A forlorn wife or girl friend.
- Another educational institution checking out an application by a present or former student.
- A reporter from the news media seeking the results of some professor's experiment.

The person answering the phone often has no idea whether or not such information may be properly divulged. Moreover, his knowledge of the affair may be incomplete or inaccurate. Yet in most cases no firm guidelines for answering such inquiries exist.

Generally, in any police matter contact will be made through the university security officer, whose office typically shares information with local and other law enforcement agencies, government agencies and often potential employers. Other government departments will generally contact the president's office, the registrar or some other officer with whom there exists an established working relationship.

It should be noted that a clear relationship is frequently seen between the disclosure of information and public ownership and control (as in publicly owned junior colleges, state colleges and universities), as opposed to the privately endowed institution. The public accountability of the local junior college or state college tends to make it more open and accessible in providing information to employers, credit bureaus, government and other investigative agencies.[15]

Records Handling

Typically there are four computerized files of student records in a modern university:
- The admissions file
- The sessional file
- The historical file
- The alumni file.

Applications for admission are accumulated on the admissions file during winter and spring. Successful candidates are notified in early summer. In August, registration materials are mailed, and in September the sessional file is built from the completed registration forms.

The sessional file is the working file on which marks (grades) are recorded two or three times a year. It originates in particular schools or departments within the college or university. When the last marks are entered for the term, the information on each student is carried over to the historical file in the Registrar's office.

In the historical file each student's record contains a list of courses taken, marks, and year point average, culminating in his final cumulative average, usually given numerically. This cumulative record becomes the "official transcript" when a student graduates.

After the awarding of a degree, selected information is carried over from the historical file to the alumni file and, frequently, to a job placement file.

The supplementary and often corresponding files kept by deans, department heads and faculty members, as well as those in such service facilities as counseling offices, medical or psychiatric offices, and security departments, are still generally manual, with considerable autonomy in each area over the control, kind and content of records.

Uses of the Computer

The universities whose data processing operations were studied had an average enrollment of 6,800 students. 85 percent of these universities used their computer to process student records.

Other uses of the computer were:

Research	73 percent
Academic Instruction	61 percent
Payroll	61 percent
Accounts Payable	58 percent
Accounts Receivable	48 percent
Library	42 percent
Staff Records	42 percent
Faculty Records	36 percent
Space Allocation	33 percent
Admissions Applications	30 percent
Budget Control	27 percent
Inventory Control	24 percent
Class Scheduling	24 percent
Alumni Records	24 percent
Research Administration	24 percent
Sale of computer services outside the university	21 percent

Less common uses included: Housing inventory, 9 percent; mailing lists, faculty-club accounts, analytical (operations research) studies, and miscellaneous uses, 6 percent; buildings and grounds, 3 percent.

The average student record file contained 36,500 records (sections added term by term are apparently not consolidated). The largest type of record kept was accounts receivable, with an average size of 2,250 characters. The average master student record (sessional file) contained 1,265 characters. The lengths of other records were:

Admissions	650 characters
Student History	558 characters
Sports-Medical	200 characters
Fee Transactions	135 characters
Residence	100 characters
Course Records	80 characters
Faculty Records	40 characters

THE ADMISSIONS CYCLE

The university admissions cycle begins when the applicant files a standardized admission application with his high school guidance officer or counselor. The guidance officer or other administrative official consults the applicant's high school record and enters the school's recommendation on the application. That recommendation is a quantitative appraisal of his overall suitability for post-secondary education: A, B, C, D, E, or F. (The last two categories practically guarantee rejection.) The application form is then forwarded to the student's university of choice.

If the student appears to be acceptable to the university on the strength of his standardized application form, the information on it is entered on the university's application file and the following additional forms (or their equivalent) are sent to the applicant:

• The university's own application form (if used)
• A personal data form
• Medical examination form
• Two reference forms
• A release form for the applicant's final high school marks and test scores.

As these forms are completed and returned, they are entered on the applicant's record in the admissions file. When a sufficient number of applicant records have been built in this way, a print-out of the admissions file is sent to the university admissions officer, who decides which applicants to accept. Successful applicants then receive permits to register along with other registration materials.

Despite the enactment of human rights legislation, some universities still collect admissions information that could be used to determine the applicant's religious persuasion, ethnic origin, or socio-economic status. These data are obtained from responses to such questions as:

- Religion
- Country of birth
- Languages spoken (as opposed to proficiency in the language of instruction)
- Father's (mother's, relative's) country of birth
- Date of entry into country
- Previous names
- Father's occupation and employer
- Are parents alumni of this university?
- Are parents (relatives) college graduates?
- Are parents (relatives) high school graduates?
- City, county and state of birth
- Number of siblings older and younger
- Marital history (divorces).

There is some ambiguity in the various laws over what data should be collected. Some data is required by the university for statistical reporting reasons. Generally, in the case of statistical data, only aggregated information is released, although there may be some disclosure of personal data by small-sample reporting.

A large proportion of most student master records (historical files) consists of information originally collected to arrive at an admissions decision. Such data include:

- High school principal's rating
- Secondary school marks
- Standard test scores
- Prior academic history
- Previous applications to university
- Previous refusals of admission to university
- Work history prior to admission
- Comments made at time of admission.

Suggestions have been made to delete data such as these from the admissions file at the time it is merged with the sessional file, in order to simplify the records-keeping task by reducing the size of the file. At present, however, most of this information becomes a part of the student's sessional file.

There are, of course, vast individual differences among university admissions officers with respect to how much data is acquired before an admissions decision is made. All that is attempted here is to indicate procedures that are widely practiced.

Student Aid or Awards

There is little uniformity among universities as to the procedure for investigating statements made in support of applications for student awards or financial aid. Such requests are common, however, and they generate their own families of records. The chief difference between such applications and admissions records is the orientation toward financial need, and the fact that information is therefore sought not only regarding the student but also regarding his parents.

Typical investigative procedures may include the following:

- Student parking permits are cross-checked against statements regarding car ownership. This may also be done any time a student's vehicle is found unlawfully parked or observed to be operated in a careless or dangerous manner.
- A cross-check is made of statements made by siblings enrolled at the same or other universities.
- The student may be asked to verify his parents' salaries. Consolidated scholarship services in the United States ask to see the IRS-1040 forms. In Canada, income tax files are checked routinely in this connection in Quebec, for instance, although the practice is illegal in the province of Ontario.
- The student may be asked to present legal papers to verify his claim of independent status. A marriage certificate, if relevant, may be required. The student may be asked to sign releases so that substantiating statements may be taken from his local clergyman and secondary-school principal. (This may be done to verify the fact of a long-standing estrangement of the student from his parents.)
- The child of an independent businessman may be required to present a certified true copy of his father's profit-and-loss statement signed by a chartered accountant.
- University payroll records may be searched to verify the salaries of staff members whose children apply for student aid. In other circumstances a father's employer or banker may be consulted.

THE REGISTRATION CYCLE

Registration represents the major data processing problem in university student records. Different institutions have different names for the component parts and officials involved, but their roles are similar. Here we are going to look at a representative although hypothetical model.

The university is made up of several *faculties* (law, medicine, engineering, etc.), each headed by a *dean*. Each faculty consists of several *departments* (civil engineering, mining engineering, chemical engineering, etc.), each directed by a *chairman* or *head*.

Each department offers several *courses* (mechanics, structures, hydraulics, etc.) under the direction of a *course chairman*. Many courses have several sections or *classes*, each taught by an *instructor*.

Students are housed (for live-in universities) in residence halls called *colleges*, each supervised by a *warden*.

The financial affairs of the university are handled by a finance officer or *bursar*. The personnel matters of the university are handled by an officer called the *registrar*. He is usually also responsible for student progress records and for electronic data processing (EDP).

There is also a *student council* elected by the students, and financed by special fees paid by the students. It publishes the student newspaper, student directory and yearbook. In recent years, with students demanding and getting more control over their personal lives within the university community, these councils have been operating *student courts*, which levy fines against students for minor offenses, and *student police* who cooperate with university security officers in keeping order at campus gatherings. In some universities the council may even operate an on-campus bar and grill or other service facilities.

At registration time, the registrant completes his registration contract, selects his courses, makes a request for living accommodations, and pays his fees. These procedures are implemented by multi-part forms. Copies of the registration form and accommodation request go to the finance office. The registration contract goes to the registrar, where class assignments are made. The accommodation request goes to the warden of the college, where living quarters are assigned.

The forms are returned to data processing, where the computer produces

1) Class lists for each instructor.

2) Course lists for each dean and department chairman.

3) Residents lists for the warden of each college.

4) A verification copy that is checked by the student and returned to EDP with corrections noted.

During the first two weeks of the term the student is allowed to shop around for his courses. Where he elects to make one or more changes, he originates a change-of-course form, copies of which go to the dean of his faculty, his department chairman, the instructors concerned, the finance officer, the registrar, and EDP, which produces change-of-course notices for the same officials and the student.

After all course changes have been made, the computer produces corrected course lists which are sent to the deans and department chairmen for verification. Corrected class lists are produced for the deans, department chairmen, and instructors. The instructors verify that all students on the list are actually attending classes and send the lists back to EDP.

The computer will also process other record chores, such as changes of address or name; the student directory, which is sent to the student council; and a comprehensive report of registration in all courses for the registrar. (In Canada such a report is sent to the Ministry of Colleges and Universities, and a similar one is produced for Statistics Canada.)

Individual receipts for fees collected are generated for the finance officer, who sends an individual receipt to each student who has paid his fees.

Proliferation of Records

Despite the establishment of central records offices, usually under the registrar, no single officer can be said to have real control over student records. A reason for this is the "typewriter syndrome." The computer is frequently used as a million-dollar typewriter rather than anything else. In records processing, its computational use is minimal.

The computer spews out a seemingly endless progression of preliminary copies, confirmation copies, verification copies, and so on—in duplicate, triplicate, and more. This uncontrolled production of multiple, unaccounted hard copies is abetted by promiscuous use of the photocopy machine.

The result is that in addition to the central records facility, every dean, department chairman, administrative aide, and faculty member builds up his own private file of information, often incorrect and quickly outdated, and maintained under conditions of dubious security.

Before a central records facility could gain control over its records, the practice of building private *ad hoc* files would have to be stopped and total reliance placed upon the central system. This suggestion, however, runs contrary to the characteristically independent temper of the academic community.

When hard copy must be produced from computer-based records and circulated for verification by the source, confirmation, collection of additional data, or input to a human decision-making process, good security practices dictate that copies should be serially numbered, protected by the recipients in secure storage, and accounted for by the central records facility if they, in fact, contain sensitive information. Reducing the number of hard copies printed, accounting for all copies circulated, and marking each DO NOT COPY would contribute substantially to the confidentiality of personal student records.

THE MARKS CYCLE

The marks cycle is repeated two, three or four times a year, depending upon the length of the basic term. Just prior to the end of the term, each instructor receives a computer-produced class list. After he grades the final examinations, he enters his marks on the list and returns it to EDP. Frequently, the examinations themselves are graded by computer.

The marks are recorded on the sessional file, and the computer prints out course lists containing a mark opposite each student's name. The course lists containing these marks are distributed to deans, department chairmen, instructors, and to the registrar. Promotion decisions based on these marks are sent to EDP from the chairman via his dean and also recorded on the sessional file.

Finally, the computer prints individual student grade reports (containing his final marks and the university's promotion decision). Copies are sent to the student, instructor, chairman, dean and registrar.

At the end of the term or year, data from the sessional file is carried over to the historical file. The student's record in the historical file constitutes his actual academic record. However, in most universities his *official* academic record is a cardboard jacket kept by the registrar.

At the end of each term or session, the registrar's copy of each student's grade report, which is often printed on adhesive-backed paper stock, is affixed to the student's academic report card. If, after his graduation, a transcript of university grades is required for employment purposes, the request is sent from the prospective employer to the registrar. The registrar makes a copy of the official transcript, personally signs and dates it, and impresses the university's raised seal over his dated signature.

When a student completes his course of study, he files a formal application for a degree. It goes to EDP by way of the finance officer (to see that all outstanding bills have been paid), the dean and the registrar (to verify that his academic record is such that a degree is merited). From these applications the computer produces a degree list, which goes to the registrar, who prepares the actual diplomas, and to the deans, who arrange for the convocation (graduation) ceremony.

Student marks are the most sensitive items of private data still kept in university files. They are treated with varying degrees of confidentiality at different universities. At one end of the scale, a student's mark is considered to be a strictly private matter; at the other it is quasi-public information. In the Faculty of Medicine at Canada's University of Toronto, for example, tradition dictates that the dean publicly declaim the final marks from the front steps of its principal building.

The contents of a student's record should provide few surprises for the student himself, except in some universities where letter grades are reported to the student while numerical grades are entered in his file.

Consideration of any claimed right on the part of each individual student to review his own record has to take into account the need to guard against unauthorized alteration of the record. It would be undesirable from a security point of view to implement any such review by instituting yet another broadside mailing of print-outs of student records.

Violations of confidentiality of student records are impossible to measure, but are not uncommon. Our own study discovered such examples as these:

- A janitor used spoiled print-outs of course lists with preliminary marks to line office wastebaskets.
- A secondary-school student learned his final grade marks before the school released them, through a source in the registrar's office at a university to which he had applied for admission.
- Lists of new admissions were given to the Student Health Service at one university before the registrar received them. As a consequence, applicants were sent an implied notice of admission in a circular mailed by the Medical Officer before official notifications were released.
- A student was able to tell his dean his class standing before standings were announced. He had obtained an advanced print-out of the course list from one of his instructors.

PRESERVING SECURITY OF RECORDS

In about half of all universities, the same staff processes administrative records as handles teaching and research computing.

Separate staff	51 percent
Same staff	42 percent
No staff	3 percent
	100 percent

An accountable administrative officer could find himself in an uncomfortable position when the computing facility for whose actions he is responsible reports to an officer whose principal responsibilities have to do with teaching and research rather than administration.

Following are the results of our inquiries regarding the locus of control of the computing facility charged with processing administrative data:

Administrative officer	49 percent
Academic or research officer	39 percent
University president	1 percent
No facility or staff	1 percent
	100 percent

Our studies showed that in the majority of cases, the same computer used to process administrative data was also used for academic instruction and research.

Same computer	64 percent
Separate computer	28 percent
No computer	8 percent
	100 percent

In general, the computer used for teaching and research is highly visible and vulnerable, as was demonstrated in 1969 at Sir George Williams University. The computer room usually has at least one glass wall. There are frequent tours by undergraduate computer science classes and local high school students. Students, graduate students, students' wives, junior faculty and staff frequently work as programmers or operators. Third-year computer science students are allowed to program the computer in machine language, frequently causing monitor crashes, that is, failure of the computer's master control routine.

Back-up tapes are often stored within the computing facility. Historical records are kept in a bewildering assortment of storage cabinets and document boxes. Little use is made of microfilm for storing these records.

Some universities don't even process their own data. Sixty-six (66) percent of universities are able to handle all their computing internally. The others use service bureaus (27 percent) or the facilities of other universities (17 percent) to handle the overflow.

The average university computer has 161,500 words of internal (core) storage and 122.5 million words of disk (random access) storage. It is a large machine capable of time-sharing operation if desired. About thirty persons are employed at the computing center. Their breakdown by job function is:

Programmers	38 percent
Operators	23 percent
Clerks	20 percent
Supervisors	10 percent
Technicians	9 percent
	100 percent

Sixty-nine (69) percent of universities use no students in their computing center operations. Thirty-one (31) percent have bonded some of their staff members.

The breakdown of computing center personnel by categories is:

Professionals	73 percent
Students	10 percent
Bonded professionals	9 percent
Manufacturers' personnel	3 percent
Part-time employees	1 percent
Other	4 percent
	100 percent

Source data is kept in the form of documents, coding forms or punched cards, with retention times varying from three to thirty-five months. Transaction (that is intermediate or working) files are kept on punch cards, magnetic tape or fixed disks, with retention times ranging from three to twenty-two months. Back-up files are kept on magnetic tape with an average retention time of six weeks.

The reason for the short retention time is that the back-up file is usually the prior copy of the master file left over when the file is updated. There is, in fact, a back-up file perpetually in storage somewhere, although copies are changed each time the master file is updated.

The protection level of files can be classified as protected (custodian on duty at all times), locked or open. These categories, by medium, are:

	Documents	Punched Cards	Tape	Disk
Protected	13%	10%	50%	33%
Locked	68%	55%	50%	50%
Open	19%	35%	—	17%
	100%	100%	100%	100%

The computer log is one vehicle that permits *ex post facto* discovery of malfeasance in the computer center if it is carefully scrutinized.
• In 61 percent of universities the log is kept automatically.
• In 42 percent, the operator keeps the log.
• In 33 percent, the supervisor keeps it.
That these figures do not add to 100% means that in some places duplicate logs are kept—a good security measure.
The following events are entered on the log with the frequency indicated:

Job start/stop times	82 percent of university centers
Job identification	79 percent
Routine file operations	42 percent
Operator on/off duty	39 percent
Tapes or disk packs mounted	36 percent
CPU-time and core per job	36 percent (extent of central processor usage)
Equipment changes	30 percent
Non-routine operations	27 percent
Core dumps	24 percent (examination of the internal information content of the computer)
Accounting file changes	21 percent
Monitor changes	15 percent (control program)
Visitors to the center	12 percent
Supervisor on/off duty	9 percent

Events less commonly reported include: power failures, and monitor crashes, 6 percent; and equipment failures, and maintenance response-time, 3 percent.
In 52 percent of the centers logs are reviewed by the director. In 33 percent

of the centers this function is delegated to lower echelon personnel (manager, assistant manager, tape librarian, etc.). In 15 percent of the centers the logs are sent to users of the center, including department chairmen and deans.

Methods used to insure the accuracy of data include:

Keypunch verification	70 percent
Confirmation copy sent to originator	61 percent
Internal consistency checking	52 percent
Sequence checking	45 percent
Sight checking	24 percent
Other (*e.g.* check digits)	6 percent

These percentages add to more than 100 because several centers employ two or more of these measures.

The customary method for producing transcripts, *i.e.*, computer-produced "sticky labels" affixed to a card, which is subsequently photocopied when a transcript is requested, is an open invitation to forgery.

The need for good computer center security dictates that the following measures be taken to insure the confidentiality of student records:

- If economically feasible, a separate dedicated computer should be utilized to process administrative data.
- The administrative computer should be installed in a secure office environment with access controlled by the custodian of records.
- Back-up tapes or disk packs should be stored off campus, preferably in a bank vault.
- Historical files should be converted to microfilm (this can now be done electronically) and stored in a secure off-campus archival establishment.
- Transcripts should be produced in a single computer pass on unalterable check stock (laced background).
- An electric shredder should be used to destroy spoiled print-outs or outdated records.
- If economically feasible, a separate staff of operators, supervisors, programmers, systems analysts, and clerks should be employed to process administrative data.
- Staff should be of good character, acceptable to a fidelity bonding company.
- In no case should students, graduate students, teaching faculty, research staff, or student wives be employed to handle confidential administrative data.
- Ultimate control of the administrative data processing function should

be vested in a senior administrative officer or in an officer sufficiently senior that his span of control subtends administration, and teaching or research.

- Detailed instructions concerning admission to the computer room, authority to accept jobs and deliver print-out or removable magnetic media, authority to mount tape on disk files, and procedures for keeping the operating log should be furnished to shift operations supervisors (or senior duty operators).
- Magnetic media should be wiped clean electronically before being reused.
- Input documents, excess print-outs, coding forms, and punched cards should be routinely destroyed as soon as back-up tapes have been created and stored.

Many of these measures save money at the same time as they enhance security.

In addition to being an educational institution, a business, and an employer, a university is also a center for research of all kinds. Generally, all classified research of a defense nature has been removed from the universities following the confrontations of the late sixties. However, some professors still do research and consulting work that may have profound implications for public policy. Other research studies may deal with information of a highly personal nature.

Measures must be taken to guard against premature or inaccurate disclosure of research results, and to be sure that such disclosure as is made is proper within the terms of the contract under which it was undertaken.

At one university, student-life officers instituted, at registration time, a room-mate compatibility study that requested answers to a wide range of personal questions. Completing the questionnaire was announced to be a voluntary act, but it was also announced that no residence accommodation would be assigned until it was completed.

In many universities, use of questionnaires like this, their custody, and the use of information obtained from them, would first have to be approved by a university committee charged with control of personal information collected for research purposes.

PROBLEMS OF TIME-SHARED COMPUTING

Universities are entering a new era of data processing. They are leaving the "typewriter" age and entering the age of the "TV tube." This is another way of saying they are moving from centralized batch processing of records to concepts of data processing which involve functioning in resource-sharing remotely-accessible computer environments.

Our survey revealed the following means currently used for processing student records:

Batch processing exclusively	37 percent
Remote capability or plans to employ remote access	33 percent
Some form of remote access	21 percent
No computer processing	9 percent
	100 percent

Among the 21 percent of universities with some form of remote access to student records, we observed several variants in processing:

Remote display of selected records	9 percent
Remote high-speed data entry	3 percent
Remote keyboarded data entry	3 percent
Remote high-speed entry, printer output, and display	3 percent
Remote display and keyboard update	3 percent
	21 percent

The 70 percent of universities using computers, but not presently using remote access, require some additional breakdown:

Plans to go remote, no existing capability	26 percent
No plans to go remote, existing capability	17 percent
No plans to go remote, no existing capability	17 percent
Plans to go remote, existing capability, some developmental work	10 percent
	70 percent

Remote access to student records presents both advantages and hazards from a security point of view. On the positive side, it does away with the multiple print-outs that probably constitute the greatest existing threat to confidentiality. On the other hand, the remote computer has no way of telling whether the user at the terminal has a right to see information he has requested, and, more seriously, to alter or update it. Nor can the computer tell, in some cases, whether the request came from a legitimate system terminal. There is also the additional hazard of wiretapping.

The average number of terminals on a university time-sharing system is twelve, with numbers ranging up to sixty. In 85 percent of the cases, a user can protect his files against any access to them by other users. In twelve percent of the cases, other users can read his files; in only three percent of university time-sharing systems would other users be able to write over a user's files.

The use of various entry control devices is as follows:

Account number	59 percent
User's name	35 percent
Password with its printing inhibited	29 percent
Password typed over a mask	12 percent
Bare password	12 percent
One-time password	12 percent
File password	6 percent

The fact that the total is over 100 percent indicates that several centers have multiple access controls.

The means of access control were found to be:

Line scanner	35 percent
User entered identification	35 percent
Direct wire	24 percent
Answer back	6 percent

Special logs of terminal activity contain the following entries:

Terminal on/off times and identification	53 percent
User's log in and out times and identification	47 percent
Number of users accessing the system at any time	29 percent
Telephone line numbers used by each terminal	29 percent
Unsuccessful attempts to obtain service	6 percent

The types of connection between terminals and the central computer is a measure of the system's vulnerability to wiretapping. This kind of attack is not currently viewed as a major threat to security of university systems.

Direct lines within a single building	59 percent
Direct lines between buildings	41 percent
Public switched telephone network	41 percent
University Centrex	12 percent
Local automatic switchboard (PABX)	12 percent
Local manual switchboard (PBX)	6 percent

The fact that the percentages do not add up to 100 indicates that answers are on a line basis, rather than by system. One system may have two or more types of line in use.

The subject of security in remotely accessible computer systems is a complex one. The following security practices would merely hit the high points:

- Truly sensitive data has no place in any resource-sharing system using existing operational security measures.
- Unless interconnecting telecommunications lines are located entirely within the premises containing the university administrative offices and connect directly into the computer with no intervening switchboard or unsupervised junction box, some possibility of wiretapping or surreptitious entry into the system must be presumed.
- The system must establish the identity of the calling terminal before any information is transmitted.
- The system must establish the identity and authority of the user before any information is transmitted.
- Records in any file containing sensitive material should be paged into sub-records so that each remote user can access only the data he actually requires to accomplish his assigned task.

Chapter 10

PERSONNEL INVESTIGATIONS

"Good name in man and woman, dear my lord,
Is the immediate jewel of their souls:
Who steals my purse, steals trash; 'tis
something, nothing;
T'was mine; 'tis his, and has been slave
to thousands;
But he that filches from me my good name
Robs me of that which not enriches him
And makes me poor indeed."

—William Shakespeare, *Othello*

INTRODUCTION

The first duty of any state is to safeguard its own existence. If the state itself cannot survive, it can do little to insure the freedom and well-being of its citizens. Similarly, the first duty of any commercial enterprise is to stay in business. If a company goes bankrupt, everyone's job is gone, individual and collective agreements notwithstanding.

At some point, security becomes the paramount consideration.

Security classification systems are usually established with one consideration in mind—to preserve the integrity of the nation. The SECRET classification is reserved for information whose disclosure would endanger the state. The

235

TOP SECRET classification is generally assigned to safeguard information whose disclosure would place the state in *grave* danger.

Lower classifications—CONFIDENTIAL, RESTRICTED, OFFICIAL USE, etc.—are used to safeguard information whose disclosure would embarrass the state, assist its enemies, or endanger individuals and organizations or their property.

The measures discussed in this chapter deal principally with investigation of persons and organizations who would have access to SECRET and TOP SECRET information. Even within these categories, not all of the measures outlined would be used in every case. There are degrees of risk to be weighed against cost, as in any security situation.

Such personnel investigations involve four general techniques:
1) Backgrounding
2) Positive Vetting
3) Polygraphing
4) Profiling.

These approaches involve a coherent progression from recording verifiable facts regarding past events to making inferential observations regarding current attitudes of the subject and probabilistic predictions of his future behavior. This, after all, is what really concerns a security officer.

Of these four measures one, Positive Vetting, is not widely used in North America. Acquisition and assessment of medical history information in connection with Backgrounding is likewise rarely used in the United States and Canada. In the latter instance, most applicants subsequently receive a complete pre-employment medical examination. At that time a government physician will take their medical histories and pursue any questionable areas with appropriate diagnostic procedures.

Polygraphing and Profiling, rightly or wrongly, encounter strong opposition in certain quarters, and their range of application is probably somewhat less than their potential contributions might otherwise dictate.

BACKGROUNDING

A complete background investigation proceeds in four steps:
1) Taking a complete Personal History Statement from the applicant.
2) Evaluating the Personal History Statement.
3) Carrying out a National Agency Check.
4) Performing a Full Field Investigation.

Personal History Statement (PHS)

A complete PHS is the cornerstone of a successful background investigation. Ideally it should require the subject to quote relevant file numbers wherever possible.

It might be argued that no applicant can reasonably be expected to remember a dozen or so relevant numbers, and that a subject who has too much detail at his fingertips should automatically be suspect. However, the situation provides evaluative opportunities that can be exploited.

The applicant can be allowed to fill out in the agency's office as much as he can of the PHS. He can then be permitted to go home and dig up the information he was unable to remember. Upon his return, he should be asked to fill out a completely new PHS. The agency would then have two statements that could be cross-checked for consistency. Inconsistencies, of course, would provide leads to be pursued in the subsequent full field investigation.

The Personal History Statement consists of fifteen sub-histories:

1) Personal history
2) Marital history
3) Residence history
4) Citizenship history
5) Availability
6) Physical data
7) Educational history
8) References
9) Employment history
10) Military history
11) Foreign Travel history
12) Court record
13) Credit record
14) Organizational memberships
15) Family history.

Essentially the PHS constitutes a complete chronology of the subject's life from birth onward, starting with the name of the registry office and his birth registration number. Remember that the legends of many illegals begin with the appropriation of an identity from birth records.

Personal history should include all those episodes in the subject's life that might recur in a critical setting or expose the subject to the threat of blackmail. These include non-medical use of drugs, chronic drug dependence even if legitimized by prescription, alcoholism, immoderate use of intoxicants, or homosexuality.

If the subject has been licensed to drive a motor vehicle, keep or carry firearms, or practice a regulated trade or profession, the appropriate regulatory agency may have relevant data showing how responsibly he has discharged the obligations incumbent on such a tradesman or professional person. To make such information readily available to field investigators, the PHS should show the jurisdictions in which the subject has been licensed and give his file or certificate numbers.

Marital history includes names, dates, places of residence, and the citizenship of present spouse, former spouses, and present and former in-laws. It should disclose the reasons for termination of each marriage with details of each marriage and divorce, annulment or separation, including the name of the registry office, liber and page numbers where such action is recorded.

Divorces and the like may provide evidence of instability on the part of the subject. They may also impoverish a man by alimony and support payments, making him receptive to offers of bribery, etc. Nor is it unknown for previously married illegals to go through a "wash divorce" so that one of them can proceed with new infiltration attempts without the disadvantage of association with the other.

Residence history should be complete chronologically and go back at least fifteen years.

Citizenship history should include all prior nationalities and reference the location of the citizenship court and nationalization certificate number. Be careful of instances where the applicant has a claim on some other nationality. Aside from the problems of conflicting alliance, such a claim can sometimes help a person evade prosecution for treasonable acts or forestall extradition proceedings. Look also for any steps the subject may have taken to change his nationality in the past or present.

Educational history should be chronologically complete with reasons given for the termination of all matriculations and the subject's release of all transcripts.

References may be subdivided into character references, social references, business or credit references, and neighbors. Each category can shed its peculiar light on some aspect of the subject's life. References should not be redundant, such as former supervisors, who would be covered under "employment." Give the subject high marks, however, if he quotes a reference who has legitimate access to pertinent files, such as his local chief of police.

Employment history should contain reasons for leaving each employment situation, starting and final salary, and starting and final position. Look for evidence of downgrading which could have been accepted as an alternative to dismissal. The name and business address of the subject's *immediate* supervisor should be given in each case, as well as the subject's consent to make inquiries of his present employer.

The chronology must account for all periods of unemployment. If the subject was out of work, where did he live? What did he do? What did he live on? His unemployment insurance claim number or welfare account number can help you to pin down such otherwise unaccounted for periods of time.

Military service history should include the subject's serial numbers, officer's file numbers, veteran's claim number if any, and types of discharge received, as well as branch, corps, and especially country served. Selective service data should be listed: local board number, location and address, subject's registration number, deferment classification, and the reason a deferred classification was assigned. If the subject has no service record and was of military age during a period of national emergency, how did he sit it out?

Foreign travel history should list all countries visited, years, dates, locations, passport numbers and visas. Note should be made of instances where the subject has traveled under foreign passports or *other travel documents,* such as those issued by the United Nations. A claim of "refugee status" has often been an effective penetration aid.

Court record would normally cover any criminal history. If the subject admits to any history of criminal involvement, he should be asked to give details of all incidents, especially date, place, agency in case of arrest, court jurisdiction and sitting of all trials, names and places of confinement with institution number, and the file identification of his criminal record (FBI number in the United States; Fingerprint Section number in Canada).

Financial history is important for several reasons. Difficulty in discharging past financial obligations may indicate a lack of responsibility. Heavy indebtedness may show not only bad judgment on the part of the subject in managing his affairs, but also a potential for breach of trust should he be admitted to a position where he might easily enrich himself unlawfully.

On the other hand, a good credit rating does not always indicate honesty. A person wholly dependent on his income who lives habitually beyond his means might be stealing from his current employer or be "on retainer" from a potentially hostile quarter. One with legitimate sources of income beyond his normal salary might subsequently find himself in a conflict-of-interest situation, or he might lack incentive in the position for which he is a candidate.

Organizational memberships can be revealing in many ways. Candidates for positions of trust who hold or have held membership in subversive organizations obviously constitute real security hazards. An applicant with too many memberships may have poor judgment in budgeting his time. Another with no apparent outside interests may actually be in hiding, possibly an illegal. Attention should also be given to potentially conflicting membership, as in the case of applicants who belong to reserve components of the armed forces (militia in Canada). Such affiliations might interfere with the candidate's availability in the event of a national emergency.

Family history should include the name, dates and places of birth, residence, and citizenship of children and close relatives. Special emphasis should be placed on any relatives who are not citizens or who live abroad, because of the possibility of conflicting alliance on the part of the subject or the risk of these relatives being held hostage to compel the subject to commit disloyal acts.

Subjects with relatives in the military or government services of foreign countries may be security hazards. And those who have relatives in the military or government service of your own country may be vulnerable to situations in which nepotism or unauthorized interdepartmental exchange of information could occur.

Evaluating the PHS

To be usefully evaluated, a Personal History Statement must be complete and verifiable. Gaps in the chronology could conceal the fact that the subject had been confined in prison, undergoing treatment in a mental hospital, serving in the armed forces of a foreign country, or even attending a subversive school operated by a potentially hostile power.

Even if there are no time sequences unaccounted for, the evaluator should exercise extreme caution in such areas as the following:

- Don't allow a post-office box number to qualify as a residence address. The subject didn't live in a pigeon hole. He should provide a real address where you can interview former neighbors or landlords.
- Be alert to the possibility that a real address may only have been a "mail drop." It is not at all uncommon for a young person to retain his parents' mailing address during periods of wandering or informal living. His use of a mail drop may keep you from probing contacts he made while living in a commune, say, on the island of Majorca.
- Be suspicious of "dead ends." If you encounter a subject whose birth record was filed in a courthouse that burned down, or who worked for

a large number of firms that subsequently went out of business, or whose prior residences for one reason or another seem all to have been demolished—look out. A postal employee in British Columbia was discovered to be supplying just such information about burned courthouses, defunct companies, and demolished buildings to a potentially hostile foreign power—information useful in fabricating "legends" or cover stories for illegal agents.
• Look for inconsistencies and ellipses: anything that is where it shouldn't be; anything that should be there, but isn't.

National Agency Check

A national agency check involves preparing a search request based on the subject's PHS, supplying recent I.D. photographs, and taking a 10-rolled, 10-flat fingerprint card. This information will be run through the files of the various national security agencies. (Fingerprint comparisons are not always made to confirm identity, since clearance is sometimes granted without fingerprints having been submitted.) The affirmative response to a National Agency Check is "nothing derogatory."

In Canada it is easy to do an agency check. The Security Services of the Department of Supply and Services sends the documentation to the RCMP, which does any necessary investigation and provides the clearance information.

In the United States, because of the complexity of the security and intelligence establishment, this is more difficult. In this study it is possible only to describe a typical pattern of procedure.

The applicant completes a Personal History Statement. He delivers it to the prospective employer's security officer, who may have him photographed and fingerprinted, using the firm's own facilities. The material is forwarded to the security office of the procurement agency with which the firm has contracted.

Depending on the level of security clearance required for the position involved, a National Agency Check alone or in conjunction with a Full Field Investigation will be ordered.

The National Agency Check consists of consulting the files of the Federal Bureau of Investigation; Army, Navy and Air Force Intelligence Commands; the Subversive Activities Control Board (formerly the House Unamerican Activities Committee); and in some cases the Atomic Energy Commission Intelligence Division. The Federal Drug Control Agency may also be checked to see if the applicant has a record of drug-related offenses or involvement.

When a Full Field Investigation is required, the National Agency Check is supplemented by having investigators verify the statements made in the Personal History Statement. These investigators are employed by the military service with which the firm has contracted.

Internal security in the United States is a mission delegated to the Federal Bureau of Investigation. The Special Agents assigned to internal security work out of Bureau Field Offices and report through the same chain of command as do Special Agents assigned to criminal investigation. They cultivate and pay informers within organizations suspected of engaging in subversive activities.

The intelligence commands of the Army, Navy and Air Force feed information upward to the Defense Intelligence Agency, an instrumentality of the Department of Defense. Prior to 1971, personalized information contributed by the armed services intelligence commands had been centralized in a computerized National Security Data Bank at Fort Holabird, Maryland. When controversy regarding this data bank developed in the United States Senate, the DOD announced that its National Security Data Bank had been abolished.

Another file of consequence containing internal security information consists of the names of persons who have made threats against the President or other high government officials, or have demanded personal interviews with them. This file is maintained by the U.S. Secret Service, an agency of the Treasury Department which has, among other responsibilities, that of protecting the persons of the President, Vice-President, and their families.

Basically, an agency check must be regarded as a *name search*. Slight variations in spelling of the subject's name can sometimes preclude a positive match with a record containing derogatory information.

It is difficult to search a file on fingerprint data or physical description alone. The RCMP was able to connect James Earl Ray with his AKA of Ramon George Sneyd only through a painstaking search of passport files. This required thousands of man-hours of effort.

The French, with their Bertillon *portrait parlé* and phonetic coding of names, have a much more effective technique for searching files containing personal information. This advantage is partially nullified by the diffusion of responsibility for security in France among at least nine different agencies.

Field Investigation

Of its very nature field investigation is a spotty operation. No nation has the resources within its security services to check out every statement made by every applicant for security clearance.

There are vast differences among security services in handling field investigations. In some services they are performed by young men newly assigned to security and intelligence after prior careers in general police work. In others they are "filler assignments" for regular agents, additional chores imposed upon the field office staff. Still other services hire relatively low-level investigators and assign them to backgrounding on a more or less permanent basis.

There is a Chinese saying that you don't use good iron to make nails, or good men to make soldiers. By the same token it is not always possible to assign top-flight agents to backgrounding. Generally, it is hard to maintain a high level of motivation in this kind of work.

Unless the evaluator spots something incongruent on the Personal History Statement and calls for a special check, the investigation will probably consist of the investigator personally interviewing some of the references quoted and the subject's more recent prior employers, while the agency itself obtains documentary verification. A resourceful investigator may also have a few knowledgeable personal contacts whose acquaintance—or often lack of acquaintance—with the subject will go a long way to confirm the investigator's judgment.

Other Uses of the PHS

The most important part of the Personal History Statement is *the last line.* Here the applicant states under pain of immediate future dismissal that he has provided a true chronology of his life. Should he subsequently abuse his position of trust, it may be a lot easier to prove falsification of the PHS than to develop evidence needed for an indictment.

From time to time every security officer encounters sticky situations in which an employee becomes a problem, but gives the security officer nothing to get hold of. A couple of examples will illustrate the value of the PHS in such situations.

- An attractive girl in the typing pool is dating an unusual number of junior analysts and asking them altogether too many penetrating questions. An investigation of her PHS may reveal that, during a time period in which she stated she lived in San Francisco, she was in fact occupying a cozy apartment on Bubbling Well Road in Shanghai. While not conclusive, that evidence is enough to place the girl where security people can keep a sharp eye on her.
- A series of security lapses occur—safes left on combination, burn bags incompletely incinerated, crypto aids mixed up. They all appear to involve a particular cypher clerk. An examination of his PHS may reveal that he forgot to mention twenty-one shock treatments (electro-convulsive

therapy) he had a year or so ago. A resultant interview discloses that he has some real or imagined grievance against the agency. He will be happier going home—and the security officer will sleep easier.

POSITIVE VETTING

One government service formerly utilized an old house situated near its training station where new officers first reported for duty. During his training period, each new man was sent there for a talk with the security officer.

The waiting room in the house was grubby—peeling paint, faded congoleum, rickety chairs, a few well-thumbed copies of old magazines. Its decor, or lack of it, was carefully calculated to erode the subject's self-confidence.

After he had cooled his heels for a while, the subject was ordered into a brightly lighted, almost antiseptic room. There he was closely questioned on his PHS by the security officer, who had previously studied it with great care, comparing it point by point with evidence developed in a National Agency Check and a Full Field Investigation.

This example illustrates positive vetting. Its essence is
- A personal interview
- Conducted under conditions of stress
- Based upon answers previously given by the subject, and
- Confirmed or denied by other information.

In such an interview the subject is not questioned to elicit information. That is obtained in a properly designed Personal History Statement. The reasons for the personal interview are
- To impeach the subject on the basis of any false statements.
- To observe his behavior under stress.
- To open avenues for exploration that he has heretofore concealed.
- To provide new leads for field investigators to follow.

Before a stress interview, the interviewer has to do his homework. It should be remembered that, if the subject is misrepresenting himself or has something to hide, it is certain that he will have rehearsed his role in the interview. The interviewer can't afford to allow him to retain that advantage.

Interrogation is an art as well as a science. All that is possible here is to offer a few suggestions:

1) Never ask a question unless you already know the answer. It is your job to surprise the subject, not to let him surprise you. Stick to the assertions made on the PHS. This is no time to go on a fishing expedition.

2) Exercise some selectivity in your questioning. The PHS may be fourteen pages long, and you have perhaps an hour to talk with the subject.

Ask questions regarding assertions that appear to be
- (a) mutually contradictory,
- (b) at variance with information received from other agencies,
- (c) different from facts unearthed by field investigators,
- (d) contrary to your own personal knowledge.

Explore areas in which the subject has failed to answer questions or appeared to equivocate in his responses.

3) Do not ask questions in chronological or any other logical order. Not doing so keeps the subject off balance.

4) Where your evaluation of the PHS has produced a few key questions, ask each of them several times, in different contexts and at different points of the interview. Compare the subject's various responses for consistency.

5) If the subject becomes expansive on some subject, let him ramble on, but not so much as to gain control of the interview. He may open interesting avenues to explore. Never deny a subject the rope with which to hang himself.

6) Be alert to inconsistencies between assertions made on the PHS and statements made during the interview, as well as differences among the subject's oral statements.

7) Don't take notes, show surprise, or, for that matter, display any other emotion. Interrogation is like a game of pinball in which the subject is the machine. Don't let *your* face light up "tilt."

8) If your memory tends to fail you, use a concealed tape recorder.

POLYGRAPHING

The polygraph is not a lie detector; it is a stress detector. A polygraph examination is an extension of, and complementary to, the interview. Even where the security officer is not authorized to conduct such tests, he should be familiar with the technique so that it can be fitted into an overall interview program.

The instruments used measure the physiological manifestations of stress: pulse (quickened), blood pressure (raised), respiration (shallow), galvanic skin resistance (lower), voice waveforms (stressed), and brain waves (jagged).

The idea is not new. Medieval trials by ordeal also measured physiological manifestations of stress. A guilty person could handle a hot iron without being burned (sweaty palms); could not whistle after eating an unsalted biscuit (dry mouth); would fail to drown if thrown into the lake (constricted air passages).

Some opposition to polygraph examinations has been voiced by organized labor, ranging from demands at the bargaining table to attempts to secure legislation adverse to its use. A few companies have agreed to contract prohibitions, and in twelve states laws have been enacted prohibiting its use. Fourteen other states, however, have enacted legislation licensing polygraphists.

It should be noted that the polygraph may be used to establish innocence as well as guilt of crime or deception. *The Polygraph Technique,*[16] edited by J. Kirk Barefoot and published by the American Polygraph Association, cites a number of examples in which suspects were cleared of suspicion of crimes through the use of the polygraph, including a woman who had signed a written statement admitting that she had "done wrong." A polygraph test indicated that she was innocent in spite of her admission, and additional questioning revealed that she had signed the damaging statement because she was frightened.

The Polygraph Technique (to which we are indebted for the substance of much of this brief review of polygraphing) describes the attachments of the polygraph as a blood pressure cuff, identical to that used by a physician, which is attached to either the upper arm, forearm or wrist; one or two rubber tubes, which are wrapped around the trunk of the body to measure and record the rate and pattern of respiration; and a third attachment, usually placed on one or two fingers or connected to the palm of the hand, to measure changes in electrical resistance of the skin.

Test Questions

Although there are at least a half dozen different testing techniques, all are similar, differing only in minor details of procedure. Most contain some built-in safeguards to protect the subject. Some individuals, for instance, tend to show a guilty response pattern to *any* pertinent question asked under test conditions. A "guilt complex" question is used to identify these rare subjects.

Another and most important safeguard is the use of one or more *control questions*. These are questions specifically formulated to induce the subject to lie. The function of the control question is to provide a response pattern which the examiner can compare to responses to relevant questions in the test, both to reveal deception and, even more importantly, to verify truthful answers. The control question has the added effect of preventing an individual from "passing" the test who is, in fact, physiologically or psychologically incapable of responding normally, which is generally true of sociopaths.

A polygraph test may consist of only eleven questions. Of these, one might be the control question, requiring an answer contrary to fact; five might be innocuous or neutral; the remainder would be relevant to the investigation.

Examiners may improvise on the neutral questions. In backgrounding, the five central questions might be such as these:

1) Is your name John Doe?
2) Are you a citizen of the United States?
3) Have you ever stolen government property?
4) Have you ever knowingly revealed classified information?
5) Is there anything in your past that might make you subject to blackmail?

No attempt is made to surprise the subject. On the contrary, the areas to be covered and the test questions are discussed in advance, and the subject is given an opportunity to qualify his responses. The examiner will then modify his questions accordingly.

After each test or "run" where a stress response is recorded, the question is discussed with the subject and amended in subsequent tests until the traces are normal (within control limits) or until the examiner has to report his findings as "inconclusive." (In our context, such a finding might be construed as unfavorable to the subject.)

The revised form of central question 5 (regarding blackmail) might be: "With the exception of an affair with the upstairs maid, is there anything else in your past that might make you subject to blackmail?"

In backgrounding, central areas of inquiry might include questions concerning theft of money or property, arrests or convictions, being fired from a job, use of drugs or alcohol to excess, applications for other positions, treatment for mental or physical disorders, indebtedness or bankruptcy, military court martial or discharge other than honorable, and similar subjects.

The Control Test

Prior to the actual test, a control test is usually given. Its purpose is to allow the subject to become used to the polygraph and to relax, and at the same time to give the examiner some indication of the subject's response pattern.

One of the most common control tests involves the use of playing cards. The subject is asked to select one card from a group of five to seven, which are displayed face down and numbered. He does not reveal which card he chooses. He is then instructed to answer "No" to *all* questions in the control test. The examiner will ask the same question regarding each card: "Did you choose card number ____?" One negative answer must obviously be untrue, and the reading on the polygraph chart will enable the polygraphist to observe before the real test how the subject responds when he lies.

The Pre-Employment Test

The vast majority of all polygraph tests administered are pre-employment tests. Such an examination typically lasts about an hour, and of this period as much as 45 minutes may be spent in the pre-test interview. During this time the subject's health and medical history and background are discussed. The subject is encouraged to explain anything in his past that might affect the wording of the test questions. A question frequently asked, for example, is, "Have you ever been arrested for anything not listed on the application?" If the subject admits that as a teenager he was caught shoplifting in a department store and turned over to the police, the question would be modified (like the blackmail question in the previous example), along the lines of, "Other than the shoplifting incident mentioned, have you ever been arrested for anything not listed on the application?"

When the interview is over, the actual examination is given. It usually includes two or more runs, each lasting only three or four minutes, normally covering ten or twelve questions, interspersing relevant questions ("Have you committed major thefts against previous employers?") with irrelevant ones ("Is your first name Richard?") and the control question or questions. All questions are answered with a "yes" or "no" response.

At the end of the first test the subject is given an opportunity to explain anything that might have come to mind during the run, triggered by the test questions and reflected in the polygram tracing. If no such explanation is offered, the polygraphist conducts the second run, after which he will discuss the results in detail with the subject, particularly with reference to any thought process that might have affected a response shown in the chart. If new information is volunteered at this time, the pertinent question will be rephrased and a new test administered.

If the subject fails to offer any explanation for a response that indicates a clear attempt to deceive, the examiner will discuss the issue openly with him, providing yet another opportunity for the subject to come forward with the true facts. If an explanation is given, a final or *clearing chart* is made.

It should be stressed that the polygraph examination includes only questions that are either completely neutral or have some specific relevance to the applicant's fitness for the job. For instance, such highly personal matters as sexual relations or conduct are never a subject for questioning in the typical pre-employment situation. Only for highly sensitive positions where blackmail might be a factor would such questions be appropriate. In general, the applicant's age and background, the nature of the job, and common sense provide reasonable guidelines for the propriety of questions. For example:

- A teenager seeking a job in the shipping department of a cigarette company would probably not be asked about chronic alcoholism but might well be questioned about any recent history of thefts.
- A middle-aged man with a ten-year record of responsible handling of large amounts of cash and merchandise would not be questioned about youthful shoplifting incidents.
- A 20-year-old applicant for a position in a hospital pharmacy could be questioned regarding illicit use of narcotics or a recent firing from another health care facility.

Specific Testing

One of the oldest and most reliable polygraph tests is the Peak of Tension (POT) test. It is rarely used in private testing, but is commonly found in follow-up and police testing.

A familiar example of the POT test occurs in police questioning of a possible suspect. Questions used in the test are based upon specific knowledge of a crime that could be known only to the criminal. For this reason facts about a serious crime, such as homicide, are frequently withheld from publication by law enforcement agencies, enabling the information to be used in suitable questions, both to identify the criminal and to clear innocent parties who might otherwise be suspect.

Periodic Testing

The periodic test is one customarily given to employees on a regular basis. Because it does not need to cover the broad range of subjects that might be included in a pre-employment test, the periodic examination is restricted to a narrow spectrum of pertinent issues, such as questions about the handling of cash or merchandise. Questions might begin, "Since your last polygraph test, have you ____?"

Voice Stress Evaluation (PSE)

The Dektor Psychological Stress Evaluation (PSE-1) detects, measures, and graphically displays specific stress-related components of the human voice. These components result from physiological tremors of the muscles of the voice mechanism. They are manifested in frequency modulation of the voice waveform at a rate of 8–14 hertz (cycles per second). These oscillations, which are in the inaudible infrasonic range, are normally present in the human voice, but are suppressed when the muscles are subjected to stress induced by fear, anxiety, guilt or conflict. This facilitates detection of attempted deception during interrogation.

There is a growing body of cases in which the PSE test has been used successfully in both public and private investigations.

- Police in Vienna, Virginia, have used voice stress evaluation in investigation of murder, rape, robbery, burglary, kidnapping, and grand larceny. Police Chief Vernon L. Jones comments that it helps to screen out innocent suspects, allowing investigators to concentrate their efforts.
- In Monterey, California, a private detective used voice stress to evaluate narrative telephone calls, permitting him to confirm and track the route of two men, one armed, involved in kidnapping an 18-month-old asthmatic child. The monitored trail, which led up the Pacific Coast and into Canada, ended in the Midwest, where the child was recovered.
- Police in Lenoir, North Carolina, have used PSE to investigate larceny, armed robbery, rape, assault, and embezzlement.
- In Baltimore, Maryland, a lawyer using voice stress evaluation found a convict serving life for first-degree murder to be innocent. Two state-administered polygraph tests confirmed the lawyer's findings.
- Police in Ellicott City, Maryland, describe four cases in which the technique was used. In two cases, charges were dropped. In a third, the test confirmed the innocence of a suspect accused of writing bad checks. In the fourth case, the results of the test induced a young accomplice to plead guilty to shoplifting.
- In Cleveland, Ohio, a private detective used the PSE to test a highly neurotic female intermittently under psychiatric care. A conventional polygraph test would have been potentially too traumatic. The PSE showed that the woman had told her husband the truth, and the finding helped to preserve a family with three children.

These examples point up several important factors about the PSE. The human voice can be transmitted over long distances by telephone and radio. It can be recorded on magnetic tape. Consequently, its use to disclose the physiological response to psychological change does not require attached sensors, elaborate equipment, or a highly controlled environment in association with the subject. The PSE can also be—and frequently is—used in conjunction with other indicators of psychological stress, such as blood pressure, heart beat, muscle movement, respiration, and brain waves.

A standard PSE costs approximately four thousand dollars and the price includes a three-day course by the manufacturer during which fifty actual cases are studied. The equipment used consists of a telephone pickup and a dynamic microphone, a four-speed tape recorder, an electronic filter and frequency-modulation detector, and a strip-chart recorder using a heated stylus and heat-sensitive paper. No connections to the subject are required, and the chart can be analyzed out of his presence.

How the PSE Works

The human voice produces three types of sound:

- *Vibration of the vocal chords* produces sound which is, in turn, a product of partially closing the glottis and forcing air through it by contraction of the lung cavity. The frequency of these vibrations varies between 100 and 300 hertz, depending upon the sex and age of the speaker and upon the intonations he applies. This sound has a rapid decay time.
- The *formant frequencies* result from the resonances of the throat, mouth, nose, and sinus cavities. They are created by excitation of the resonant cavities by a sound source of lower frequencies: vocalized sound produced by the vocal chords, or the partial restriction of the passage of air from the lungs in unvoiced fricatives.

  The frequency of the formant is determined by the resonant frequency of the cavity. The formant frequencies generally appear above 800 hertz in distinct frequency bands. The lowest formant is created by the mouth and throat cavities and is notable for its frequency shift as the mouth changes volume in forming vowel sounds. The higher formant frequencies are more constant, because of the more constant physical volume of the cavities.

  The formant waveforms are ringing signals. When voiced sounds are uttered, the voiced waveforms are imposed upon the formant waveforms as amplitude modulation.
- *Infrasonic frequency modulation*—which is measured by the PSE—is present in both the vocal chord and formant sounds. It is typically between 8 and 14 hertz, and is inaudible to the human ear. As frequency modulation it is not directly discernible on time base/amplitude chart recordings.

To observe infrasonic frequency modulation, any of the techniques for demodulation of frequency modulation may be employed. For example, pulses of the amplitude modulation of formants by a voiced signal of 190 hertz, after 2.5 kilohertz high-pass filtering of the normal voice, can be seen to contain infrasonic frequency modulation observable in the center-of-mass waveform. A simple slope detection can be made of the unlimited infrasonic waveform of a syllable utterance.

When slight to moderate psychological stress is created in a subject, the muscles associated with the vocal chords and cavity walls are subject to mild tension. This tension, indiscernible to the subject, is sufficient to virtually eliminate the muscular undulations present in the unstressed subject, thereby removing the basis for the carrier frequency vibrations that produced the infrasonic frequency modulation.

Additionally, diction stresses may be evident as a progressive change in an individual pattern. This may be audible as the subject exerts abnormal control over his diction to try to maintain a static speech pattern. These indications include minor changes in syllable stress and changes in the concatenation patterns in the separate responses.

The opposite configuration may also occur. The stress may be indicated by high amplitude and a multi-form trace, while relief may be shown by a drop in amplitude and more simple pattern. These effects depend upon whether an individual responds to psychological stimulus with excitation or depression. Infrasonic indicators remain constant from test to test and from individual to individual.

Users of PSE

There were, at the time of this writing, approximately 500 users of the PSE, including ten laboratories and clinics, doctors, lawyers, nine police departments, eight retail companies. King Hussein of Jordan has five of them.

The PSE has been used in insurance matters, industrial losses, retail-store employee honesty checks, pre-employment screening, casualty and property claims, studies of employee morale and efficiency, and investigation of internal and external industrial thefts.

PROFILING

One way to predict how a person will react in a future critical situation is to determine what kind of a person he is. This can be done by observing his behavior, interviewing him, or analyzing his responses to a questionnaire. Frequently all three approaches are used.

The scientific basis behind these techniques lies in the correlation between the responses given by many previous subjects and their subsequent behavior, or in correlations found when the test is administered to persons whose past actions have shown what kind of people they are, such as convicted felons or inmates of correctional institutions.

The Reid Report

One such report has been developed by John E. Reid and Associates, a consulting firm, for use in an applicant testing program conducted for clients.

The principal function of the Reid Report is the evaluation of the subject's attitude toward honesty. This is accomplished by asking approximately 100 questions to which the subject must answer "yes" or "no." These questions reflect the subject's basic attitude towards dishonesty by other persons and by himself. His answers are scored and given individual weights, which are then computed to provide an overall score.

The report also provides a detailed analysis of the subject's entire employment history, armed service history, medical history, and financial history and present status. His arrest and conviction record, if any, is asked for, and he is requested to agree to various conditions which will assist in subsequent investigations if losses occur. These include having his photograph and fingerprints taken, submitting handwriting samples for questioned document examination, and agreeing to undergo polygraph examinations under various conditions.

George W. Lindberg of the Reid organization comments:

"The experience we have gained by conducting over 20,000 pre-employment polygraph and Reid Report examinations has indicated to us that approximately 30 percent of the population has an attitude that will not tolerate dishonesty in the area of theft.

"It would be a most desirable situation if it were possible to employ only that 30 percent. The economics of the employment market are such, however, that an additional 40 percent are permitted to obtain positions of trust with but a reasonable degree of risk. The character of the persons in the 40 percent group is such that with reasonable security precautions they will not become involved in theft.

"The final 30 percent, however, will actually create an opportunity to engage in theft. It is this group that the Reid Report is designed to eliminate."[17]

In analyzing the Reid Report, Dr. Philip Ash of the University of Illinois has noted that it consists of three main sections. The first is a Yes-No questionnaire that measures attitudes toward punishment for theft ("Do you believe there are some special cases where a person has a right to steal from an employer?"), as well as the individual's own attitudes and behavior relating to theft ("Did you ever think about committing a burglary?").

The second section of the report consists of a detailed biographical history, while the third includes a list of questions to which an affirmative response constitutes an admission of a committed theft ("Did you make a false insurance claim for personal gain?").

Ash adds these comments on the report:

"In the typical employment use of the report, an applicant completes the form in the employer's personnel office. Part 1 is scored and all three sections analyzed by a staff member of J.E. Reid and Associates. On the basis of the item score, plus evaluation of responses to the *bio-data* and the *admissions* questions, an evaluation is made. Norms exist for the score itself, but the bio-data and the admissions questions are also taken into account.

"Incredible as it may seem, applicants in significant numbers do admit to practically every crime on the books. Furthermore, on the first part 'faking good' seems to be rare.

"In the absence of data, it may be speculated that response to the questionnaire is strongly determined by the individual's own practices:
- Someone who steals approves of punishment only for persons who steal more than he does.
- He sees as admissible more 'thoughts about stealing' than do rigidly honest respondents."[18]

Other Studies of Profiling

A particularly interesting study of profiling as a means to discern an individual's adaptability to certain kinds of work has been carried out by Michael Maccoby of Harvard University. The study is based on interviews lasting as long as six hours with more than 250 executives, lower-level managers, and engineers at a dozen corporations in the United States. Roughly half of the sample was drawn from two of the largest and most successful companies; the remainder were also employed by companies which generally hire people right out of college and expect to keep them.

In the context of his study Maccoby adopts the psychoanalytic concept of character as referring to the emotional attitudes that determine how an individual responds to a situation—what he likes or dislikes, what he finds stimulating or frustrating, exciting or depressing—and how he relates to himself and to others.

In essence Maccoby takes a step beyond the familiar Peter Principle, which asserts that the level to which people will rise in a work situation is determined by their intellectual competence. His study suggests that an individual will do well in a job only if his character is adaptive to the work involved; he will rise to a level of achievement determined by his emotional attitudes. A profile of those attitudes will therefore identify the potentially successful—or unsuccessful—candidate for a particular job.

As Maccoby concludes, "Successively promoted until their personalities no longer fit the requirements of work, even the most brilliant are likely to fail. A character type adaptive to a high level in one kind of organization may not fit another."[19]

Maccoby's study employs an extensive questionnaire of 150 items, administered during the personal interviews and supplemented by both dream interpretation and Rorschach (ink blot) tests. The questionnaire is divided into five parts:
• Work situation
• Attitudes to work
• Personal problems and values
• Sociopolitical attitudes
• Family life.

In addition to the questionnaire-interview (normally lasting about three hours), the individual's relationships with those closest to him both inside and outside of work are also probed.

Four distinct character types have been identified in the study:
1) The Craftsman
2) The Gamesman
3) The Company Man
4) The Jungle Fighter.

Although this study was carried out in the context of high technology industry, these character types can readily be recognized in other settings as well. Their profiles are shown in the appendix.

Personality Questionnaires

One form of profiling, already in widespread use particularly in large companies, is the personality questionnaire administered to young professional people seeking their first career job. A typical such questionnaire consists of 520 questions, including a number of redundant questions designed to eliminate "faking good" by cross-checking for consistency.

Half of the questions deal with activities at different ages, and the other half with attitudes and relationships. A rough subject breakdown is shown in the accompanying table.

	Percentage of Questions
SCHOOL ACTIVITIES (33%)	
Grammar School	1
High School	25
College	7
GENERAL ACTIVITIES (17%)	
Childhood	3
Adolescent	4
Adult	10
INTERPERSONAL RELATIONSHIPS (42%)	
Home Father	4
(21%) Mother	3
Parents	10
Siblings	4
Outside Teachers	4
(21%) Others	9
Self	8
ATTITUDES (8%)	
Work	7
Anger	1
Total	100

Figure 10-1: Question Subjects in Personality Questionnaires

ORGANIZATIONAL INVESTIGATIONS

There are instances (for example, in conducting a security survey) when the security officer may be called upon to investigate an organization such as a business firm or agency, as opposed to investigating individuals.

In organizational investigation five techniques have been found useful:
1) Profiling
2) Request for a brief or statement

3) Questionnaire
4) Interview
5) Special studies.

Since any such investigation may take place over a long period of time, it is expedient to maintain a *control form* and a *face sheet.*

The control form is used to record dates of contacts with the target organization and the names of persons in your organization and the target firm who were parties to these contacts, including members interviewed during site visits. Note also what kind of contact was made—meeting, letter, Telex, teletype or telephone call—and furnish a reference to the file location in which the substance of the contact is preserved. This file would include copies of record communications, minutes of formal meetings, memos summarizing informal meetings or telephone calls, and references to the location of any recordings of them.

The face sheet is used to keep an inventory of the documents held in the case folder, which is opened when an investigation is started.

Profiling

The agency profile consists of situational information, which is neutral in nature, and background information having potential impact upon the purpose of the investigation.

Situational information includes identity and infrastructure; ownership and organization; and operations. The source should be noted for each item of information. If an estimate is submitted, indicate who made it.

Data on identity and infrastructure includes:

1) Corporate name of the target organization and other names by which it is known.
2) Corporate headquarters.
3) Principal office if different from its headquarters. (The legal headquarters of some Delaware corporations, for instance, is nothing but a pigeon-hole in a lawyer's office in Wilmington.)
4) Location and function of all major establishments.
5) Location and function of all major information-handling centers.
6) Network interrelationships. On an outline map of the organization's area of operations, illustrate the following where applicable:
   (a) Corporate information network, including major data-processing centers, data-collection centers, and teleprocessing links.
   (b) Rights-of-way, identifying the trunk lines, switching centers and feeder lines.

(c) Resupply routes, warehouses and distribution centers.

(d) Flow of product: raw material supplies and pre-processing, primary processing (extraction) plants, secondary processing (manufacturing) plants and service centers.

Information on ownership and organization may include:

1) Principal owners (largest stockholders, directors).
2) Chief executive officer.
3) Principal operating executive.
4) Officer responsible for handling corporate information and his title.
5) Your principal working contact within the target organization and his title.
6) Type of incorporation: federal agency, state or provincial agency, regional or local agency, federal incorporation (charter), state or provincial incorporation, foreign incorporation, other (partnership, proprietorship, etc.).
7) Objective: profit-seeking or non-profit.
8) Principal subsidiaries and function of each.
9) Relationship or affiliation with foreign organizations, including identity of each, relationship to target organization, and its nationality.
10) Responsible regulatory agencies, function regulated, relevant act, level of government interested (identify states, provinces or lesser units).
11) Organization chart (simplified), showing the target organization's place within a larger organization or group if such exists.
12) Organization chart (simplified), showing the lines of management control within the target organization. Identify on this chart the position of the information-handling function.

Operational information should include the following:

1) Principal function. Use Standard Industrial Classification (SIC), if appropriate to your investigation.
2) Principal products or services and estimated percent of income realized from each.
3) Total assets in dollars (quote exchange rate if applicable).
4) Latest measure of total annual revenue in dollars (operating budget if an agency, gross sales if a manufacturer or distributing firm, insurance in force if an insurance company, resources if a financial institution, etc.).
5) Latest annual earnings in dollars.
6) Total number of employees, classified according to (a) whether they

are hourly rated or salaried (non-professional or professional), and (b) to which operating branch or division they belong.

7) Total number of clients, customers, subscribers, etc., classified according to the product or service delivered to them.

8) Relative importance of the organization in its field and in the general scheme of things, including growth record (shown graphically if possible), current financial health and prospects, and any evidence of the extent of its influence.

In presenting situational information about a foreign corporation or agency, it is frequently useful to make a point-by-point comparison between the target organization and a domestic corporation or agency whose structure and levels of activity are known to the intended recipients of your report.

Background information includes recent developments related to organizational structure, financing, operations, litigation, labor and community relations, and any additional documentation.

- Organization: Look for reports of mergers, consolidations, acquisitions, disposals, new ventures and joint ventures. Recent personnel changes should be reported, including hirings, dismissals, promotions, reallocation of responsibilities, retirements, resignations, transfers and deaths.
- Financing: Look for stock issues, mortgages, bond issues, debentures, tenders and take-over attempts, conversions, loans and grants.
- Operations: Look for major capital improvements, new products, new services, entry into new lines of business, and acquisition of real estate or other major assets.
- Litigation: Record pertinent judicial decisions, regulatory actions, relevant legislative actions, class action suits, anti-trust suits, suits for patent and copyright infringement. Report suits filed both by and against the target organization.
- Labor: Give attention to strikes, wildcat strikes, near strikes, slowdowns, work-to-rule movements, widespread abuse of sick leave, sabotage, demonstrations, imminent bargaining talks, union certification elections, organizing drives, lockouts, major layoffs, boycotts, problems related to environmental protection, and local controversies regarding zoning regulations.
- Additional documentation may include the following:
  1) Directory entries (attach photocopies)—Dun & Bradstreet, Moody's Manual, Standard and Poor's, Poor's Directory of Officers and Directors, Congressional Directory for agencies or corresponding government

directories in other countries, and the national computer census of the country involved.

2) Company reports, such as the latest annual report, this year's quarterly reports, stockholder notices, proxy statements, or pertinent line items from the national budget.

3) Company propaganda, including public relations brochures, image-promoting advertisements, sales literature, recruiting literature, internal and external house organs, take-home flyers distributed to employees, and speeches or press interviews given by officers.

4) Press reports concerning the target organization that might appear in national or local newspapers; national general, news and business magazines; national specialized news, technical and trade magazines; national trade newspapers and local business newspapers; national financial newspapers and magazines.

5) Public documents, including patents, papers by employees of the target organization published in professional journals, judicial decisions, pleadings, entries in the *Congressional Record* or *Hansard,* reports of Congressional Committees or Royal Commissions, etc.

6) Intake forms, such as employment application, application for consumer credit, order blanks, requests for service, etc.

7) Quasi-public documents—policy statements, contract proposals, technical reports made publicly available, pricing and specification sheets, maintenance and operating manuals dealing with company products.

8) Adverse publications, including reports in international or local union newspapers, items in "Action Line" columns, articles in undergraduate student newspapers or the underground press, "confession"-type books or articles by former employees, interviews granted by defectors.

In reviewing an agency profile, mark all items about which you feel you have insufficient information or which require a deeper look. These include the names of personnel about whom you may want to check vanity directories (*Who's Who,* etc.) or order a personal investigation.

The composition of a request for a brief or a questionnaire, if either is to be used, should be weighed heavily by what you have learned or failed to learn in preparing the profile.

Briefs

The target organization may be invited to submit a brief or statement telling its position on the subject matter under investigation. The composition of that brief can be channeled so as to fulfill your information requirements by such methods as enclosing a position paper outlining areas of concern along with your invitation to submit a brief; asking several open-ended questions in your letter of request; or holding a conference between members of your team and representatives of the target organization to sharpen the focus on various issues.

Questionnaires

The questionnaire is the principal information-gathering instrument used in an *overt* investigation. It confirms information developed in the profile. It pursues sweeping and possibly self-serving statements made in a brief in order to elicit hard, factual material. It relieves the members of the site interview team of the need to gather a lot of numerical data, freeing them to probe management's perceptions, attitudes and plans. And it provides a factual base from which to launch Special Studies.

Each questionnaire has to be tailored to fit the particular subject under investigation. It should be as long as necessary, but it is a fact of reality that the acceptable length of the questionnaire tends to grow in direct proportion to the amount of political muscle behind the investigation.

A multiple-choice format is better than a free-form, essay, or fill-in-the-blanks questionnaire, because non-directed questions frequently elicit surprising and totally unusable responses. If an adequate profile study has been prepared, it should be possible to bracket the choices between concrete values in a knowledgeable fashion.

Default choices, such as "not available," "does not apply," and "other," are appealing to subjects with something to hide and are, therefore, not recommended. *Blue-sky choices,* such as "greater than" or "less than," are not especially informative to the evaluator of the questionnaire.

One such questionnaire developed by the author contained 124 questions. Of these only the first three required the respondent to fill in blanks. They had to do with confirming the name of the respondent, identifying the specific individual who answered the questionnaire, and confirming the respondent's mailing address. The remaining 121 questions required specific choices.

The body of the questionnaire consisted of five types of question:

1) *Factual questions* (29) elicited factual information. They were to be answered by selecting from bracketed numerical choices (e.g., 0–100, 100–250, etc.). These questions were constructed to confirm or deny information previously estimated during the profile study.

Questions in this area common to most questionnaires would include those dealing with the target organization's legal structure, its profit-seeking objectives, its standard industrial classification (SIC), number of employees and customers, activities of the organization, composition of its product line, volume of activity, amount and kind of equipment used, and the like.

Factual questions answered the question: "Does the target organization have what it takes to do its job?"   .

2) *Perception of requirements* (28) questions were dichotomous choices to be answered "yes" or "no." In the study mentioned these dealt with perceived threats to security, needs for safeguards, use of error control techniques, impact on the target organization of recent changes in its pattern of activities, and any management preference for manual over automatic controls.

Perceptual questions answered the question: "What does the target organization think it should be doing?"

3) *Operating procedures* (19) questions were of the "Do you ever?" kind. They were to be answered by making a choice from a three-point scale: "frequently," "occasionally," or "never."

Procedural questions answered the question: "What is the target organization actually doing?"

4) *Implementation of policy* (27) questions were to be answered by selecting choices from a four-point scale: "All," "most," "some," or "none." In effect these questions forced the respondent to reveal how religiously the target organization practiced what it preached. The responses provided a cross check on the information elicited earlier regarding the target organization's perception of its requirements.

Implementation questions answered the question: "How does the target organization reconcile any discrepancies between what it thinks it should be doing and what it is actually doing?"

5) *Management attitudes* (18) questions were to be answered by choosing responses on a five-point attitudinal scale: "strongly agree," "agree," "neutral," "disagree," or "strongly disagree." Each question stated some principle related to a new policy or regulation under consideration by the consultant or currently finding acceptance in organizations similar to the target organization.

Attitudinal questions answered the question: "Does the management of the target organization really give a damn?"

Site Interviews

A site interview should be undertaken by a team whose specialties cover all fields of interest in the investigation. It should be carefully planned. Each member of the team should review the company profile, brief, and answers given to the questionnaire before going out on the site visit. These preliminary results should be discussed thoroughly among the team members.

The key document in a site interview is the *Site Interview Guide*. Its first page makes reference to preliminary documentation—the agency profile, brief, and answered questionnaire. It also contains an itemized descriptive inventory of additional documentation obtained during the site interview. This would normally include copies of data intake forms used by the target organization; control reports produced within the organization's documentation system; policy statements and procedural guides used; and other relevant materials, including photographs and sketches produced by members of the site visit team or artifacts acquired at the site.

The technique of the site interview may best be seen by examining a particular interview guide. The one to be discussed here was used in an investigation of information-handling practices. However, the elements included could comprise an important part of nearly any in-depth study of an organization. The structure of the interview guide could, of course, be expanded to include other items of interest in a specific investigation, such as production processes, research and development, usage of materials, etc.

The sample site interview included nine categories of inquiry:

1) *Processing Problems:* (data or anything else).
   - Composition of the staff as engaged by function and by category.
   - Activities carried out (shown in a flow-chart).
   - Input and output requirements (products, quantity of each).
   - Current problems of management.
   - Direction of future developments.
2) *Identification of Items:* Files, products, materials.
3) *Item Description:* This section should be repeated as many times as necessary, giving a description of each item identified in section 2. When the items under consideration happen to be files, as in our sample, this information included:
   - Cross reference to section 2—identifying number.
   - Number of records held.
   - Size of each record in characters.
   - Medium in which the file was held.

- Purpose of each record.
- Itemization of data entries.
- Back-up provisions (ancestor tapes, hard copy, microform, etc.).
- Security provisions (need-to-know policy, vaults, etc.).
- Controls over accuracy (checksums,[20] batching, circulation of confirmation copies, etc.).

4) *Description of Processing Equipment:* This should be repeated for each major item of equipment, covering computers or other equipment relevant to the investigation. In the example this included:
- Number of units.
- Manufacturer and model.
- Available core storage in words, main memory and extended core storage (computers only).
- Number of disk drives (computers only).
- Number of tape drives (computers only).
- Year installed.
- Security provisions (access control, audit log, etc.).
- Perceived threats to security.

5) *Field or station operations:* A separate form was used for each major station operated by the target organization.
- Telecommunications terminals used (number and type).
- Data-base accessed (organization responsible for maintaining this data base, type of data contained in it).
- Information collected at the station.
- Information transmitted to the station from center.
- Information transmitted from the station to center.
- Use made of this information at station and center.
- Security provisions (terminal identification, access, control, line security measures, etc.).

6) *Known compromises:*
- Number, nature and dates.
- Mechanism for handling compromises with examples of actions taken.

7) *Collection of information:*
- Usual sources.
- Collection of extraction practices.
- Security measures applied to new data.
- Validation and field evaluation procedures.

8) *Access and Output:*
- Types of reports prepared.

- Release policy and normal recipients of information (addresses for action and information).
- Policy governing access to raw data and to agency files.
- Means of authorizing dissemination of information.
- Controls over dissemination (security classifications in use).
- Security Manual (if available).

9) *Management Attitude:*
- Concept of security.
- Appreciation of potential threats.
- Attitude of personnel toward existing and proposed security measures.
- Plans for future developments.

Special Studies

The fifth phase of an organizational investigation will involve special studies. These are often carried out by personnel operating separately from the formal team organization. The studies are directed toward specific areas of interest, such as instances of compromise or security lapse (discrepancies), incidents associated with some specific operation carried out by the target agency, details surrounding some personnel change, or the agency's response to some specific counter operation.

Frequently the source of information will be a former employee (or, unofficially, a present employee) of the target organization, a relative of such an employee, a member of the public or a group representing the public interest who has had specific contact with the target organization, a competitor, or someone who regards himself as a "victim."

Leads may come from items reported in the news media or even local gossip. One such lead in an investigation came from a partially incinerated roll of microfilm found in a town dump. These leads are normally pursued by interviewing the individuals involved, sometimes under highly informal circumstances.

Information derived from special studies should be evaluated with great care. Each case should be assembled in a *case documentation form,* headed by the name of the researcher developing the case and a case identifier.

The typical case documentation form will include the name of the target organization, the location where the case was developed, and the type of information acquired. It should itemize the name, age, and sex of any principal informant, the category to which he belongs (ex-employee, etc.) and his present or former relationship with the target organization. Space should be provided for comments by the researcher and identification of sources other than the principal informant. The comments section should include an inventory of any additional documentation submitted in connection with the case.

EVALUATING THE ORGANIZATIONAL INVESTIGATION

At this point the five-phase investigation will probably have produced a great deal of paper and little else. There may be a control sheet, face sheet, agency profile, brief, completed questionnaire, site visit notes, one or more case documentation forms, collateral documents and document surrogates (i.e., films, tapes).

There are three other essential steps in assembling and evaluating the results of investigation. These are (1) documentary control, (2) content analysis, and (3) report preparation.

Documentary Control

Organizing and safeguarding case materials developed in an investigation is achieved by submitting all documents and document surrogates as they are received to a document control officer (DCO). Part of his responsibility is to assign to each document or surrogate a *case identifier,* which may be a code word, a mnemonic or a number; a unique *serial receipt number; page numbers* for each page of each document; and a *security classification.*

The security classification is denoted by the color of a cover sheet attached to each document: red and white striped (TOP SECRET), red (SECRET), yellow (CONFIDENTIAL), or green (RESTRICTED). The cover sheet may incorporate the routing and sign-off list of authorized recipients of the document. The security classification is stamped, written or printed at the top and bottom of each page.

Identification and storage of document surrogates presents special problems. These arise in connection with automatic data processing (ADP) media, photographic film, analog recordings, and documents too large for the case folder.

ADP media include punched cards, punched paper tape, print-out stock, magnetic tape, magnetic cards and disks. In addition to external identification, the identity and security classification should be recorded *in the medium itself,* so that it will appear at the top and bottom of each page when the information is printed out.

The colors of punched cards, punched paper tape, and print-out stock should be appropriate to their security classifications. The security classification should be preprinted at the top and bottom of each punched card and each print-out page, as defined by perforated page boundaries. In the cases of punched paper tape and imperforate print-out stock, the security classification should be printed at least at 10-inch intervals along the strip.

Decks of punched cards and reels of paper tape can be marked with crayon in the appropriate color on their edges, and on the first and last card or the tape leader. Other external identification depends upon the physical shape of the document surrogate. Flat cylinders, for instance, holding magnetic tape reels, magnetic disks, motion picture film, etc., should be marked with identification and security classification on top and bottom of hubs or reels and on edges or keepers. Long cylinders (map and blueprint tubes, film canisters) can be marked on the top, bottom and side, while box-shaped storage containers should be identified on top, bottom and two edges.

Security classification and identity should be stamped on slide frames and scratched into *photographic film* in leaders and periodically between frames. If possible, they should also be part of the silver-halide or dye image.

Analog recordings encompass audio tape reels and cassettes, video tape reels and cassettes, and strip-chart recordings. Here, too, identity and security classification should be recorded using the medium of the document surrogate. The same general rules hold for external physical marking. Use the letters A and B to differentiate between sides of a tape reel or cassette.

In general, the application of the serial receipt number system to document surrogates is analogous to that used with documents. Each surrogate (film, tape, fingerprint card, blueprint, etc.), if it contains original data, should be regarded as a document. Each recognizable subdivision of the document surrogate (a frame of film, a foot of tape, view of a blueprint, etc.) should be treated as if it were a page of a document.

All document surrogates should be stored under secure and controlled conditions—for example, the place of storage should be fireproof, air conditioned and shielded against electrical and magnetic fields when tapes and disks are stored.

Copies create special problems. They should not be made unless necessary. Four common kinds of copies encountered are transcriptions or extracts of tapes, prints of photographs, translations, and photocopy reductions of oversize documents. Each copy should be identified by the serial receipt number, classification, and "page" numbers of the original document or document surrogate, with a suffix appended to indicate that it is a copy and which of how many copies it is.

Bookkeeping Procedures

There are four sets of records normally maintained by the Document Control Officer: a document register, activity log, station serial file, and case folders.

The *document register* is a bound copybook in which the DCO enters the serial receipt number, classification, case identity, a brief description of each incoming document or document surrogate, and specifies where it is filed. The register affords space to record the date any document was destroyed and the signatures of the officers authorizing and supervising destruction.

The DCO creates the *station serial file* by feeding each incoming document page by page, cover sheet first, through a copy-flow microfilm camera. This provides a security back-up file of all information contained in the case folders.

The *station activity log* is another bound copybook in which all case documents are checked in and out by analysts working on them. Each entry records the date, time out and in, document serial number, and signature of the analyst taking it. The DCO signs on and off duty in the log. Such a log indicates where any document is at any given time.

The *case folder* is the color of the highest security classification attaching to any document in it. The folder carries the case identifier prominently displayed. The DCO inter-files all documents or copies of document surrogates in the proper case folder. Each entry is recorded on the face sheet.

Transfer of Documents

Documents to be transmitted between stations or from station to center should be sent by registered mail, certified mail, or courier. A separate letter of transmittal should be mailed and a copy of it stapled to the document.

Documents should be sent in double wrappers with the security classification stamped top and bottom, front and back on the *inner wrapper only*. The inner wrapper should be regarded in part as a backup in case of damage to the outer covering, but principally its purpose is to regularize internal handling.

Personalized or *eyes only* documents should be transmitted in *triple wrappers*. The inner wrapper should be prominently marked, top and bottom, front and back, with the name of the recipient and the "eyes only" designation. This is a protection against improper opening by, for example, the intended recipient's secretary.

Content Analysis

The customary steps in analyzing the content of an organizational investigation include highlighting, targeting, amplification, verification, and cross reference.

Highlighting means nothing more than having one or more knowledgeable analysts review the file, marking each significant passage or recurring theme with a translucent yellow highlighter crayon.

Targeting (red lining) means reviewing the file a second time and underlining in red all references to specific people, places and events.

Amplification begins with stamping a red star opposite any reference (commonly a person's name) that appears to require a deeper look—which may mean calling for a personal investigation.

Verification involves stamping a black question mark opposite any reference that appears to be questionable. Later, when and if the reference is confirmed, a red "V" will be stamped next to the question mark.

Cross referencing involves stamping the letter "R", enclosed in a box, in the margin opposite any reference that is to be amplified, confirmed, denied, or otherwise mentioned in some other part of the file. Document serial numbers and page numbers of appropriate reference locations are subsequently recorded within each of these reference boxes.

In the process of amplifying a starred item, a cross reference might be made to a subsequent report on the person targeted. This report would, in turn, be marked with a cross reference which would contain the location of the starred mention of the subject's name.

Report Preparations

After the documentation developed in each major phase of the case (profile, brief, questionnaire, site report, and any special studies) has been analyzed, the principal investigator should write a *synopsis* of that phase and add it to the case folder.

The synopsis of the *site report* should be circulated to each member of the team that made the visit and returned to the principal investigator with any additional comments and observations appended to it. This is called the *round-robin* procedure.

When the case is substantially complete, the principal investigator will normally write a ten-page *summary* of it, followed by a *briefing* for his superiors.

The briefing typically consists of a talk lasting approximately twenty minutes.

It may involve making up a visual presentation of the information contained in the summary. usually to be shown as 35mm slides, but possibly as Vu-graphs or flip charts. Such a presentation would normally require from 14 to 18 slides.

The principal investigator generally composes the briefing and usually presents it alone. He may, however, present it in concert with one of his team members.

A wise principal investigator usually tries out his presentation on the members of his investigative team before putting it on for his superiors. In this way he can get their criticism and make any necessary revisions.

When the report is presented to management by the principal investigator, he may take his senior analysts and some of his team members along, even if they are not to be presentors. The basic presentation is usually followed by a question period during which the investigator may find it useful to field questions to his staff.

If the object of the investigation was, for example, a security survey for a client, the executive in charge of the account will probably integrate the report with his own recommendations for new or improved equipment, procedures and practices, and arrange for a further presentation to the client.

APPLICATION OF TECHNIQUES

The parts of an organizational investigation carried out in any specific case will depend upon the setting.

When the target organization is friendly and open, and the investigation is authorized and *overt,* such as a security survey undertaken for a client, all parts of the procedure described in this chapter will be used, with particular weight given to the contents of the brief and the replies to the questionnaire. In a security survey, the site visits may sometimes be unannounced and perhaps even unobserved if the security of the target organization is not alert.

When the target organization is unfriendly, open, and the investigation is overt, as in the case of a regulatory agency investigating a regulated company, the contents of the brief and questionnaire should be regarded as potentially self-serving. In this situation greater reliance should be placed upon profiling and site visits. Special studies, if performed, would have to be done with discretion because of the potentially adverse publicity.

When the target organization is unfriendly, open, and the investigation is *covert,* such as an investigation of a competitor by a corporation, solicitation of briefs and submission of questionnaires are out of the question. Site visits would have to be selective and highly informal. In these circumstances, reliance would be placed principally on profiling and special studies.

When the target organization is unfriendly, closed, and the investigation is covert, such as a national secret service investigation of one of its rivals, security considerations would be paramount. Site visits, if carried out at all, would have to be highly imaginative in concept. Opportunities for special studies might also be limited. In this kind of investigation, profiling becomes extremely important. Hopefully other techniques would become available from time to time to provide points of confirmation.

A complete paradigm of various possible types of organizational investigations is suggested in the accompanying table.

Computerized Investigations

Some exciting new developments in the investigative process involve use of the computer. Their use in documentary control becomes practical when more than 10,000 cases are being handled annually. Their need in organizations having case loads lower than 10,000 may be dictated by high levels of activity in acquiring and coordinating information. And when the case load approaches 100,000, the computer could probably be considered essential.

Computers are especially useful in analysis. *Highlighted* or *red-lined* (targeted) information can be entered into the computer system along with case, document and page identifiers. The sorting power of the computer can then be utilized to prepare concordances and indices. These can be keyed upon personal names, place names, dates or key words extracted from the marked passages.

These techniques can facilitate cross referencing to star amplifications, query verifications, and parallel observations of the same incidents. They can be used to impeach witnesses on the basis of conflicting testimony and to point up inadequacy of information by cross comparison of the facts known about similar but distinct subjects.

Although the technique is still essentially in the research stage, the computer can be used to perform highlighting and red-lining automatically. The technical name for this operation is *key-word extraction.*

Progress in *automatic language translation* has been made to the point where an analyst can be provided with a word-for-word translation, with alternative choices printed out by the computer where ambiguity could exist. In these cases the analyst must use his knowledge of the language to obtain the sense of certain passages. Smooth translations must still be done manually by linguists.

DESCRIPTION OF SITUATION

Posture of Organization

O = open
C = closed

Type of Investigation

N = normal (overt)
U = undercover (covert)

Attitude of Organization

F = friendly
I = unfriendly

COMPONENTS OF THE INVESTIGATION

P = profile
B = brief
Q = questionnaire
V = site visit
S = special studies
( ) = covert operations

SITUATION	COMPONENTS	HYPOTHETICAL EXAMPLE
N, F, O	P, B, Q, V, S	Security survey by a consultant
U, F, O	(P), (V), (S)	Investigation of conditions at a field station
N, I, O	P, B, Q, V, S	Anti-trust investigation
U, I, O	P, (V), (S)	Industrial espionage
N, F, C	P, B, Q, V, (S)	Investigation of allegations against police agency
U, F, C	(P), (V), (S)	Investigation of the activities of an allied secret service
N, I, C	P, B, Q, V, (S)	Some congressional inquiries
U, I, C	P, (V), (S)	Organized-crime investigations, espionage

Figure 10-2: Types of Organizational Investigations

Computers can also be used to disseminate information selectively among analysts. This is accomplished by use of *interest profiles*. The process is called Selective Dissemination of Information (SDI).

Whenever an analyst requests information on a subject, the search terms of his request are added to his profile of interests. This profile is normally started when he joins the agency and is continually modified. Each time a new document becomes available for circulation, the indexing terms assigned to it are compared by the computer with those contained in each analyst's profile (including his clearance level or need-to-know), and, if a sufficient degree of commonality is sensed, that analyst is sent a card containing a brief abstract or summary of the document.

Progress in using computers to prepare abstracts, a technique called *automatic abstracting,* has been disappointing so far. Similarly, little help from the computer can be expected by a principal investigator in preparing his reports. So-called *text-editing systems* are available that assist in the mechanical details of report preparation, but they operate with such a low level of protection from interception that most organizations do not use them for highly sensitive work.

Two interesting techniques for estimating the capabilities and predicting the future behavior of rival and inaccessible organizations have received considerable attention.

One of these is called *mathematical modeling.* A set of equations is written that interrelate the facts of interest. Into these are then plugged probability estimates based upon what the rival has done in the past. In this way it is possible to generate by computer a large number of random plays of the "game." Tabulations of the results make it possible to assign probabilities to the various possible outcomes of whatever situation is under study.

The second of these techniques is called *gaming.* Here the computer is set up to perform on paper whatever process is being studied (such as invasion of a country). Instead of plugging in decisions based upon what the rival has done in the past, or making some probabilistic decisions, human teams are put together to play the role of the rival "firm." These human "adversaries" are specialists, selected from the primary organization's own people to match the psychological characteristics of real adversaries as far as they can be known. These people then play the game with the computer to win. Their behavior is observed—in the hope that it corresponds to what their real-life counterparts are doing or would do.

Chapter 11

THE ISSUE OF PRIVACY

> "The principle with which we are now dealing is that
> one which is called Expediency. The usage of this word
> has been corrupted and perverted and has gradually come
> to the point where, separating moral rectitude from
> expediency, it is accepted that a thing may be morally
> right without being expedient, and expedient without
> being morally right. No more pernicious doctrine than
> this could be introduced into human life."
>
> —Marcus Tullius Cicero, *Concerning Moral
> Duties*, Book II, Chapter III

The issue of privacy of personal records has caused worldwide contention, distinguished more by the generation of heat than light.

There is a tendency to lump at least five separate issues together, where the only common bond between them is that they all involve the handling of sensitive information concerning or describing individuals or groups of individuals. These issues are: privacy, confidentiality, secrecy, freedom of information, and security.

Since the single issue of *privacy* has captured the spotlight of public attention, it is natural for anyone interested in the proper handling of sensitive information to force his special concern to conform to the general rubric of privacy. The net result is frequently utter confusion. However, a simple paradigm

275

may place matters in proper perspective. One can think of sensitive information as either *public,* that is, information of concern to the nation or one of its political subdivisions; or *private,* that is, information concerning or describing individuals or groups of individuals.

Moreover, one can consider as an objective either the proper *use* of information; or the *non-use* of information except within a very restricted group.

These concepts provide a neat schema for classifying four of the issues central to the "privacy" debate.

	USE	NON-USE
PUBLIC	Freedom of Information	Secrecy
PRIVATE	Confidentiality	Privacy

In this context of the fifth issue, *security* is the mechanism that keeps each type of sensitive information within its proper category.

Public Information

Regarding the dichotomy between freedom of information and secrecy in the area of public information, there are two divergent philosophies.

In countries such as France and the British Commonwealth, the philosophy is: "All that is not permitted is forbidden." In such countries there is a broadly drawn Official Secrets Act. Furthermore, those charged with enforcing such an Act frequently possess extraordinary powers of investigation permitting them to search, seize, and arrest without warrant, while those charged under the Act are often denied the usual rights of accused persons such as habeas corpus, the presumption of innocence, public trial, disclosure of prosecution evidence, and exclusion of hearsay.

In countries such as the United States, the German Federal Republic, and the Scandinavian countries, the philosophy is: "All that is not forbidden is permitted." There is no all-encompassing Official Secrets Act. Instead there are several specific acts such as the Atomic Energy Act, the National Defense Act of 1947, and the Espionage Act of 1917.

The spectrum of what is forbidden varies widely from a great deal in the United States to almost nothing in the Scandinavian countries. In general, prosecution under any specific secrecy act follows the same procedures as for any criminal offense.

Lest we imply that countries having an Official Secrets Act are in any way closed societies, it is only fair to state that most of these countries are parliamentary democracies where the cabinet ministers sit in the legislature and where they are subjected daily to potentially embarrassing questions by members of the opposition. Although they can take refuge behind the Official Secrets Act, to do so too often becomes a serious political liability and could even lead to a parliamentary vote of non-confidence in the government followed by a general election.

Private Information

Regarding the dichotomy between confidentiality and privacy in the area of private information, where an individual or group gives up certain items of sensitive information to expedite a desired relationship, in expectation of a benefit or in compliance with law, and this information is subsequently misused by the recipient to the detriment of the subject, what has occurred is a violation of confidence, not an invasion of privacy. However, when the information in question arises from objective and overt observation of the subject by the information recipient, it is by no means clear that the subject retains any residual interest in it whatsoever.

Concepts of Privacy

Privacy seems to have eluded precise definition. Probably the most succinct definition is "the right to be left alone."[21] But this definition is also probably the worst to work with.

Jerry M. Rosenberg puts forward a more useful definition: "The right (of an individual) to determine how, when, and to what extent data about oneself are released to another person."[22]

Clearly, there are several practical exceptions. The individual must take reasonable measures to secure his own privacy. One customarily pulls down the shade to have privacy in the bedroom.

There are other situations where, in our society, the individual cannot control when or to whom information concerning or describing him will flow. This is true if he is observed committing a crime, although any felon would doubtless relish the opportunity to charge an arresting officer with invading his privacy.

Less facetiously, one has to file tax returns, respond to a census enumerator, and convince a prospective employer of his qualifications for the job he seeks. One has to establish that he is sufficiently skilled in operating a vehicle if he wants a license to do so, and he must similarly establish his possession of certain skills before being admitted to any number of trades or professions.

Alternatively, if he does not apply for a job or establish himself as a member of some profession, he had better be able to establish his statutory eligibility to receive welfare benefits.

And, of course, when we enter into a business agreement, the other party, especially if he is extending credit, wants to know something about us, especially whether we are ready, willing, and able to repay. Conversely, we want to know something about the seller. Is he able to carry out his end of the agreement before and after sale and is his product or service all that he represents it to be? (Today it is not always possible to find out these things. However, with the rising tide of consumerism, the disclosure of sensitive information in the marketplace is rapidly becoming a two-way street.)

Privacy and Freedom

Practically speaking, the realities of modern society very quickly transmute privacy questions into ones of confidentiality, which is a somewhat different breed of cat. Only in a society in which each person would receive whatever benefit or privilege he desired without surrendering any information about himself could the idea of privacy entertained by some persons be achieved. To many proponents of strict protection of privacy, their advocacy is seen as a way to approach such a closed and nurturing society. However, any such social synthesis lies in the far distant future, if at all.

Privacy and freedom have been conjoined in public conception ever since Professor Westin's book by that name appeared. However, empirical observations do not always support the claim that privacy necessarily leads to freedom, nor that lack of privacy need lead to repression. In fact, just the opposite can sometimes be shown.

In Bulgaria and other East Bloc countries, one does not have to file income tax returns, nor does one have to give personal information in order to obtain automobile insurance, medical care and treatment, or retirement benefits. In the Soviet Union, people enjoy what some would regard as the ultimate privacy: no telephone directories are published.

On the other hand, Sweden is perhaps one of the most open societies. A computer is used to provide public access to the address of anyone in the country whether he has a phone or not. Belgium is following suit.

Of course, these examples do not prove the point. However, a firm link between privacy and freedom has yet to be established by objective and systematic research. And there is reason to believe that concepts of privacy may turn out to be too culture dependent and possibly too transient to permit any valid conclusions to be achieved were such studies to be undertaken.

Privilege vs. Law Enforcement

Looking specifically at the subject of confidentiality, we observe one immediate conflict of rights: the national interest versus privilege.

By national interest we mean those activities carried on by public bodies which are directed toward protecting the security of the nation state and its political subdivisions, and the lives and property of its citizens.

Among those public bodies, the police come to mind first, but just as important in more specialized ways are fire marshals, medical officers of health, health of animals officers, food and drug inspectors, and building inspectors.

Depending upon the local political system or climate, various constraints may be placed upon some or all of these officers, and their pursuit of information relative to their mission may have to be authorized by warrant, subpoena, or writ of assistance (British Commonwealth only, although the Drug Control Agency comes very close to having this power, provisions of the U.S. Bill of Rights notwithstanding).

However, within these constraints the field of pursuit is wide open, and even use of wiretapping and electronic surveillance can be authorized in some cases.

This pursuit stops only at the barrier of privilege. Generally only two kinds of privileged relationships are recognized: wife-husband and lawyer-client. Despite the hopes of many reformers, there is as yet no such thing as medical privilege, psychological privilege, journalistic privilege, or even "the seal of the confessional."

The defense of self incrimination (Fifth Amendment) is also a kind of privilege, but it exists only in the United States and even there can be circumvented by a guarantee of immunity from prosecution.

Another doctrine that requires some comment is that of sealing records. The details of infant adoptions are sealed; the records of pardoned criminals are sealed; and certain judicial actions may also be sealed.

Sealing a record does not mean that it is erased or destroyed, nor does it mean that information regarding the event cannot be discussed. It simply means that whatever document is needed for legal proof of the matter—birth certificate or certificate of conviction—is not producible in court. Essentially this means that persons concerned with an event can deny its occurrence without fear of prosecution for perjury.

TYPES OF SENSITIVE INFORMATION

Administrative Information

Administrative information is public information and has already been discussed at some length. The only additional comment necessary is that security agencies have a two-fold duty: to see that secret information is not disclosed to unauthorized persons; and to see that information necessary to assess the performance of elected officials is not improperly withheld from the public.

The exchange of personal information between administrative agencies creates a good deal of concern on the part of citizens. Some examples include the use of census responses and agricultural allotments in the collection of taxes, and the use of immigration information to establish eligibility for educational and welfare benefits.

With the exception of law enforcement agencies, who have a paramount right to pursue evidence of fraud, perjury, or attempted espionage wherever it may be found, the exchange of administrative information should be constrained by legislation or executive order and the protocols for such exchanges should be well publicized. In this way, the subject would know at the time he divulged information just what use would eventually be made of it.

It is, of course, encumbent upon each agency to take all necessary measures to see that the letter and the spirit of laws and regulations compartmentalizing administrative information are carried out.

Security agencies should have the responsibility of seeing that these laws and regulations are obeyed just like any others. The nature of the laws and regulations must be left to the customary legislative and administrative processes of government.

Trade Secrets

Technical information. includes all of what are commonly regarded as trade secrets: inventions not covered by patents, processes, procedures, formulae, computer programs, etc. Generally, these are regarded as private property and their misappropriation is punishable as theft. There is, however, a corollary requirement that the owner exercise reasonable security precautions and put persons on notice as to what is his property.

Here we encounter another instance in which information gathered in one context should not be used in another context to the detriment of the subject.

Frequently trade secrets must be disclosed in proposals to government procurement agencies. It is certainly injurious to the subject for the government to use such information without compensation to the owner except in assessing his competence to perform the contract he seeks. Likewise, it is irresponsible for the government to allow building plans, engineering drawings, formulae, computer programs, exploration maps and the like to be made public or to fall into the hands of competitors.

The government, or the prime contractor as the case may be, has a clear obligation to protect the security of such information and to compensate the owner in the event of its loss.

Business Data

Commercial information concerns the affairs of businessmen. Here violation of confidence is often punishable only by private sanction, for theft of business secrets is difficult to prove, except in the case of substantial files such as mailing lists. Between businessmen and bankers, insurance agencies and the like, confidentiality becomes a matter of self interest. One is not going to continue to deal with a blabbermouth.

Quite probably the most serious potential leak of business secrets is to be found in census data, where an astute investigator can perhaps use mathematical logic to obtain shipment and value-added data regarding some specific company. This is a problem that must be carefully monitored. In general, the legal responsibility rests with census officials to insure non-disclosure, but the implementation is by their administrative edicts. The problem is exceedingly tricky now that most national census offices are making certain detailed data available to social scientists.

Another source of disclosure, not so evident, is the release of data regarding government contracts, detailed departmental budgets, and contractors lists. However, here the right of a businessman to keep his business to himself conflicts with the right of the taxpayer to know what he is getting for his tax dollar.

Similarly, a stock prospectus may disclose more than some businessmen would like, although there are vast differences internationally in disclosure requirements—Canada, for example, tends to require much less information than the United States. Again, the right of the businessman conflicts with the right of the general public to know what it is getting when it buys a new stock issue.

The U.S. anti-trust legislation and the Canada Combines Investigation Act give enforcement officials vast powers to rummage through all kinds of business files in carrying out their statutory responsibilities. While they undoubtedly need this power to uphold the law, there is a parallel responsibility, covered by the concept of administrative privacy, that information so gained should not be released unnecessarily in such a way as to give the subjects' competitors an unfair advantage.

Associations and Their Secrets

Organizational privacy refers to associations: their membership lists, command structure, contributors, and internal secrets.

Contrary to some public pronouncements, there is no such thing as the freedom of association. There is, however, the right of people to assemble peacefully and petition their government for redress of grievances. On the other end of the scale, there are laws against criminal conspiracy.

The various elections acts wisely require that principal contributors to political campaigns be made known so the public can judge whether any politician may be under undue influence.

But there are broad areas for controversy: it is widely considered right to infiltrate counter-intelligence agents into the Communist Party or Canada's *Front Liberation Quebecois,* but not into the New Democratic Party (Canada) or the Democratic Party (U.S.). It is correct to steal the internal protocols of the Minutemen and, possibly, the John Birch Society, but not the Freemasons or the Knights of Columbus. It is okay to place the headquarters of the Weathermen and the Black Panthers under electronic surveillance, but a crime to break into Watergate. Visitors to the Soviet Embassy are photographed but not, we hope, those visiting the Canadian Embassy.

The underlying principal is, of course, the right of a nation state to protect its own existence—call it insuring domestic tranquility or keeping the Queen's peace or whatever. And, naturally, the measures taken must themselves be secret to be effective.

However, this area is fraught with danger to human liberty and to the political system. At some point, the decisions taken with respect to the surveillance or proscription of an organization must receive public attention, open debate, and popular sanction. Whether this occurs through a parliamentary question period, congressional hearings, or judicial proceedings depends upon the particular political arena.

In any event, the sooner such decisions are taken publicly the better, because the decision of what is and what is not subversive can be made by a single man or group of men only at the ultimate cost of everyone's liberty.

Medical Information

Medical information creates a problem in that information extracted from the patient in a care-and-treatment situation may later be used to his disadvantage, perhaps in causing the denial of some benefit or opportunity. Another problem is whether a patient may be allowed to see his own records, contrary to the advice of his doctor.

Normally, entry into patients' medical records is denied as a matter of medical ethics, and a breach of confidence in this regard becomes a breach of ethics subjecting the physician to civil liability and to professional sanction. West Germany has enacted these strictures into law.

However, insurance companies, credit grantors, and prospective employers frequently are able to coerce subjects into giving a third party consent to inspect their own records.

In general, there seems to be some danger to the individual here. Institutional physicians who would inspect records tend to be conservative on behalf of their institutional clients and to look pessimistically at a subject's chances for complete recovery from some earlier illness or trauma and upon the effectiveness of prosthesis or medical control of chronic conditions.

It would seem fairer if some publicly appointed medical ombudsman could be employed to review records upon request of a patient and then furnish to the patient and the third party requiring information a statement of the patient's insurability, life expectancy, capability to perform the duties of the position he seeks or whatever question is at hand.

The medical ombudsman could also be called upon to audit a patient's record and deliver a summary of the significant facts to the patient and his doctor in cases where these two persons disagree as to whether it is or is not in the patient's interest to see his own record.

It might also be well to make it a criminal offense to obtain or use any personal medical data, unless obtained from the ombudsman.

There are other questions such as those regarding the use of patients as teaching subjects or as subjects of research reports. However, the medical profession has over a long period of time developed effective techniques for protecting the privacy of patients in these settings and needs only to revive traditional guarantees.

These guarantees (*i.e.,* removing names, blanking out faces, avoiding small sample disclosure, etc.) should be made part of the codes of administrative procedure of teaching hospitals.

Personal Information

Personal information has been the cause of much contention regarding the activities of investigative credit-reporting agencies. Starting in 1970, legislation has been passed in several jurisdictions regarding personal credit reporting. Comparative data for three such statutes are shown in Appendix 9. One is the U.S. Fair Credit Reporting Act and two are Canadian Provincial Statutes.

If anything, the trend is to become more restrictive, and it may be expected that the U.S. law will be strengthened.

Security men, of course, obey the law. It looks as if it will become increasingly dangerous to do any of the following:

1) Report any criminality on the part of the subject, short of an actual conviction.

2) Report any judgments or writs unless one is able to obtain a statement from the creditor or assignee as to its current status.

3) Make any report based upon neighborhood interview information, unless one is able to confirm the basic facts and clearly identify the source.

Finally, we came to the question of the dissemination of arrest records. In most countries, one's criminal records consist only of convictions and there is considerable pressure to make this the norm in the United States also.

Actually, the problem is one of administration of criminal justice. Only in the United States might an individual amass a record of 20 or 30 arrests with no convictions. This is primarily because of the difficulty in obtaining convictions in court. There are legal technicalities, seemingly endless routes of appeal, and the uncertainty of the jury system. Even in Canada, a judge can throw out a jury verdict if he considers it absurd and either ask the jury to reconsider or empanel another jury. The prosecution also can appeal if it is not satisfied that justice has been done.

On the continent, of course, there is no adversary system of law. Instead, the judge, prosecutor, and defense counsel are united in a search for the truth.

It would be ideal if criminal records were to contain only actual convictions. It would greatly reduce the possibility of diminishing the life chances of innocent people.

However, concurrent with such restrictions on the dissemination of such information, there would have to be improvements in the criminal justice system all the way from more professional investigation through more effective prosecution to better and quicker adjudication, so that a conviction record could truly be said to reflect the subject's behavior.

CONCLUSIONS

The privacy issue is one manifestation of a worldwide malaise. A steadily rising general level of formal education, coupled with the phenomenal growth of mass communications media, has aroused in the inhabitants of all democratic countries expectations which are becoming increasingly difficult for most national economies to fulfill.

Today, everyone wants the perquisites that were formerly available to only a few in the upper classes and upper-middle classes. The man on the street, not just in North America but all over the free world, wants a home in the country with an acre of land, a rich and varied diet, an automobile, color television, modern home appliances, first-rate medical care when he is ill, a college education for his children, a vacation abroad, and a financial buffer against loss of any of these things should he lose his job.

And he wants his privacy protected.

It is a tall order for any government to deliver. And when the government fails to deliver, the average voter has no compunction against turning the incumbents out. Almost everywhere it can be observed that neither of two traditional parties is able .o command a working majority. Governments tend to form coalitions with smaller and more radical parties or groups of the left or right to obtain a working majority.

National leaders all over the free world must govern with one eye on an election that is, in most countries, just around the corner. They tend to respond to any apparently popular demand for greater personal freedom or well-being.

And today ideas spread throughout the free world with jet speed. A new, liberalizing concept originating in some obscure place is soon heard as a demand at chancelleries and government houses of the largest countries.

Discrimination is an ugly word, and employers are pressed to hire their fair share of blacks, women (including pregnant women), men over forty, youths, and so on. It seems quite probable that they will one day be asked to hire their fair share of criminals as well, and their share of men and women crippled mentally and physically as well as morally.

And what about records in such a climate? They will still be around, but they will become increasingly hard to use for security reasons. Privacy is viewed as a liberal virtue for a liberal time. No organization is going to be able to draw a sanitary cordon around itself. The fortress concept is a dying one.

But that does not mean security is impossible. It will, however, have to be based upon internal partitions and a check-and-balance system. All of this calls for the use of more information, not less. And more intensive use of information as a planning and assignment criterion, not as a perimeter barrier.

In such an atmosphere, the security officer will have to work harder and think smarter. His knowledge and use of records systems will continue to be an invaluable tool, helping him to meet the challenge of an increasingly sensitive, difficult and important role.

APPENDIXES

Appendix 1
Individual Questions and
Their Occurrence in Records

IDENTIFIERS AND LOCATORS

Question	Percent of Files
Name in Full	100
Residence Address (street and number or rural route)	100
Sex	100
Usual Signature	85
Date of Birth (DOB)	74
Residence Telephone Number	37
Place of Birth (municipality)	33
Social Security Number	22
Alias (AKA)	17
Citizenship	15
Height and Weight	11
Photograph	9
Physical Description (color of eyes and hair)	7
Port of Entry	4
Address to Which You are Moving	4
Fingerprint Card	4
Drivers' License Number	2
Military Serial Number	2
Medical-Surgical Insurance Number	2
Hospital Insurance Number	2
Numbers of Previous Passports and Issuing Country	2
Welfare Account Number and Agency	2
Fingerprint Section Number	2
Place of Death (municipality)	2

EMPLOYMENT, EDUCATION, AND SKILLS

Question	Percent of Files
Occupation and Title	61
Employer's Name and Address	43
Date of Employment	24
Educational History (schools attended, dates, degrees or certificates earned)	20
Business Address	17
Business Telephone Number	13
Armed Forces Service History (country, branch, rank, dates, type of discharge)	7
School Marks (transcripts)	7
Languages Spoken, Read or Written	4
Professional Organizations of Which You Are a Member	4
Other Skills Possessed	4
Aptitude Test Scores	2
Apprenticeships Completed	2
Professional Publications of Which You Are an Author	2
Type of Employment Promised Upon Immigration	2

MARRIAGE AND IMMEDIATE FAMILY

Question	Percent of Files
Marital Status (married, never married, widowed, divorced, separated, common law)	39
Spouse's Name and Address	39
Dates of Children's Births	17
Names of Children	15
Number of Other Dependents (besides spouse and children)	15
Spouse's Employer (name and address)	13
Closest Relative (NOK)	13
Spouse's Salary	11
Spouse's Date of Birth	11
Names of Persons Unrelated to You Living in Your Home	9
Date and Place of Marriage	9
Number of Children	9
Date of Spouse's Employment	9
Places Where Your Children Were Born	9
Maiden Name of Wife	7
Names and Addresses of Other Dependents	7
Name and Address of Closest Relative not Living in Your Home	4

Parents-in-Law (names and addresses)	4
Previous Marriages (marital history)	4
Spouse's Business Telephone Number	2
Spouse's Occupation	2
Children's Schools or Occupations (names and addresses of schools or employers)	2
Previous Marital Status of Spouse	2
Dependents' Incomes	2
Incomes of Relatives Legally Liable for Your Support	2

FINANCIAL STATUS

Question	Percent of Files
Salary	31
Bank Accounts (institution's name and address and your balance)	22
Other Assets (describe and give value)	15
Bank or Other Loans Outstanding (institution's name and address and balance owing)	15
Other Debts Owed Including Liens	15
Insurance Policies (company, type, face value and cash surrender value)	13
Automobiles Owned (make, body style, year)	13
Stocks and Bonds Owned (description, value, and annual yield)	11
Real Estate Owned (description and market value)	11
Accounts Payable (names and addresses of creditors)	9
Credit Cards	7
Cash on Hand	7
Your Mortgage Payment (amount owing, name and address of institution)	7
Monthly Income	4
Monthly Living Expenses	2
Merchandise Inventory	2
Inheritances Expected	2
Assets to Follow Immigrant	2
Income Tax Form (copy required)	2

HEALTH STATUS

Question	Percent of Files
Physical Disabilities	20

Names of Hospitals and Medical Practitioners Who Have Treated You (address and permission to release medical records)	11
Results of Physical Examination Report	9
Vision Examination Report	2
Injuries or Surgical Procedures (names and addresses of hospitals and medical practitioners and permission to release medical records)	2
Psychiatric Report	2
Medical Details of Your Birth	2

HOUSING

Question	Percent of Files
Do You Own Your Own Home?	17
Number of Years at Current Home	9
Name and Address of Landlord	7
Previous Homes Owned or Rented	7
How is Your Home Financed?	4
Health Conditions in Home	4

LIFE HISTORY

Question	Percent of Files
Previous Employment and Dates (employment history)	28
Previous Addresses (residence history)	15
Criminal Convictions (date, court, and jurisdiction)	11
Foreign Travel (countries, dates, reasons for going)	6
Court Proceedings Pending Against You	4
Recent Transfers of Property	4
Annual Income the Last Full Year You Worked	2
Marital Status of Mother	2
Length of Time in Country	2
Names of Natural Parents	2
Have You Ever Been on Welfare?	2
Previous Electric Utility	2
Names of Other Agencies Who Might Be Interested in Your Case	2
Record of Paying Bills (credit rating)	2

Automobile Accidents You Have Had
in the Last 3 Years   2

Name and Address of the
Previous Owner of Your Car   2

PERSONAL HABITS

Question	Percent of Files
Leisure-Time Activities	11
Purpose of the Loan (for which you are applying)	2
Pets Harbored	2
Do You Fly (other than as a paying passenger on scheduled airlines)?	2

ASSOCIATIONS

Question	Percent of Files
Personal References (names and addresses and length of time known)	7
Organizations (non-professional) of Which You Are a Member	4

Lawyer's Name and Address   2

ANCESTRY AND RELIGION

Question	Percent of Files
Parents' Names (natural or adoptive mother and father; stepmother or stepfather; or legal guardians)	22
Religion	17
Parents' Ages	15
Parents' Birthplaces (municipalities)	15
Parents' Addresses	13
Parents' Religions	7
Maiden Name of Mother	7
Parents' Occupations (names and addresses of their employers)	7
Names and Addresses of Brothers and Sisters (natural, step- or half-siblings)	7
Father's Nationality	6
Citizenship History	2
Ethnic Origin	2

Appendix 2

Retail Credit Company Data

A. LIFE INSURANCE REPORT

Account number_____ District, agency or branch_____,
Policy number_____. Office_____ Date_____.
Name, address, occupation and employer of subject.
Account number.
Amount of coverage, family or individual, date.
Date of birth, place.
Health insurance applied for, dollars per_____.
Hospitalization insurance, major medical.

1. Significant features.
2. Date of inspection.
3. (a) How many years has each of your sources known applicant?
   (b) How many days since you or sources have seen applicant?
   If not within two weeks, explain fully.
4. Is there any reason to doubt accuracy of date of birth?
5. (a) Estimate of net worth.
   (b) Annual earned income from work or business.
   (c) Has applicant any income from investments, rentals, pension? If so, state source and amount.
6. (a) Does the occupational job differ in name from that given?
   (b) Does applicant change jobs frequently?
   (c) Any part-time or off-season occupation. Does applicant plan work or travel in foreign countries?
   (d) Does applicant sell or manufacture beer or wine or liquor?
7. Is applicant a fast, reckless or careless driver?
8. (a) Has applicant taken flying lessons either as a member of armed forces or as a civilian, owned or piloted a plane, or flown in planes not operated by scheduled airlines?
   (b) Does applicant engage in hazardous sports?
   Racing, skin or scuba diving, sky diving, snowmobiling, big-game hunting, mountain climbing, cave exploring, dune buggying?
9. (a) Is there anything unhealthy about his appearance, such as being very thin or having excess weight?
   (b) Any deformity, amputation, blindness, deafness or other defects?
10. Did you learn of any illness, operation or injury in the past or present?
11. Did you learn applicant was ever rejected for military service or discharged for medical reasons?
12. Did you learn of any member of family (what relationship?) having had heart trouble, cancer, diabetes, tuberculosis, or mental disease? If so, who, and which disease?
13. Is applicant a steady, frequent drinker? Daily or almost daily, several times a week, how often?

How many drinks does applicant take on these occasions?
What does applicant usually drink?

14. Does applicant now or has applicant in the past used intoxicants to excess?
15. Anything adverse about living conditions or neighborhood?
16. Any of the following apply to this applicant?
    Heavy debts, domestic trouble, drug habit, connection with illegal liquor, irregular beneficiary?
17. Is there any criticism of character or general reputation?
18. If family policy. anything adverse on health or physical condition of other family members?
19. (a) Business: Employer's name, line and size of business, name of applicant's job, how long so employed. Cover any indication of frequent job changes or instability of employment.
    (b) Married, single or divorced. Any children? Type of associates. If woman, name of father or husband, his occupation, net worth and income.
    Signature of person making report.
20. (a) Does applicant appear unhealthy? Complexion, weight.
    (b) Describe if over- or underweight. Give details.
21. Nature of illness or injury.
22. Approximate date injury occurred.
23. How long confined or laid up. Is he completely recovered?
24. (a) Attended by doctor, name, address.
    (b) Confined to hospital. If so, name and address.
25. Any facts on present health. Details.
26. When, where and under what circumstances does applicant drive in a fast and reckless manner? Open highway, congested areas, etc.
27. Any evidence of unsupervised racing? Submit details.
28. Any arrests? Approximate date.
29. Charges? If convicted, approximate date.
30. Any accidents? If so, approximate dates and details.
31. License ever suspended or revoked? If so, cause, date and whether applicant drove without a license.
32. Living conditions:
    (a) Overcrowded, dirty, unsanitary, etc.
    (b) If apartment, dark or dirty halls, broken or littered stairs, etc.
33. Neighborhood: Deteriorating, poor sanitation, crime, vandalism.
34. Classify excessive drinking. Present, past, how often? Once a week, once a month, etc. Classify as:
    (a) Getting drunk, stupefied, entirely out of control of usual facilities.
    (b) Boisterous, loud, or obviously under influence of liquor although mostly still in possession of faculties.
    (c) Mild excess, just getting feeling good, or stimulation.

B. INDIVIDUAL CREDIT REPORT

Account number_____. File number_____. Report made by
RCC _____ office.
Report from _____. State whether former address_____
Date_____.
Name and spouse_____. Address. _____
Employment: occupation, business address. _____
Transaction: amount, monthly amount. _____
• Time known at each source. _____
• Are names and addresses correct?_____
• Is subject known to file? _____
• About what age? If around 21, verify._____
• Is applicant married, single, divorced, widowed? Number of dependents.___
• Name of employer._____

• Name of business. _____
• Position. How long with present employer? If less than one year, explain._____
• Work full-time steadily? If not, how many days per week? _____
• Are prospects for continued employment good? _____
• Estimated net worth? _____
• Of what does this worth consist? Real estate, cash, stocks. bonds, etc. _____
• Does applicant own home, rent, or board?_____
• What is his earned income from work or business?_____
• Added annual income from investments, rentals, pensions, disability?_____
• If spouse employed, get name of employer. _____
   (a) Position held, approximate annual income_____
   (b) Approximate number of years employed. _____
• Is general reputation good?_____
• Did you learn of any failures, bankruptcies, mortgage foreclosures, suits, judg-
   ments against him?_____
• Any factors that affect doing business with applicant on a credit basis?
• Credit record. _____
• Business finances. Comment on past and present business connections. Irregular
   employment or lack of stability. Subject's financial position, giving breakdown
   on worth. _____
• Personal: How long has subject lived at this address and former addresses?
   State any unusual information such as domestic difficulties, illness learned or
   other features that would affect earnings or paying abilities.
• Credit table: Date checked. Kind of business. How long selling. Highest credit.
   Terms of sale. Amount owing. Amount past due. Paying record. Specify 30, 60,
   90 days, etc. Is this in accordance with terms? If contract account, so state.

Appendix 3
Dun & Bradstreet Commercial Credit Report Data

Reference Book Line Entry
Prefix A — entered in past sixty days
      C — change in listing during past sixty days.
(Note: In Canada there are more than 370 changes daily.)
Standard classification code _____.
Business name used in buying _____.
Asterisk if business is incorporated _____.
Abbreviation for line of business _____.
Year started _____. Last digit of year within the last ten years _____.
D & B composite rating _____. Financial strength and appraisal _____.

D & B Business Information Report
SIC code _____, data universal numbering system assignment _____, date
of rating _____, date started _____, D & B composite rating _____,
name of firm _____, line of business _____, address _____, telephone number _____, names of owners _____.

Summary:
Payments _____, gross sales _____, net worth _____, number of
employees _____, record _____, condition _____, trend _____.

Trade Section:
High credit _____, amount owing _____, amount past due _____,
terms _____, method of payment _____, remarks _____.

Financial Condition:
Date and source of statement, period of statement.

BALANCE SHEET:
Cash _____, accounts receivable _____, merchandise _____, total
current assets _____. Fixed assets _____, other assets _____, total
assets _____. Accounts payable _____, notes payable _____, total
current liabilities _____. Notes payable deferred _____.
Net worth _____.
Total _____.

PROFIT AND LOSS STATEMENT:

Annual gross sales _____, gross profit _____, net profit _____.
Fire insurance on property _____, merchandise _____, fixed assets
_____.

Annual rent _____, lawsuits _____, court records including liens
_____, court judgments _____, bank loans _____, contracts
_____, outlook _____, banking relations _____, bank balances
_____, loans outstanding _____.

History:

Personal history of partners _____, owner's experience _____, method
of operation _____, business terms _____, accounts _____, employees _____, housekeeping.

D & B Market Identifiers:

Dun's number _____, SIC codes _____.
Name _____.
Mailing address and street address _____.
Date started _____.
Line of business _____.
Sales volume _____.
Rating _____.
Employees at this location _____, total employees _____.
Headquarters: ☐ yes   ☐ no.
Manufacturing: ☐ yes   ☐ no.
Branch: ☐ yes   ☐ no.
Single location: ☐ yes   ☐ no.
Subsidiary: ☐ yes   ☐ no.
Headquarters Dun's number _____.
Location codes: National _____, state _____, city _____, standard
metropolitan trading area _____.
Dun's number of parent _____.
Telephone number _____.
Chief executive _____.
Net worth _____.

Appendix 4

Proposed International Standard Identifiers for Machine-to-Machine Information Interchange

A. STANDARD IDENTIFIER FOR INDIVIDUALS (SII)

The first data element of the Standard Identifier is the Identification Code Designator (ICD). The designators are as follows: 02 Social Security Number (SSN), 04 Social Insurance Number (SIN), 08 Birth Number (BN), 09 User Agreed Code for Individuals (UACI).

The second data element is separated from the ICD by a space and consists of the numeric code number designated by the first data element.

The third data element is separated from the numeric code by a space. It contains the individual's name, consisting of the following elements: surname, first name, and middle name, in that sequence.
- Religious names are not considered names or portions of names unless the change in name has been authorized by a civil official.
- Titles are not considered names or portions of names.
- The use of "Mrs." and the husband's given names by a woman is not acceptable.
- Surname suffixes such as Jr., III, etc., are not part of the surname.

The surname, first given name, and second given name are all terminated by commas. Each name part therefore contains three commas regardless of the presence of other characters in any given field.

No punctuation marks are used except the comma, which functions as a separator. Hyphens and apostrophes may be used if they are part of the name. Spacing appears only when it is a part of a name word, as in a compound name which contains a space rather than a hyphen.

The following examples illustrate the application of these rules to specific cases:

1) Punctuation marks	O'Neil,Thomas,Patrick,
2) Word prefixes	DiAngelo,Anthony,Joseph,
	St Germain,Joseph,Anthony,
3) Compound names	Smith-Harding,John,Thomas,
	Medina y Lopez,Juan,Pablo,
	Wilson,Jo Anne,Elaine,
4) Initials for given names	Johnson,William,R,
	Johnson,W,Robert,
	Johnson,W,R,
5) Name does not contain three elements (no middle name)	Johnson,William,,

B. STANDARD IDENTIFIER FOR ORGANIZATIONS (SIO)

The SIO consists of three parts, an Identification Code Designator (ICD), a code part and a name part, in that order.

- The designators are as follows: 00 User Agreed Code for Organizations (UACO), 01 Employer Identification Number (EIN), 03 Data Universal (D-U-N-S), 05 Statistics Canada Central List (CLID).
- The code part of the SIO is separated from the ICD by a space and consists of the particular numeric code number as designated by the first data element.
- The name part of the SIO is separated from the numeric code by a space.

The period is not used even if part of the name. When the decimal point is part of the organization name, substitute "PNT" for the character itself.

The slant ends the name part of the SIO. If this character is part of the name, substitute "SLT" for the character itself.

The number sign terminates the record name within the name part of the SIO. If this character is part of the name of the organization, substitute "NBR" for the character itself. When the cent sign is part of the organization name, substitute "CNT" for the character itself.

The semi-colon is used only to distinguish organizational relationships. It may not be used even if part of the name.

Do not use the articles "A," "An," and "The" when the article is the first word of the name. Use the word if it is not an article as in the case of the initial "A" in a person's name or when it is the trade style. For non-English names, the articles remain.

The following examples illustrate these rules:

John W Doe/	All Fuels SLT Natural Gas/
N J Grocery/	5 & 10 CNT Store/
D'Vinci Co/	Independent Order of Ground Hogs/
Van-Husen Iron Works/	Mid-West Hardware Co/
Dr Doe Pain Killer/	Cie Generale Transatlantique/
NBR 17 St Louis Post/	Luxury Island Hotel Corporation/
3 PNT 2% Loan Company/	

The number sign is used to separate the record name from other names:

Healy's Inc#Healy's Tours#Healy's Travel Agency/

Sub-units may be named after the organization name and preceded by a semi-colon:

Northern Iron Works Limited; Westside Foundry/

Appendix 5
Standard Numeric Codes

1. Calendar date

$$\underbrace{NN,NN,NN,NN}_{\substack{a \quad b \quad c \quad d}}$$

a = century
b = year
c = month
(01 = January , . . . , 12 = December)
d= day

2. Time Zone References

TIME ZONE REFERENCE CODE	STANDARD TIME	LOCAL TIME DIFFERENTIAL FACTOR
NST	Newfoundland Standard Time	+0330
AST	Atlantic Standard Time	+04
EST	Eastern Standard Time	+05
CST	Central Standard Time	+06
MST	Mountain Standard Time	+07
PST	Pacific Standard Time	+08
YST	Yukon Standard Time	+09
HST	Hawaiian-Alaskan Standard Time	+10
BST	Bering Standard Time	+11
GMT	Greenwich Mean Time (Universal Time)	+00

3. Time

The following examples represent a local time of two hours, nine minutes, and twenty-three seconds past noon in the U.S. Eastern Standard Time Zone.

	Representation
Universal Time	190923Z
Local Time with a Time Differential Factor	140923+05 or 140923+0500
Local Time with a Time Zone Reference	02:09:23P EST

4. Place Names (U.S.A.)

Each named place within a state is assigned a standard code consisting of five digits. This code is used with the two-character state abbreviation or code for identification of states. The standard representation of the code is in the form AANNNNN or NNNNNNN (A= alphabetic character and N=numeric character) where the first two characters represent the state abbreviation or code and the last five numeric characters represent the place within a state. For example, the code for Jamestown, Virginia, might be represented as VA-44400 or 5144400 where VA and 51 are the state abbreviation and code and 44400 might be the place code for Jamestown.

5. Occupations

The Dictionary of Occupational Titles (DOT) is the base for the occupational classification structure in which individual occupations are identified by a 6-digit code.

All occupations are grouped into nine categories, which, in turn, are divided into divisions and groups. The nine occupational categories are as follows:

0.) Professional, technical, and
1.) managerial occupations.
2. Clerical and sales occupations.
3. Service occupations.
4. Farming, fishing, forestry, and related occupations.
5. Processing work occupations.
6. Machine trade occupations.
7. Bench work occupations.
8. Structural work occupations.
9. Miscellaneous occupations.

These categories are divided into

eighty-four 2-digit divisions, and the divisions, in turn, are subdivided into 603 distinctive 3-digit groups. Example:
2 — Clerical and sales occupations.
20 — Stenography, typing, filing, and related occupations.
201 — Secretaries.

The next three digits of the code are based on job requirements that cause workers to function in relation to Data, People, and Things. The following are the hierarchies of the 4th, 5th, and 6th codes:

Data (4th digit)

0 — Synthesizing	5 — Copying
1 — Coordinating	6 — Comparing
2 — Analyzing	7 — No significant
3 — Compiling	relationship
4 — Computing	8 — No significant
	relationship

People (5th digit)

0 — Mentoring	5 — Persuading
1 — Negotiating	6 — Speaking-
2 — Instructing	Signaling
3 — Supervising	7 — Serving
4 — Diverting	8 — No significant
	relationship

Things (6th digit)

0 — Setting-Up	4 — Manipulating
1 — Precision	5 — Tending
Working	6 — Feeding-
2 — Operating-	Offbearing
Controlling	7 — Handling
3 — Driving-	8 — No significant
Operating	relationship

6. Languages

INTERLANGUAGES

089.2	Esperanto
089.6	Interlingue (= Occidental)
089.7	Interlingua

GERMANIC LANGUAGES

20	English
30	German
393.1	Dutch
393.6	Afrikaans

396	Norwegian
397	Swedish
398	Danish

ROMANCE LANGUAGES

40	French
50	Italian
590	Romanian
60	Spanish
690	Portuguese

LATIN, GREEK

71	Latin
75	Greek

SLAVONIC LANGUAGES

82	Russian
83	Ukrainian
84	Polish
850	Czech
854	Slovak
861/862	Serbo-Croat
863	Slovenian
867	Bulgarian

INDIAN LANGUAGES

912.3	Sanskrit
914.3	Hindi
914.31	Urdu

SEMITIC LANGUAGES

924	Hebrew
927	Arabic

TURANIAN LANGUAGES

943.5	Turkish
945.11	Hungarian
945.41	Finnish

ASIAN LANGUAGES

951	Chinese
956	Japanese
957	Korean

LANGUAGES OF OCEANIA AND INDONESIA

992.21	Bahasa, Indonesia, Indonesian

7. Summary of North American Numeric Codes

ICD	NAME OF CODE	ABBRE-VIATION	ISSUING ORGANIZATION	STANDARD DISPLAY STYLE
00	User Agreement Code for Organizations	UACO		
01	Employer Identification Number	USA-EIN	USA Internal Revenue Service	NN-NNNN-NNN
02	Social Security Number	USA-SSN	USA Social Security Administration	NN-NNN-NNNN
03	Data Universal	D-U-N-S	Dun and Bradstreet Inc.	NN-NNN-NNNN
04	Social Insurance Number	CDN-SIN	Canadian Dept. of National Health & Welfare	NNN-NNN-NNN
05	Statistics Canada Central List	CDN-CLID	Statistics Canada	—
06	RESERVED FOR FUTURE USE	—	—	—
07	RESERVED FOR FUTURE USE	—	—	—
08	Birth Number	BN	State and Local Registrars of Vital Statistics	NNN-NN-NNNNNN
09	User Agreement Code for Individuals	UACI	—	—

8. Interpretation of Individual Numeric Codes

U.S. Social Security Number (SSN)

$$\underset{a}{\underline{N}},NN\text{-}NN\text{-}NNNN$$

a = issuing office

Canada—Social Insurance Number (SIN)

$$\underset{a}{\underline{N}},NN\text{-}NNN\text{-}NN\,\underset{b}{\underline{N}}$$

a = province where issued

b = Luhn check digit

France—Numero National D'Identite (NNI)

$$\underset{a}{\underline{N}},\ \underset{b}{\underline{NN}},\ \underset{c}{\underline{NN}},\ \underset{d}{\underline{NNNNN}},,\underset{e}{\underline{NNN}},\ \underset{f}{\underline{NN}},$$

(Display style: NNNNNNNNNNNNNNN)

a = sex (1 male, 2 female)
b = year of birth
c = month of birth
d = place of birth
e = serialization
f = French check digit

Sweden-Personnummer (PN)

$$\underset{a}{\underline{NN}},\ \underset{b}{\underline{NN}},\ \underset{c}{\underline{NN}},\ \underset{d}{\underline{NNN}},\ \underset{e}{\underline{N}},$$

(Display style: NNNNNN-NNNN)

a = year of birth
b = month of birth

c = day of birth
d = serialization
    (odd units digit = male)
    (even units digit = female)
e = Luhn check digit

Denmark-Central Personal
Registration (CPR)

NN, NN, NN, N, NN, N,
a   b   c   d   e   f

(Display style: NN NN NN-NNNN)

a = day of birth
b = month of birth
c = year of birth
d = century of birth
e = serialization
f = Danish control figure also
    stating sex

Ontario—Motor Vehicle Operator's
License Number

A, NNNN, NNN, N, N-N, NN, NN
a   b   c   d   e   f   g

(Display style: ANNNN-NNNNN-NNNNN)

a = last initial
b = numeric code derived from
    last name
c = numeric code derived from
    first given name
d = numeric code derived from
    middle initial
e = year of birth
f = month of birth and sex
    (add 5° if female)

g = day of birth

Check digits and Control Figures

French control figure = 97 − (sum of
first 13 numbers from right).
    The Luhn check digit is obtained as
follows:
- Start with the low order digit (units
position).
- Double the value of every other digit
(all odd positions).
- Add all the digits of these products
to all of the even digit values.
- Subtract the sum total from the next
higher value of 10.

Example:

$$9 \quad \begin{array}{cccccc} 7 & 4 & 3 & 2 & 1 & 6 & 0 \\ \times 2 & & \times 2 & & \times 2 & & \times 2 \end{array}$$

$$9 + 1 + 4 + 4 + 6 + 2 + 2 + 6 + 0$$

$$= 40$$

Complete Social Insurance No = 34(−)
    6

974321606

Calculation of the Danish Control Figure:

$$\begin{array}{ccccccccc} 0 & 3 & 0 & 6 & 3 & 6 & 1 & 1 & 7 \\ \times & \times & \times & \times & \times & \times & \times & \times & \times \\ 4 & 3 & 2 & 7 & 6 & 5 & 4 & 3 & 2 \end{array}$$

$$0+ \; 9+ \; 0+ \; 42+ \; 18+30+ \; 4+ \; 3+14 = 120$$

120:11 = 10
110
 10 (rest)

Control-Figure: 11÷rest=11÷10=1

9. REMINGTON SOUNDEX CODE

1. Always retain initial character of the name as a letter.
2. Drop the vowels (A,E,I,O,U) and the letters: W,H,Y.
3. Drop the second letter of every two-letter pair.
4. Assign numbers to remaining letters as follows:

B,F,P,V	= 1
C,G,J,K,Q,S,X,Z	= 2
D,T	= 3
L	= 4
M,N	= 5
R	= 6

5. Zero fill to field length desired.

Appendix 6
Headings Used in
ICPO General Special Information Index

PROPERTY

1. Passports (file by NUMBER, ignore prefix letters, sequence in numerical order; the point is used as a thousands separator. E.g. file Passport No. 9-PA-3567 under No. 93 · 567.
2. Cars, etc. (file by REGISTRATION NUMBER),
3. Cars, (file by ENGINE NUMBER),
4. Cars (file by SERIAL NUMBER),
5. Cars (file by CHASSIS NUMBER),
6. Weapons (REGISTRATION NUMBER),
7. Gold bars (NUMBER),
8. Objects found (DATE FOUND),
9. Objects lost (DATE LOST),
10. Bodies (PLACE DISCOVERED, alphabetically),
11. Bodies (approximate DOB).

FILED BY NUMBER

12. Radio, TV,
13. Typewriters,
14. Watches,
15. Cameras,
16. Paintings (ARTIST, alphabetical and by type):
    1 = Animals
    4 = Groups of persons
    7 = Still life
    10 = Landscapes
    13 = Portraits
    F = Allegorical or abstract themes,
17. Stamps (COUNTRY, alphabetical),
18. Place of offense (TOWN or COUNTRY, alphabetical).

FILED BY NAME OF FIRM

19. Brokers, 20. Banks, 21. Jewelers, 22. Cafes, 23. Entertainments, 24. Agencies, 25. Insurance, 26. Cooperatives, 27. Schools, 28. Garages, 29. Printers, 30. Publications,

31. Pharmacies, 32. Resorts, 33. Museums, 34. Shops, 35. Boats (NAME, alphabetical), 36. Aircraft (AIRLINE and flight #), 37. Identity cards (NUMBER), 38. Checks (NUMBER).

CRIMES (file by date of offense)

THEFT

39. Animals, 40. Cameras, 41. Radio-TV, 42. Silverware, 43. Weapons, 44. Cars, 45. Aircraft, 46. Luggage, 47. from Camp Grounds, 48. from Hotels, 49. from Trains, 50. from Aircraft, 51. from Ships, 52. from Parked Cars, 53. Boats, 54. Jewelry, 55. Money, 56. Checks, 57. Documents, 58. from Shops, 59. Furs, 60. Clothing, 61. Typewriters, 62. Watches, 63. Musical Instruments, 64. Art, 65. from Castles, 66. from Churches, 67. from Galleries, 68. from Museums, 69. Identity Cards, 70. by Sleight-of-hand, 71. Drugs, 72. by Substitution, 73. Stamps, 74. by Picking Pockets, 75. Securities, 76. Aggravated Theft, 77. ARSON, 78. FRAUD, 79. Fraud using Classified Ads, 80. Insurance Fraud, 81. by Fake Jewelry, 82. in Gambling, 83. by Impersonating priests, 84. by Impersonating police, 85. by Marriage, 86. involving Cars, 87. Bad Checks.

FORGERY

88. Gasoline Coupons, 89. Documents, 90. Insignia, 91. Passports, 92. Art, 93. Stamps, 94. Money Orders, 95. Securities.

TRAFFICKING

96. Weapons, 97. Jewelry, 98. Cigarettes, 99. Lotteries, 100. Foodstuffs, 101. Currency, 102. Furs, 103. Clothing, 104. Watches, 105. Gold, 106. Cars, 107. Counterfeit Currency, 108. Drugs.

HUMAN LIFE

109. Accidents, 110. Murder, 111. Kidnapping.

INDECENCY

112. Rape, 113. Homosexuality, 114. Pornography, (file by TITLE and date), 115. Prostitution.

SUPPLEMENTAL (file by date of occurrence)

116. Poison pen letters (date written), 117. Large gatherings, 118. Clandestine drug laboratories and plantations, 119. Chinese Commercial Code, 120. Fraud involving airplane tickets, 121. Forged travel tickets, 122. Aircraft hijacking, 123. Discovery of bodies, 124. Unusual modus operandi.

Appendix 7
Comparative Profiles of Character Types

WORK SITUATION			
CRAFTSMAN	GAMESMAN	COMPANY MAN	JUNGLE FIGHTER
Not satisfied in a large corporation	Likes to run a high-powered team	Identifies with a large organization	
Likes to work in small groups	Likes pushing the troops	Likes to know where he fits in	
Likes to stick with a job all the way	Likes a wide range of problems	Satisfied with large hierarchical projects	
Enjoys technical involvement	Facinated with new techniques and methods	Not adaptable to change	
Doesn't like competition except with materials	Bored and passive without competition	Sees competition as the price of success	Kill or be killed
Likes to be first among equals	Likes to be boss	Submissive bureaucrat or authoritarian boss	Dominate or be dominated
Not strongly motivated by money	Likes winning all the games	Desires acceptance by authority	
Dislikes being pushed around	Dislikes controls; circumvents, rules	Likes a tight schedule	Thinks fear stimulates better work
Likes limited aspects of a well-defined market	Likes challenge	Good salesman	
Pleasure in building	Likes excitement		
Enjoys working with knowledgeable people	Discusses work in game terms		

ATTITUDE TOWARDS WORK

CRAFTSMAN	GAMESMAN	COMPANY MAN	JUNGLE FIGHTER
Respect for craftsmanship	Innovative (others say grandiose)	Does his job well	
Respect for quality	Flexible (others say superficial)	Responsible	
Can be trusted in the crunch	Remains cool, thinks hard under pressure	Loyal	Self-serving
Difficulty making decisions	Turned on by pressure and crisis	Afraid of failure	
No business sense	Sees work as a game		
Likes to get away from work	Gets pleasure in winning		Gets pleasure in crushing opponent
Believes in the work ethic	Dislikes taking orders		
Interested in his work	Detached attitude		
	Sees work as win or lose; triumph or humiliation		

SOCIOPOLITICAL ATTITUDES

CRAFTSMAN	GAMESMAN	COMPANY MAN	JUNGLE FIGHTER
Respects others	Not respectful of others	Courteous	
Concerned about social implications	Does not consider social values	Concerned about people	
Likes to see everybody happy	Inconsiderate of others	Makes himself attractive to others	Takes pride in being feared by others
Dislikes disagreements	Lacks commitment to people		
Lone wolf		Does not like to be off by himself	
	Contemptuous of losers		
	Tends to be very fair		

FAMILY LIFE

CRAFTSMAN	GAMESMAN	COMPANY MAN	JUNGLE FIGHTER
	Lacks capacity for love		Hard hearted
	Lacks understanding		

PERSONAL PROBLEMS AND VALUES

CRAFTSMAN	GAMESMAN	COMPANY MAN	JUNGLE FIGHTER
Values thrift	Takes risks		
Man of his word	Lacks commitment to principles		
Highly independent	Not an independent person	Malleable	
Closed person, hard to get to	Lives in a semi-fantasy world	Centerless person	
Goal is to perfect his technique	No goals beyond winning	Fears falling behind	Lusts for power
Tinkers as a hobby	Lacks capacity to create		
Overly anxious	Becomes worried and apathetic	Fears losing momentum	
Perfectionist	Unsound		
Keeps feelings to himself	Controlled aggression, suppressed anger		Strong sadistic tendencies
Would like a picture of a lone pine tree	Likes pictures of football players		Likes pictures of lions and tigers
Emotional problems	Less prone to emotional problems	Emotional problems	
Enjoys sailboating	Watches pro-football		
Likes hiking	Plays poker		
Finicky	Lacks patience		
Suffers from insomnia, psychosomatic ailments	Becomes depressed, goalless		
Not ambitious	Excessively competitive		
Too cautiosu	Adolescent rebelliousness	Modest	
Stick-in-the-mud	Go-go spirit Self contempt, sense of guilt and self-betrayal	Has dreams of being chased, falling, or being a top	

Appendix 8
Standard Industrial Classifications

A. U.S. SURVEY OF MANUFACTURERS INDUSTRY GROUPS

20. Food and kindred products
21. Tobacco Manufactures
22. Textile mill products
23. Apparel and other textile products
24. Lumber and wood products
25. Furniture and fixtures
26. Paper and allied products
27. Printing and publishing
28. Chemicals and allied products
29. Petroleum and coal products
30. Rubber and plastics products

31. Leather and leather products
32. Stone, clay and glass products
33. Primary metal industries
34. Fabricated metal products
35. Machinery and allied products
36. Electrical equipment and supplies
37. Transportation equipment
38. Instruments and related products
39. Miscellaneous manufacturing
    industries
19. Ordnance

B. CANADIAN STANDARD INDUSTRIAL CLASSIFICATION

1. Agriculture
2. Forestry
3. Fishing and trapping
4. Mines, quarries and oil wells
5. Manufacturing Industries
   1. Food and beverage industries
   2. Tobacco products
   3. Rubber and Plastics
   4. Leather
   5. Textile
   6. Knitting mills
   7. Clothing
   8. Wood
   9. Furniture and fixtures
   10. Paper and allied industries
   11. Printing, publishing and allied
       industries
   12. Primary metal industries
   13. Metal fabricating
   14. Machinery
   15. Transportation
   16. Electrical products
   17. Non-metallic mineral products

18. Petroleum and coal products
19. Chemical and chemical products
20. Miscellaneous manufacturing
6. Construction industry
7. Transportation, communication and
   other utilities
8. Trade
   1. Wholesale trade
   2. Retail trade
9. Finance, insurance and real estate
10. Community ,business and personal
    service industries
    1. Education and related services
    2. Health and welfare services
    3. Religious organizations
    4. Amusement and recreation
       services
    5. Services to business management
    6. Personal services
    7. Accommodation and food services
    8. Miscellaneous services
11. Public administration and defense
12. Industry unspecified or undefined

Appendix 9
Comparative Fair Credit Reporting Act Data

A. U.S. Fair Credit Reporting Act of 1971

SCOPE:
Investigatory credit bureaus reporting on persons, as opposed to businesses.
ENFORCEMENT:
Federal Trade Commission
USES OF INFORMATION:
Credit, empolyment, insurance, licensing, or other business transactions.
Excludes:
   Credit over $50,000
   Insurance over $50,000
   Employment over $20,000
PROHIBITED INFORMATION:
(1) judgments after **seven years**
(2) bankruptcies after **fourteen years**
(3) **paid** tax liens after **seven years**
(4) debts charged to profit-and-loss **after seven years**
(5) arrests, etc. after **seven years**
(6) other adverse items after **seven years.**

RIGHT TO INSPECT ONE'S OWN RECORD:
(1) with a friendly witness
(2) must waive some rights to sue
(3) can charge for disclosure
RIGHT TO INFORMATION:
(1) nature and substance except medical information
(2) sources except when used only in preparing an investigatory report.
PENALTIES:
Non-compliance: actual damages, punitive damages, cost of action and attorney's fees.
Negligent non-compliance: actual damages, cost of action, and attorney's fees.
Obtaining information under false pretenses: one year and $5,000 fine.
Unauthorized disclosure: one year and $5,000 fine.

B. The Manitoba Investigations Act of 1971

SCOPE:
Excludes: government agencies, police
ENFORCEMENT:
Director employed to enforce the act.
USES OF INFORMATION:
Excludes:
   Employment over $12,000
   Selection of business partners
   Life insurance over $25,000
PROHIBITED INFORMATION:
(1) reasonable effort to corroborate information
(2) judgments unless creditor is named
(3) bankruptcies after **fourteen years**
(4) statute-barred judgments

(5) writs after **twelve months** unless current status is given
(6) other adverse information after **seven years** unless voluntarily supplied
(7) race, religion, ethnic origin, or political affiliation, unless voluntarily supplied
RIGHT TO INSPECT ONE'S RECORD:
Disclosure within 24 hours
RIGHT TO INFORMATION:
(1) source and detail of factual information
(2) nature of investigatory information
PENALTY:
Personal: $500 fine
Corporation: $2,500 fine

C. The Ontario Consumer Reporting Act of 1973

SCOPE:

In-file and investigatory credit bureaus reporting on persons, as opposed to businesses

ENFORCEMENT:

(1) Executive Director, Business Practices Division, Ministry of Consumer and Commercial Relations, enforces the act and directs investigations

(2) Registrar of Consumer Reporting Agencies registers all credit bureaus and their investigators

(3) Commercial Registration Appeal Tribunal adjudicates appeals from administrative action

USES OF INFORMATION:

Purchase or collection of debts, tenancy, employment, insurance, credit, updating files.

PROHIBITED INFORMATION:

(1) credit information that is not best evidence

(2) uncorroborated personal information

(3) judgments after **seven years**

(4) judgments unless creditor is named

(5) bankruptcies after **seven years**

(6) statute barred judgments

(7) **unpaid** fines or taxes after **seven years**

(8) convictions after **seven years** from release

(9) writs after **twelve months** unless current status is given; **seven years** if status is given

(10) criminal charges dismissed, set aside, or withdrawn

(11) other adverse items after **seven years**

(12) race, creed, color, sex, ancestry, ethnic origin, or political affiliation

(13) information given orally

RIGHT TO INSPECT ONE'S OWN RECORD:

(1) without charge

(2) without waiver of rights to sue

(3) with a friendly witness

(4) can make an abstract

RIGHT TO INFORMATION:

(1) nature and substance of record

(2) sources

(3) names of recipients

(4) copies of reports furnished

PENALTIES:

Personal:

   One year and $2,000 fine

Corporation:

   $25,000 fine

NOTES

1. John M. Carroll, *Personal Records: Procedures, Practices, and Problems* (Ottawa: Department of Communications, 1972).
2. *Ibid.* Data source is the Privacy and Computers Task Force Questionnaire, designed and analyzed by the author.
3. U.S. Department of Commerce, "Compilation and Use of Criminal Court Data in Relation to Pre-Trial Release of Defendants: Pilot Study." NBS Technical Note 535, August, 1970, p. 78.
4. The combined sales of Simpson's Limited and Simpson-Sears in 1969 was in excess of $915 million.
5. The Lacombe Law is an act passed by the Quebec National Assembly that provides for an expedient discharge in personal bankruptcy.
6. James B. Rule, *Private Lives and Public Surveillance* (New York: Schocken Books, 1974), pp. 97–121.
7. Carroll, *op. cit.*
8. *Ibid.*
9. E. R. Gabrieli, *Computerization of Clinical Records,* Vol. 1 (New York: Grune & Stratton, Inc., 1970).
10. Carroll, *op. cit.*
11. *Ibid.*
12. *Ibid.*
13. *Ibid.*
14. Ontario School Counsellors Association, *Report of the Committee on Ethical Standards,* Elmer Huff, Chairman (Toronto: November 9, 1967).
15. For a more detailed study of open- and closed-record policies in colleges and universities in the United States, see Burton R. Clark, "The Dossier in Colleges and Universities," *On Record: Files and Dossiers in American Life,* Ed. Stanton Wheeler (New York: Russell Sage Foundation, 1969), pp. 67–93.
16. J. Kirk Barefoot, Ed., *The Polygraph Technique* (American Polygraph Association, 1972).
17. George W. Lindberg, "A Test for Truth," *Security World* (January, 1968), pp. 27–28.
18. Philip Ash, "Attitude of Work Applicants Toward Theft," *Procedures of the 17th International Congress of Applied Psychology* (Brussels, 1972).
19. Michael Maccoby, "Character Types and Work Environment Relationship," *Spectrum* (July, 1973), 39–48.
20. Checksums are a computer technique for insuring the integrity of an identifying number.
21. This issue was raised in Sidio v. F-R Publishing Co., 113F 2d 806 (2d Cir. 1940). The case involved the detailed disclosure, in a *New Yorker* profile, of the personal life of a one-time child prodigy who manifestly wished in adulthood "to be left alone." Here, as the logic of Judge Clark made inexorable, there was no liability. Cited by Harry Kalven,

313

Jr., in "Privacy in Tort Law—Were Warren and Brandeis Wrong?" *Law and Contemporary Problems (Privacy)*, Vol. 31, No. 2 (Duke University School of Law, Spring, 1966).
22. Jerry M. Rosenberg, *The Death of Privacy* (New York: Random House, 1969), p. 194. See also p. 139.

A SELECTED BIBLIOGRAPHY

PRIVACY

Baran, Paul, *Remarks on the Question of Privacy Raised by the Automation of Mental Health Records,* Rand, 1967.

Brenton, Myron, *The Privacy Invaders,* Fawcett, 1964.

Carroll, J.M., Baudot, J., Kirsh, Carol, and Williams, J.I., *Personal Records: Procedures, Practices and Problems,* Communications Canada, 1972.

Carroll, J.M., and Williams, J.I., *The Privacy of Student Records,* Second Ontario Universities Computing Conference, 1971.

Compilation and Use of Criminal Court Data in Relation to Pre-Trial Release of Defendants: Pilot Study, U.S. Department of Commerce, NBS Technical Note 535, 1970.

The Computer and Invasion of Privacy, U.S. House of Representatives (3 parts), 1966.

Computers: Privacy and Freedom of Information, Communications Canada, 1970.

Gotlieb, C.C., and Borodin, A., *Social Issues in Computing,* Academic Press, 1973.

Invasions of Privacy, U.S. Senate (6 parts), 1966.

MacLean, C.H., *Consumer Protection and the Law,* University of Toronto, 1974.

Miller, Arthur R., *The Assault on Privacy,* Signet, 1971.

National Survey of the Public's Attitudes Toward Computers, Time, 1971.

Packard, Vance, *The Naked Society,* Pocket Books, 1964.

Privacy (Law and Contemporary Problems), Duke, 1966.

Privacy and Computers, Info Canada, 1972.

Privacy Issues in Data Protection, Organization for Economic Cooperation and Development, 1975.

Report of the Committee on Ethical Standards, Ontario School Counsellors Association, 1967.

Rosenberg, Jerry, *The Death of Privacy,* Random House, 1969.

Rule, James B., *Private Lives and Public Surveillance,* Schocken Books, 1974.

Sackman, Harold, and Mumford, Enid, *Human Choice and Computers,* North Holland, 1975.

315

Sharp, John M., *Credit Reporting and Privacy*, Butterworths, 1970.
Skils, Edward A., *The Torment of Secrecy*, Collier, 1956.
Ware, Willis H., *Records, Computers and the Rights of Citizens*, U.S. Department of Health, Education and Welfare, 1973 and Massachusetts Institute of Technology, 1974.
Westin, Alan F., and Baker, M.A., *Data Banks in a Free Society*, Quadrangle, 1972.
Westin, Alan F., *Privacy and Freedom*, Athereum, 1967.
Wheeler, Stanton, *On Record*, Russell Sage, 1969.
Younger, Kenneth, *Report of the Committee on Privacy*, United Kingdom Civil Service Department, 1972.

CRYPTOLOGY

Carroll, J.M., *Protection Methods for Real-Time Systems*, University of Western Ontario, 1974.
Gaines, Helen Fouche, *Cryptanalysis*, Dover, 1939.
Ingemarsson, I., Blom, T., and Forchheimer, R., *A System for Data Security Based on Data Encryption*, Linkoeping, 1974.
Johnson, S.M., *Certain Number-Theoretic Questions in Access Control*, Rand, 1974.
Kahn, David, *The Codebreakers*, MacMillan, 1967.
McLellan, P.M., *Privacy Considerations in Resource-Sharing Computer Systems*, University of Western Ontario, 1970.
Pratt, Fletcher, *Secret and Urgent*, Blue Ribbon, 1934.
Smith, L.D., *Cryptography*, Dover, 1943.
Wheeler, R.M., *An Infinite Key Security Transformation for Shared Random Access Files in a Resource Sharing System*, University of Western Ontario, 1972.

SECURITY

Ash, Philip, "Attitude of Work Applicants Toward Theft," *Procedures of the 17th International Congress of Applied Psychology*, Brussels, 1972.
Barefoot, J.K., *The Polygraph Technique*, American Polygraph Association, 1972.
Bergart, J.G., Denicoff, M., and Hsiao, D.K., *An Annovated and Cross-Referenced Bibliography on Computer Security and Access Control in Computer Systems*, Ohio State, 1972.
Bergart, J.G., *Computer Security, Access Control and Privacy Protection in Computer Systems*, University of Pennsylvania, 1972.
Canning, Richard, *Computer Fraud and Embezzlement, EDP Analyzer*, September, 1973.
Carroll, John M., *The Third Listener*, Dutton, 1969.

Greene, Richard M., *Business Intelligence and Espionage*, Irwin, 1966.
Hamilton, Peter, *Espionage and Subversion in an Industrial Society*, Hutchinson, 1967.
Hamilton, Peter, *Computer Security*, Cassell, 1972.
Hoffman, Lance J., *The Formulary Model for Access Control and Privacy in Computer Systems*, SLAC, 1970.
Hoffman, Lance J., *Security and Privacy in Computer Systems*, Melville, 1973.
Hoffman, Lance J., *Security Ratings for Computer Systems*, University of California, 1974.
Hunt, M.K., and Turn, Rein, *Privacy and Security in Databank Systems: An Annotated Bibliography, 1970–1973*, Rand, 1974.
Lindberg, George W., "A Test for Truth," *Security World*, January 1968.
Maccoby, Michael, "Character Types and Work Environment Relationship," *Spectrum*, July 1973.
Parker, D.B., Nycum, S., and Ouera, S.S., *Computer Abuse*, SRI, 1973.
Reed, I.S., *The Application of Information Theory to Privacy in Data Banks*, Rand, 1973.
Renniger, Clark R., and Branstad, D.K., *Privacy and Security in Computer Systems*, NBS, 1974.
Turn, Rein, and Shapiro, N.Z., *Privacy and Security in Databank Systems*, Rand, 1972.
Turn, Rein, *Towards Data Security Engineering*, Rand, 1974.
Turn, Rein, *Privacy and Security in Personal Information Databank Systems*, Rand, 1974.
Van Tassell, *Computer Security Management*, Prentice-Hall, 1972.
Watters, Carolyn Rose, *A General Information Retrieval System with Privacy Controls*, University of Western Ontario, 1972.
Woodward, F.G., and Hoffman, Lance J., *On Worst-Case Costs for Dynamic Data Element Security Decisions*, University of California, 1973.

SYSTEMS

Agency Coordination Study, U.S. Senate, 1962.
Becker, Joseph, and Hayes, R.M., *Information Storage and Retrieval*, Wiley, 1963.
Bourne, Charles F., *Methods of Information Handling*, Wiley, 1963.
Cooper, Gary, *Proceedings of the International Symposium on Criminal Justice Information and Statistics Systems*, LEAA, 1972.
Coordination of Information on Current Scientific Research and Development Supported by the U.S. Government, U.S. Senate, 1961.
Davenport, W.P., *Modern Data Communications*, Hayden, 1971.
Dunn, Edgar S., *Review of Proposal for a National Data Bank*, Bureau of Budget (U.S.), 1965.

Gabrieli, E.F., *Computerization of Clinical Records,* Grune & Stratton, 1970.

Geddes, E.W., Enrich, R.L., McMurray, J., *Feasibility Report and Recommendation: A New York State Identification System,* S.D.C., 1963.

Holm, Bart E., *How to Manage Your Information,* Reinhold, 1965.

International Survey of Standards for Individual and Organizational Identification— Structure and Use—Analysis and Summary, ISO/TC97/SC14 (Sec. 15) No. 67, September, 1974.

The ICPO—Interpol Criminal Records Department, ICPO, 1970.

Kent, Allen, *Textbook on Mechanized Information Retrieval,* Wiley, 1962.

New York Times Information Bank, New York Times, 1972.

Parker, John K., *Delaware Valley Law Enforcement Information Network,* University of Pennsylvania, 1966.

Proposal for a Central Data Bank on Students and Resources, Council of Universities of Ontario, 1969.

Salton, Gerard, *Automatic Information Organization and Retrieval,* McGraw-Hill, 1968.

Smith, M.E., Schwartz, R.R., and Newcombe, H.B., *Computer Methods for Extracting Sibship Data from Family Groupings of Records,* Atomic Energy of Canada, Ltd., 1965.

INDEX

INDEX

In addition to its hard cover books on security subjects, Security World Publishing Company publishes *Security World* and *Security Distributing & Marketing (SDM)* magazines; produces booklets, manuals and audio tape cassettes on security; and sponsors the International Security Conference, held annually in Chicago, New York and Los Angeles. Books and other materials are available from Security World Publishing Co., Inc., 2639 So. La Cienega Blvd., Los Angeles, Calif. 90034.